TRAVELS
IN A
BLUE CHAIR

TRAVELS IN A BLUE CHAIR

✦

Alaska to Zambia
Ushuaia to Uluru

A series of short stories

WALT BALENOVICH

"North America's Disabled Adventurer"

iUniverse, Inc.
New York Lincoln Shanghai

TRAVELS IN A BLUE CHAIR
Alaska to Zambia
Ushuaia to Uluru

Copyright © 2007 by Walt Balenovich

All rights reserved. No part of this book may be used or reproduced by any means, graphic, electronic, or mechanical, including photocopying, recording, taping or by any information storage retrieval system without the written permission of the publisher except in the case of brief quotations embodied in critical articles and reviews.

iUniverse books may be ordered through booksellers or by contacting:

iUniverse
2021 Pine Lake Road, Suite 100
Lincoln, NE 68512
www.iuniverse.com
1-800-Authors (1-800-288-4677)

Because of the dynamic nature of the Internet, any Web addresses or links contained in this book may have changed since publication and may no longer be valid.

ISBN: 978-0-595-46149-3 (pbk)
ISBN: 978-0-595-90449-5 (ebk)

Printed in the United States of America

The views expressed in this work are solely those of the author and do not necessarily reflect the views of the publisher, and the publisher hereby disclaims any responsibility for them.

Edited by
Wayne Cloughton
Cyril Stickney
Catherine Jenkins
Back cover photo of Walt and niece Rebecca courtesy of
www.vbphotography.net

To

Mom, Dad and my entire family

All the friends I visited, met, or who encouraged me to write this book

And to my friends who are no longer with us, but are greatly missed

Bill Reade

Tom Milledge

Carel de Mol

D. John Murrant

Tony Sanderson

And most importantly, to you for reading this book

Contents

FOREWORD . . . . *xiii*
UP THE HUMAN ELEVATOR IN TOKYO 1
ULURU, THE THORNY DEVIL IN THE OUTBACK 6
HOTEL CHÂTEAUNEUF AND THE SHOWERS OF
THE RIVIERA 14
SWIMMING WITH DOLPHINS IN A RUBBER
CHAIR 19
PACHAMAMA—THE MOTHER EARTH 25
GLOBAL WARMING IN THE YUKON AND
FOLLOWING OUR WAY TO ALASKA 35
MAKING LOVE ON THE REEF 42
STUCK IN THE GRAVEL BY THE SIDE OF THE
ROAD 48
NO SEATBELTS, BRAKES, OR BRAINS BUT WHAT A
VIEW! 55
STORMY TIMES IN THE CANOE ON TEA LAKE 60
TARRED AND SOAKED WITH FRIENDS IN
CORDOBA 67
A FEW PINTS AND A PUSH TO THE M.C.G. FROM A
FRIENDLY VEGETARIAN 75

MY FRIENDS AT THE ARK IN THE ABERDARE
MOUNTAINS 81

A NIGHT AT THE OPERA ON CLARKE QUAY 87

UP MT. WELLINGTON IN A YELLOW
SUBMARINE 92

THE EXCITEMENT OF A TIDAL BORE WHILE
LOOKING FOR MOOSE AND WHALE 98

CRUISING BETWEEN THE LAKES IN THE ALPS 105

DUSKY LODGE WITH THE WHALES AT
KAIKOURA 111

A RAINY AUTUMN WEEKEND IN THE BIG
APPLE 117

THREE HIGH FLIERS IN THE WILD, BLUE
YONDER 125

"AR MATEY, COME AN' SPEND THE NIGHT W'
ME" 132

THE BAHT IN MY HAT 137

A WALK WITH A COYOTE IN STANLEY PARK 144

DOWN ON ST. PATRICK'S DAY AND UP TO THE
ANDES 149

A WARM CHRISTMAS WITH A GOOD FRIEND IN
SYDNEY 157

ALL THE LIVING LAWN ORNAMENTS ON LAKE
NAKURU 163

I TOOK MY TIME IN TAI MEI TUK 170

MALCOLM AND THE QUOKKAS AT ROTTNEST
ISLAND 176

THE BUTCHER, THE BAKER AND THE
CHEESEMAKER 182

NEW YEAR'S EVE Y2K IN WELLINGTON, N.Z. 189

ON THE ROAD WITH THE OTHER COLOURED
CHAIRS 194

THE BLUE MOUNTAINS AND THE MEGALONG
VALLEY 200

PAYING THE TOLL TO CROSS THE BLUE
DANUBE 205

THE PLASTIC FOOD LOOKED GOOD ENOUGH TO
EAT 211

SURVIVING THE CAMPING AND COTTAGE
ADVENTURES 218

THE SOUTH AND THE NORTH OF IT 226

RELAXING IN MOMBASA DESPITE THE MALARIA
AND YELLOW FEVER 232

THE PIZZA, THE MARKET AND THE MOON
RAINBOW IN KOROTOGO 237

BORDERING ON AN ILLEGAL ALIEN 245

KURANDA, THE ATHERTON TABLELANDS AND
THE CROCS 255

SLALOMING MY WAY UP THE
CHAMPS-ÉLYSÉES 261

AOTEAROA, THE MAINLAND AND THE ISLAND 266

GRASS SKIRTS IN THE PARADISE OF THE PACIFIC 271

THE GIRLS, THE KNIGHT AND THE HOT CARS 277

THE RELATIVES AND ROASTED LAMB OF GORSKI KOTAR 284

CHINESE NEW YEAR'S EVE AT WAT CHALONG 292

ACROSS TO THE PACIFIC ALONE IN MY OLD BUICK 299

THE BEACHES, FERRIES AND TRAINS AROUND THE HARBOUR 310

QUITE A RHUBARB AT MIDSUMMER IN THE MIDDLE OF SWEDEN 316

CAMPING AT THE MASAI MARA ON THE SERENGETI 329

DON'T SHOOT DOWN MY PLANE! 334

SUNRISE WITH A SORE BUM AND A BROKEN MOTOR 340

THE END OF THE WORLD AND THE START OF EVERYTHING 347

AFRICA ENDS WITH THUNDER, A THUD AND A CRACK 354

THE HAPPY ENDING 364

Appendix 379

FOREWORD

Ever since I was little I had yearned to travel. I think it started when my dad and I would sit at the T.V. and watch the old animal and nature programs, such as *Wild Kingdom*. I thoroughly enjoyed observing the different species, but it was the odd and unusual landscapes and native peoples that really caught my imagination.

I had polio when I was twelve weeks old and spent the majority of my first five years in the hospital, although I did get to go home for Christmas. I was ultimately released to enter kindergarten, eat non-flaked potatoes and use coloured towels on a permanent basis after I had mastered getting around on crutches and leg braces, which I used with modest success (broken arms and legs) until my late 20's. I finally switched to the wheelchair full time when I moved out on my own and far from being confining, the blue chair has allowed me the freedom to do whatever I want to and when, including backpacking the world alone when time and finances allow.

I never really thought much of actually travelling when I was younger, but once I started flying around in planes during my wheelchair basketball days, it finally occurred to me that I could travel if I wanted to. Of course, travelling requires money and luckily I was able to make ends meet in my job as an I.T. consultant. The beauty of being self-employed was that once my contract was over, whether it be a year or six-months, I then had enough money to travel again. My time was my own and when I came back I could look for work again. Travelling internationally only started when my good friend Wayne invited me to visit him in Africa. I can still remember the panic I was in the night before the flight.

During each of my stints abroad I would compose a monthly report on the experiences I had encountered and e-mailed it out to all my friends back home. Invariably, the response from them when I got home was the same, "you should write a book about your adventures". It finally took a long snowy winter in Ontario for me to sit down (one of my best things) and actually type the adventures out.

So, here it is. I hope you enjoy it. My suggested reading format is just to read one or two stories before bed. I hope you will not be asleep too quickly after starting a story.

For me *Travels in a Blue Chair* isn't about the chair. The chair is in many ways just a prop to get me from point A to point B, just like your shoes. The real story is about the smiling people I've met all over the world who trip all over themselves to help me out when I need it and then remain in contact with me to become life-long friends. That is one of the special bonuses of my adventures, many new friends are still in contact with me and I sometimes get to reunite with them well after our initial meetings.

I hope you enjoy reading the stories as much as I enjoyed living them.

UP THE HUMAN ELEVATOR IN TOKYO

The thing I hate about being in a wheelchair and taking long flights is that I never get to pee. Most of the time the flight staff are more than willing to assist me into the narrow washroom, but for some reason, I prefer to save them the bother. The unfortunate consequence is that I'm bursting by the time I get off the plane, even after drinking as little as possible.

As I anticipated my date with the white throne, I watched the film shown at the end of the flight, demonstrating the ways of getting around the airport and into town. I was shocked to hear that Narita airport is about one hour away from Tokyo by taxi, and the ride would cost 30,000 yen. I wasn't too familiar with the currency, but even I could figure out that was over $300 Canadian. I had to figure something else out, and fast.

After clearing customs, I attended the washroom, which luckily had an oversized stall for the disabled. As I left the stall, I was surprised to see an elderly woman with a handmade broom, sweeping out the men's room. She worked diligently and took no notice of me, but what surprised me were the men at the urinals, going about their business, taking no notice of her. My notions of the staid Japanese were immediately challenged and I realized that Asia was going to be a totally unique experience.

I knew from the in-flight video that there was a subway station on the lower level of Narita. I enjoyed the chance to take in a bit of

Japanese life, even if it was only from the airport. The signs were in a different script, although most were in English as well, and the faces were different, but otherwise it resembled an Asian neighbourhood in any large town. I finally broke down and asked for directions to the subway and luckily for me, when I found it, there was a ramp to the entrance. People entered by inserting their stubs in a machine adjacent to the turnstile, going through and then picking the stubs up on the other side. I had no idea how to read the subway map, which was written in Japanese Kanji script, but I knew I had to get to the Asakusa train station, which is where my hotel was located.

I usually stay at cheap and clean youth hostels, which fit my budget, allowing me to meet other travellers and hopefully start conversations with other backpackers. This is important to me since I travel alone in my blue chair and it can get pretty lonely on the road in exotic, non-English speaking locales. Unhappily for me, I was arriving early in November, on a national holiday, so the youth hostel was closed. This is unusual for hostels, as most of them are open three hundred and sixty-five days a year. I was lucky to have my hotel arranged for me by Aileen, a fellow Canadian of Japanese descent, working as a computer consultant for the last year or so. Aileen was a friend of a friend of mine in Toronto and had sent an e-mail giving me the address of the hotel, but the problem was that the directions weren't in Japanese.

My immediate dilemma was trying to purchase a ticket to the Asakusa station. Since there was no one available to manually buy a ticket from, I asked a fellow commuter if she would assist me. The $10 fare was much less than the hundreds of dollars it would have cost had I taken a taxi. After going up the long ramp to the train platform, I was pleased that the train was a modern one, well lit and designed to accommodate wheelchairs. The young girl who had assisted me with my ticket was very interested that I was travelling alone. It turned out that she worked at the airport in one of the cafés and was headed back into the city on her way home from work. As I looked around at the people riding with me, I noticed that many of them were fast asleep, taking a catnap before going home for dinner. It seemed like a good idea to me. The train ride took about forty minutes and frankly, I was exhausted after sixteen hours on a plane. I needed a comfortable bed and a place to stretch out.

Upon arriving at Asakusa, I was confronted with another problem: there were no ramps or elevators to get me up to street level. I asked a local to find someone who worked for the trains who might be able to assist me up the stairs. It wasn't long before a middle-aged man, dressed in a white uniform and wearing glasses, took up the challenge. He was equipped with a hand-held radio and quickly summoned his co-workers to help me up. Now the Japanese are not a big, powerful people; they are generally short in stature. I was surrounded by six eager, but slightly overwhelmed guys, who began to lug me up the narrow stairs to the outside world. I soon realized the task was going to take a while. There must have been six flights of stairs, and at the top of each level, my assistants were out of breath and gasping for air. I have to confess feeling a bit helpless and a bit like a piece of luggage, but after a short rest at each level they dutifully resumed the assault at the summit. Thankfully, we finally made it to the top and the exit. I thanked everyone for the help and looked for a cab to get me the rest of the way to the hotel.

I was finally out in the cool autumn air of Tokyo and it felt great. I knew that the worst of the trip to my hotel was now behind me. It was early evening and this part of town wasn't especially memorable. The streetlights were on and there were a few shops, but other than that, there wasn't much to it. The man from the subway who had coordinated my elevation out of the underground, summoned a cab from the long queue of vehicles that waited for commuters at the station's exit. A cab pulled up and I prepared to continue my search for the hotel. I took the opportunity to thank the subway official for all his help and he bowed to me graciously.

The taxis in Tokyo are small and immaculate. The drivers are dressed in a military-styled uniform and are eager to assist. I tried to pronounce the name and address of the hotel, but I think my Japanese was pretty terrible as I was answered by a perplexed stare. The driver took my piece of paper and got back into the front seat, after placing my chair into the trunk. We soon arrived at a police station, called a "koban", which is more like a local police office rather than a station. These seemed to be located throughout the city every few blocks. I remained in the back seat and observed as the driver and all the police officers discussed the situation and looked at the piece of paper I had given the driver. After some time, one of the officers, an older gentlemen, carried a wooden chair over to a bookcase, stood on it and reached up to a large book on the top shelf. Apparently, it was a map of the area, and it was so old, it looked like it had been the original plan when the area was built. They all scrutinized the book and it was not until all of the men in the koban agreed and bowed to each other, that the driver emerged with a big smile on his face.

The two of us resumed our drive and I noticed that the nightlife had picked up. There was far more pedestrian traffic on the sidewalk, but we were still not in a downtown environment. It seemed to me that we were in an area that marked a border between residential and commercial areas. It just took another five minutes to arrive at my hotel.

I entered the lobby with my bag on my lap and my knapsack with the Canadian flag on it hanging from the back of my chair. The hotel was quite nice and the driver helped me into my chair, as well as helping to carry my bags past the entrance. It was a small establishment, with only four floors, but the lobby was immaculate and it was obvious that the staff were happy to see me, since they had been expecting someone in a chair from Canada to arrive. I was registered and told I had a nice room on the third floor. There were three small steps up to the elevator, but I knew they would be the smallest problem I had to deal with on this day.

I had arrived in Asia!

ULURU, THE THORNY DEVIL IN THE OUTBACK

It was my fourth visit to Australia and I was finally making a trip to the famed Outback. I had heard all the stories over the years, seen pictures of the empty spaces and wondered what I would find when I got there.

The plane from Perth to Alice Springs would fly over Uluru, the monolithic rock that rises above the dull, flat scrubland that surrounds it. The formation went by the name of Ayer's Rock during the time of European colonization, but has correctly reverted to its Aboriginal name in recent years. Fortunately, I had a window seat and was on the right side of the plane to get my first glimpse. In the sunshine, Uluru sparkled and shone and seemed to reflect a ruby hue. The pilot graciously tilted the plane for passengers on the other side, so that they too could strain their necks to try to see it. What luck! I was still unsure whether I would be able to go on a bus tour to see it up close. During my years of travel, I've had little success asking bus lines for assistance on and off the vehicle when travelling on my own. Bus lines are reluctant to allow their drivers to help due to insurance concerns and this means that most bus tours are of little use to me. At least now I could say that I had seen Uluru once in my life, even if it had been from 25,000 feet.

The airport was small and bright and I obtained a taxi to take me the short distance into town and the youth hostel. I must confess that when I arrived, I was happy to see that the hostel appeared to be almost brand new. One of the dormitories had been renovated from an old motel with lots of stairs. The office area was new and my room was in the back and had only recently been constructed. The washrooms and toilets were completely designed for the disabled and were excellent. The self-catering kitchen facility was a bit older and was up one large step. Since they had billed the facility as accessible for the disabled by using the blue, international sign of access in their travel guide, I shamed them into building me a wooden ramp. I also suggested that after I left, they should erect a permanent, concrete one. Since there were no beaches in the middle of the Outback, the facility also had a beautiful pool and pool deck. I don't swim, but I knew that where there was a pool, it would usually be the hub of hostel social activity and you would inevitably find young bathing beauties lying nearby.

I decided to wheel around "Alice" to see what it looked like and get a bit of a feel for the surroundings. Alice Springs definitely isn't a big town and there are very few people in the whole of the Northern Territory. Darwin, the capital, is in the north in what is called the "Wet Top" and Alice is in the south in the "Red Centre". I could wheel all around town in nearly forty-five minutes and it was quite nice. There were a lot of administrative offices and shops that seemed to cater primarily to tourists. The centre of town had an open square with a number of gum trees. In the heat of the day, many of the Aboriginal inhabitants of Alice Springs and surrounding area, used this as a focal point for community conversation, while retreating from the sun.

Behind the hostel was a dry riverbed. Apparently the only time the river ever runs is when there is a rare deluge of rain. I was told by an Aboriginal man that it hadn't happened in over ten years.

I took the opportunity on my trip about town to stop at the store and buy some supplies, namely food and beer, the two staples for surviving the Outback while in a blue chair. I returned to the hostel's kitchen to prepare a cup of tea and met a middle-aged Canadian woman named Deanna, who looked to be in a bit of a daze. I asked if she was all right and whether she would like to share my pot of tea with me. It turned out that when she and her husband, Allen, had been flying into Alice from Adelaide her husband had experienced chest pains and collapsed. Luckily for them, a doctor was on board and administered prompt medical care and asked the pilot to radio ahead for an ambulance to be waiting at the airport on arrival. Allen was now in stable condition in intensive care and I had to admire this brave woman, who was alone with her worries.

In time, I discovered that they were both born-again Christians. They had a strong faith in God and knew everything would work out for the best. I hope that in some small way that pot of tea and a bit of sympathetic conversation helped. I went down to the hospital the next day to check on his condition and the lady informed me that he was improving and had been moved onto a regular ward. Allen was in the hospital for a few days and seemed to have suffered no permanent damage to his heart. We became quite good friends during the rest of our time together in the hostel and shared many meals. They visited me in Vancouver for brunch when I concluded my drive across Canada a few months later. A great thing about travelling is the many new friends that you make from all over the world.

During the time that I spent at the hostel, I had only one roommate in the four-bed dormitory. I must confess that I have forgotten his name, but he was from the U.S. and I referred to him as "the phantom" when talking with my new friends at dinner. He seemed to come home in the early evening, be asleep when I arrived to go to bed, and then when I woke up in the morning, he would be long gone. I'm not one to sleep in and am generally up by seven o'clock, so this fellow was quite energetic. He seemed nice enough and we spoke once. I asked him where he had gone off to at such an early hour and he told me that he had been booked on a sunrise balloon ride over the Outback. That sounded great and I asked him if a guy in a chair could do it. He thought about it for a short while, but then told me that there were small compartments in the basket and that the sides were quite high. He didn't know how I would manage.

Later in the week as I was wheeling around, I met him again as he came out of a store with a six-pack of beer. I thought he might offer me one to be polite, but he just waved at me and then left with his beer. I guess that you can't become close friends with everyone you room with. I would soon find out about those early morning excursions for myself.

I'd finally been able to find a tour company that would take me on their bus. I outlined my dilemma to a woman at the tourist kiosk in the middle of town and she thought she knew a small company that might take me. Sure enough, the company said that they usually had two people assigned to each tour and that they could assist me onto the bus. I was all set. The company, called "Emu Run", would drop by my hostel to pick me up for the trip to the Outback. They told me that it would be a long day as it was almost a six-hour drive to Uluru. I was instructed to be outside the hostel at 5:30 a.m. for pick-up and that I would not be back until 12:30 a.m. the next day.

The next morning seemed to come very quickly and I waited with my bleary eyes for the bus to arrive. In time, it did, and a man with a clipboard asked if I was going on a camel safari. I asked if I looked like the type to spend a day on a camel and pointed to some other early rising backpackers who were nearby. Finally my transportation arrived, the two fellows introduced themselves and said they would be happy to lend a hand up the stairs. One of them was tall and thin and the other was bearded and burly, with a friendly smile. The tall man grabbed me under the arms while the other held my legs and we went up into the bus backwards. That didn't seem too difficult and I told them that I could get off myself by crawling on the floor and scampering down the stairs. After picking up the rest of the tourists, we were off on our trip to the Outback.

I took the opportunity to resume my sleep schedule as the bus was not fully booked and I could stretch out across three seats. After an hour or so, I perked up again and observed the sun rising over a vast emptiness. The bus was equipped with a speaker and the driver gave us informational tidbits and trivia as we made our way along. He stated that this had been one of the rainiest periods they had experienced for a long time. The dry riverbed back in Alice didn't seem to support his assertion, but he mentioned that if you looked out across the red earth, there were numerous green plants and shrubs. Usually there aren't any or they're quite brown. It did look a lot greener than I'd expected.

The bus had taken on about fourteen passengers and it would be a long trip to our destination. After three hours, we stopped at a petrol station and restaurant to add more fuel and pick up breakfast or coffee. I stayed on the bus, but did ask the driver if he could grab a coffee for me. We were soon on our way and were starting to chatter amongst ourselves. After another hour or so, the burly fellow named Ron, who was now driving the bus, suddenly came to a screeching halt, opened the narrow door and ran off the bus onto the side of the road. A few seconds later, he brought back a cute little reptile called a "thorny devil". It was multi-coloured and fit into the palm of his hand. Ron gave each of us a chance to pose with it for a picture, at least those who weren't afraid. It lay motionless because that was this small animal's way of protecting itself, playing dead. I was still trying to figure out how the driver had seen the darn thing from the road. It was either his experience or an eagle eye because the critter seemed to be perfectly camouflaged. Ron returned the thorny devil to the side of the road and we resumed our trip to Uluru.

Our first view of a major geological formation was one that was nicknamed "the toothbrush". Actually, we were quite far away and as it came into focus, I thought at first that it was Uluru. We continued on past more featureless landscape and then finally, approached our destination. It was amazing, even from a relatively long distance. I had read many articles and reports on the way the rock changes colour as sunlight strikes it from different angles through the day. Sadly, the sky was covered with clouds, so our chances of seeing this phenomenon were slim.

Our admission to the National Park had been included in our fare and the bus passed directly through the gates, into the car park. We were informed at the entrance that the walk to the top of the rock was closed due to winds. Personally, I was pleased about this, as the Aborigines consider Uluru a sacred place and walking on it is considered a desecration of the site. Only three people in our group had wanted to go up and they didn't seem too upset that it was closed. The other thing most people do at Uluru is walk around it. Ron and the other driver gave everyone the option of staying with them for their commentary or going off on their own. Of course I stayed with them and five other people did as well.

Ron was very helpful and wheeled me around. We visited a pool, where local Aborigines came to drink and above the pool were some ancient drawings. The pictures were rudimentary but did convey the attachment of the early inhabitants with the animals to be found in the region. The Aborigines believe the world was dreamt into being by God in the "Dreamtime" and that He then put all animals on the earth as well. In Aboriginal culture, each animal in Australia has a special place and significance in relation to the spirit world.

We walked past two especially sacred areas, where cameras were not allowed. One was for women to gather and the other for men. The rock itself was a distinctive red and very smooth. It was interesting to investigate the nooks and crannies and observe how many imperfections there were. When you looked at Uluru from a distance, it seemed smooth along the rim, but it was just the opposite.

It was lunchtime and we were given an excellent boxed lunch and then trundled back onto the bus to visit our next stop, "Kata Tjuta", which used to be known as "the Olgas". These are a series of hills with valleys between them. Their colourful striations were perpendicular to the ground. We were given the chance to walk through the vicinity and Ron wanted to push me up to the "Valley of Wind". I was very appreciative and admired his tenacity, but since the ground consisted of broken rocks, I didn't think he could do it and I was concerned that I would end up with a flat tire. We stayed at Kata Tjuta for another hour and then it was time to head back to Uluru for our sunset champagne barbeque.

As I mentioned, the sun wasn't visible, so we were unable to see the changing colours of Uluru that the dusk brings. That didn't deter us from having a great time. We were the first to arrive at the picnic area that was soon overrun with tour busses, so we were able to get the prime location. For dinner, we had cold salads and condiments, while on the barbeque hamburgers and sausages (known as snags) sizzled away. The champagne was cracked open and everyone toasted our hosts and the great day we'd had together. We watched the sunset and Uluru did treat us to a bit of colour change to see us on our way.

Our bus was one of the first to leave in the darkness and we had the open road ahead of us for another six hours to settle down and get some rest. I was dropped off just after midnight and thanked the two gentlemen for their help in getting me out to Uluru. I'd always wanted to visit that spiritual sight and tonight, in my own dreamtime, I would probably relive the wonderful experience all over again.

HOTEL CHÂTEAUNEUF AND THE SHOWERS OF THE RIVIERA

As the afternoon train from Paris pulled into the train station at Cannes, I thought of all the famous movie moguls and actors who had seen the same sight of the Côte d'Azur that I was viewing now for the first time. I had wanted to visit the Mediterranean resort town of Nice, since my brother John told me how beautiful it was and of all the lovely women who populated its beach. Cannes, famous for its annual film festival, was one of the last stops on the way there. My sense of anticipation grew as I looked out at the blue-green sea and admired the boats that had spread their tall, white sails, covering the water.

My usual worry about finding suitable accommodation took over my thoughts. Normally, I try to arrive in new cities in the mornings. Early arrival maximizes my ability to find a cheap place to sleep, and it being August, all of France was on holiday in what is called "the great vacation". I was concerned that the French holidayers, coupled with backpackers like myself, would leave me wanting for a hostel. The tourist information booth was conveniently located in the station and I had no problem maneuvering through the doors and inside. I took a number and waited until it was my turn to be served. In my best high-school French, I explained that I needed a chair-friendly place to sleep and that it needed to be affordable. I wasn't too optimistic. But in no time, the tourist officer had phoned around and handed me a map with a hand-drawn circle on it. The Hotel Châteauneuf on Boulevard Châteauneuf was expecting me and had the room I needed. It didn't look too far away, was reasonably priced, included breakfast and had an elevator. What more could I ask for? I thanked her and went on my way.

The summer of 1996 was a cool one, and after my first two stops of Amsterdam and Paris in the north, it was great to be in a warm, sunny southern resort. The Riviera is the playground of the rich and famous, and a Royal family live nearby in the Principality of Monaco. I was neither, still I couldn't say I felt out of place as I wheeled along the narrow streets to find the hotel. Small cars zipped along barely stopping for traffic signals and it almost seemed mandatory to honk the horn at all times. Shop windows were filled with the most expensive wares from France, Italy, Spain and Germany. From my glances inside, there was no lack of fashionable women, poodles in tow, exercising their credit cards. After thirty minutes, I finally came to the hotel and was surprised at how nondescript it was. In North America, it would have been mistaken for a storefront. I had expected it to be separated from other buildings by a lot of space, but it was jammed between others of similar design. The Hotel Châteauneuf was a multi-floored building with a beautiful old plaster façade of a light yellow colour. The windows were high and each unit had a walkout balcony, too small for furniture. I guessed they were mostly for getting a breath of fresh air or having a cigarette. The street was typically European, noisy and narrow, I felt I could reach out and touch the buildings across the street.

The owners of the hotel greeted me with big smiles and quickly took the bag from my lap. He was late middle-aged and she seemed to be about ten years younger. They checked me in and showed me to the elevator. It was very small and I had to remove my protruding footrest to fit. The fellow couldn't come up with me, but asked me to go to the fourth floor. As I struggled to open the manual door of the lift and squeeze my way out, I was met by the hotelier who had taken the stairs. The room was surprisingly spacious for such a small hotel and had shutters in place of windows, customary in this mild climate. The bed had tube-shaped French pillows like nothing I'd slept on before and I wondered what they would be like. The entrance to the washroom presented a problem; there were two stairs and even had it been level, it wasn't wide enough for my chair. It looked like I'd be able to crawl in, so I wasn't too concerned. There was a shower in the main room, off to one side, so I knew I'd be able to get into that at least.

It was only a few blocks to the Promenade des Anglais, which runs parallel to the Mediterranean. On the north side of the boulevard, the shops and cafés were always busy. I wheeled the length of the street on the south side, which overlooked the beach. I observed that the "beach" at Nice is not a sand beach at all, it consists of a short space between the promenade above and the sea below, filled with golf-ball sized stones. Amazingly, sun worshippers were lying on their backs under tiny towels! To me, it looked like a painful way to get a tan, and it sure must have toughened up their backs, but most of them were bronzed and looked like they were happy with the trade-off.

As a single man, in my mid-thirties at the time, what interested me most was the topless aspect of the beach. I'd seen similar beaches in Australia, so it really wasn't anything new to me, but what I did notice was that the Europeans were not bashful about walking around on the beach, or on the promenade for that matter, with their tops off. In Australia, the women are generally more conservative; while they'll go topless, they will replace their tops to go to the shower, canteen or washroom. But, as the saying goes, "you have to take the good with the bad", and in Nice, there was plenty to challenge my ideal of the perfect tan. There were numerous seventy-year-old women with their tops off walking around as well. Actually, I had to hand it to them, they were confident, walked unapologetically and I think I was the only one who took any notice. Mind you, years in the sun had definitely taken a toll on their skin, but they weren't spending much time worrying about it.

I started the next day with the breakfast that was included with the room. It consisted of a wonderfully huge, almost soup bowl, of café au lait and a large portion of cheese, some piping hot, fresh rolls, butter and jam. I didn't see many other guests in the main foyer, so I ate alone, but enjoyed it immensely. The night had not been a restful one. The noise of cars on the street and the fact that I didn't have any earplugs were bad enough, but that rounded, tubular pillow was not my cup of tea. It was not flat and cushy enough for me and the height of it had given me a sore neck. By the middle of the night, I was forced to give up and retrieve a towel to fold in its place. That seemed to do the trick.

I ventured out to wheel around the town before the heat of the day made leering along the beach the thing to do. Nice is a beautiful town and has a wonderful pedestrian mall along the Boulevard Jean, where I could relax under a tree with a picnic lunch or, as I loved to do, watch the many buskers who liven up city life, earning a few francs for their efforts. One of the most popular street entertainers I'd seen in Europe that summer, was a person outfitted in gold or silver clothes, with makeup of the same colour. He or she would pretend to be a statue and could maintain a pose for a long time without moving. If you took a photo or wanted him or her to move, you'd make a donation and he or she would slowly move into a new position. There was also the usual assortment of musicians, magicians and tricksters on unicycles. I stayed to enjoy my lunch.

On the way back to the beach for the afternoon's viewing pleasure, I looked into the Casino. It was the first time I'd ever entered one and it was long before they became as ubiquitous as they are these days. The entrance was marble and the bouncers were dressed in tuxedos. I wheeled through the doors and after observing how well dressed the clientele was, started to feel a little self-conscious. After all, I was in jeans and a T-shirt and as usual for me, my hands and arms were filthy black from wheeling around. I chickened out and left, probably saving myself some francs that I couldn't afford to lose anyway.

I crossed the street in front of the Jaguars, BMWs and Porsches waiting at the red light. I found a shady tree near a shower that topless sun-bathers used to wash the sand off their bodies. I certainly wasn't in a tuxedo, but the first young girl who smiled at me, as I sheepishly looked at her from behind my sunglasses, made me feel as though I'd hit the jackpot!

SWIMMING WITH DOLPHINS IN A RUBBER CHAIR

New Zealand is a wonderfully green country and one of the reasons it's so green, is that it's further south than its neighbour, Australia. Due to the maritime climate, winds roar along and showers can occur at any time of the day. Many times these showers are brief, but temperatures cool off suddenly as the sun drops out of sight. With all this in mind, I decided to head to the far northern part of the country, which is New Zealand's resort area for holidayers trying to get away from the hustle and bustle of Auckland's busy lifestyle. The latitude is more in line with southern Australia and the weather is the best in the country.

From Auckland, I boarded a fourteen-seat Air New Zealand Link flight to the small town of Kerikeri and was met on the ground by a taxi that transported me to the main beach resort of Paihia, where I'd booked my accommodation. The elderly taxi driver was a very friendly man named Bruce and in addition to taking me to my hotel, he gave me a bit of a tour around the area. Kerikeri is known as one of the best wine growing regions in the country and it reminded me of my native Niagara Region back home in Canada. We headed south toward Paihia, and Bruce, who trained as a pilot in Calgary, Alberta prior to W.W. II, showed me some of the mangrove swamps that grow in many of the local waterways. We passed by the town of Waitangi where the "Treaty of Waitangi" was signed, ending hostilities between the Maori tribes and the English settlers, helping found the peaceful modern-day relationship between the two cultures. Today, the treaty is still very controversial, as the indigenous peoples contend that the original terms of the treaty were never met and many are now challenging the government with land claims in court. Further along, Bruce stopped the taxi on a cliff overlooking a beautiful beach that was populated only by seabirds. "As you look out across the Pacific, the next land you would be able to see from here would be Chile", he stated as a matter of fact.

I had not found a hostel in town and my accommodation in the Northland was part of a package I'd bought with my air ticket back in Auckland. The lodging was in a motor hotel, not the scruffy type that you find by the side of the road in North America. The quality standards here are surprisingly high for the price you pay, and my bedroom came as part of a suite, which included a kitchen complete with pots, plates, cutlery and a kettle, as well as a living area and a washroom. Bruce dropped me off and I thanked him for the great tour. He gave me his card and told me to call him if I needed a lift to explore some more. The hotel was about one kilometer from the main wharf of Paihia and the surrounding town, at the side of a little highway. I can't say that the road was all that busy, but the speed limit was over sixty kilometers per hour, so wheeling into town was a little scary, especially because I always wheel on the left side of the road, since my right shoulder is weak and I can let my left shoulder do most of the work. In Canada, as I wheel on the road, I'm facing traffic, which is the safest option, but in New Zealand, they drive on the left, so the traffic was speeding up from behind me, which I found quite unsettling. This, coupled with the fact that there was a bend in the highway near the hotel, meant that as I made my way home from town, drivers couldn't see me. I always made sure to stay well away from the shoulder when I got to that part of the road, and never wheeled back in the dark.

Paihia is a lovely little resort town with a beautiful harbour. Over the years, as the area has become more popular as a holiday destination, the town has increased in size and some of the larger, more modern hotels, which cater to upscale tourists, have started to spring up. The wharf, where I spent much of my time, offered lovely views of the Bay of Islands, and in the distance a series of rounded green volcanic hills seemed to sprout out of the blue waters.

I booked a ferry ride across the small bay to the little town of Russell. Though New Zealand is generally a quiet country, even up here in the Northland, Paihia can get a bit hectic with the rush of the tourist industry, to which I was contributing. Russell is a laid back community and as we approached the landing, the ferry entered a small, sheltered harbour with dozens of white-sailed yachts and boats. Some New Zealanders claim that sailing is the national sport of the country, but certainly the rugby enthusiasts would beg to differ. If any country in the world has perfect conditions for sport sailing it's this one, as their success in the America's Cup attests.

I left the dock with not much on my mind other than spending a few quiet hours and possibly enjoying a snack. The town was quite small and well kept. Some cafés were evident, as well as a post office and bank. I wheeled away from the water for a short time to see what the homes were like. In the immediate vicinity of the main street, the houses were small, some with white fences and lovely gardens. As I rode by, an elderly lady greeted me as she stooped to weed her garden and commented on what a nice day it was. I came upon a small museum maintained by the local historical society. It was free, so I hopped up the short step and went inside.

The building held a number of artifacts of the town's long naval history. Russell used to be the location of a fort where the local British governor resided. An old wooden steering wheel from a naval vessel, and other maritime objects, were displayed. There was an interesting exhibit of photographs and the story of how the local Maori chief hated the British flag. At every opportunity, the chief would chop down the wooden flagpole and confiscate the flag. This continued for some years until the governor sent a request to Britain for a metal flagpole. Once this was erected, the Maori leader finally gave up and a lasting peace prevailed.

Returning to Paihia, I checked the forecast for the following day and learned that good weather was expected. I booked my Dolphin Discovery tour for the next day. The trip was billed as an opportunity to "swim with the dolphins", and although I can't swim, it sure sounded interesting. I'd be happy just for the chance to see a dolphin up close in the wild for the first time in my life.

I rose early the next morning and brewed a cup of tea with the supplied kettle. I dressed warmly and in a rainproof jacket, owing to my experience with New Zealand's weather. I pushed back to the pier, purchasing an egg and tomato roll for breakfast along the way. There was another, more expensive, tour I could have chosen, which went further out to an island with a natural bridge called "Hole in the Rock". The boat would sail right through the hole but I've always been a nature lover and for me, seeing some aquatic wildlife would suffice.

Boarding the boat was no problem as they had a large ramp onto the deck. The seats onboard rapidly filled up and we were soon pulling away from the calm morning waters of the bay at Paihia. We began the tour of the Bay of Islands by navigating past Russell, where I'd been the previous day, and then continued into the open waters in the direction of the "Hole in the Rock". As we moved out of the bay, the waves of the open South Pacific began to roll the ship gently. The green countryside of New Zealand, which has most recently been seen in films such as *Lord of the Rings,* looked like a carpeted golf course as it faded into the distance. We were having no luck finding any dolphins to cavort with, even though all the tour boats are in radio communication with each other. If one boat spots a school of dolphins, they will alert the fleet. This benefits all the tourists and it gets the word out that if you book one of these tours, you will likely see what you're looking for. The promotional literature indicated that the success rate was well over eighty-five percent, which is quite good.

Having not seen any wildlife other than some birds, we stopped for lunch on one of the islands. A middle-aged couple asked me if I wanted anything from the canteen, which was up a large hill from the pier. I asked if they could pick me up a cup of coffee, and when they returned, they also brought me a scone with jam and cream, and insisted that it was their treat. That was very nice. We chatted for some time and it turned out that the two of them had been to Canada a number of years previously and had taken a train across the country, through the Rocky Mountains.

We boarded the boat again in search of dolphins and each of us tried to keep our eyes peeled for anything jumping out of the water in the distance. After about another hour, word came over the radio that dolphins had been spotted. We turned ninety degrees to port and made our way to meet them. At the same time, interested guests were assembling at the stern to put on their wetsuits for their attempt at swimming with the dolphins. We finally spotted about eight of them and it was quite amazing how playful they were. The bottlenose dolphins came right up alongside the hull and I was able to get some relatively good footage of them with my camcorder, despite all the churning and jerking of the waves.

The swimmers took the opportunity to jump into the water with the mammals, but just as they did, it seemed the dolphins had other ideas and decided to take leave of us. I felt sorry for those who'd jumped in after all the waiting and I could see that it was very important to them. I know that swimming with the dolphins has proved to be an effective medical treatment for autistic and withdrawn children and these people were hoping for that type of extra special experience. Interestingly, not one of them seemed displeased and one said that she had been able to touch a dolphin. The crewmates were insistent that on many occasions the dolphins will stop and play for up to ten minutes with people in the water.

Still, there were smiles all around that afternoon, and as the dolphins sped off into the distance, we knew we'd shared a very special moment with one of the most intelligent animals on our planet, one that would forever change our relationship with the Pacific.

PACHAMAMA—THE MOTHER EARTH

I had always dreaded going to South America, but I'm not really sure why. It was probably a combination of the fact that I had always been very bad at learning languages and I knew almost nothing of Spanish, as well as the fact that if I went, I would be in a non-English environment for quite a long time. Despite these misgivings, however misguided they were, I finally decided to escape the winter of 2005 and make my way to the continent

I had tried to locate a backpacker's hostel in Santiago, Chile that would be wheelchair friendly, but without success. Finally, one of the hostels emailed me that I could try out their facility. They mentioned that they had a few stairs to get into the hostel but that once inside I would have no problems with the flat layout. I had no other options and they seemed enthusiastic to help so after an 11 hour flight and my first glimpse of the Andes from the airplane, I left the terminal and emerged to 32C temperatures and scrambled into a mini-van (with much help) to find La Casa Roja hostel.

The hostel was just as advertised, and although it was a bit of a bother getting used to finding someone to help me up the first few stairs. The lady in the hostel's travel agency, Susi, a friendly German woman, who always greeted me with a kiss, came to an arrangement with the parking lot attendants next door, that I could go and ask them for help and they would go up the stairs and buzz for help. The inside was completely flat and the wooden floorboards creaked as the blue chair glided over them. The washroom stalls were just wide enough to use but the showers had a step up to them. I would be using my facecloth for my first hostel visit in S. America.

My dorm roommates were quite friendly, including Sarah, a pretty blonde Englishwoman who had just arrived after impressively trekking the largest mountain in South America. By the evening two of the guys asked me if I wanted to go out with them for supper and a bit of drinking. It sounded good to me. We didn't get far. The hostel is located in Barrio Brasil, a bohemian neighbourhood in Santiago with a wonderful park that many families enjoyed. As evening fell, the temperature started to drop and a bit of a breeze came up. We settled on an outdoor restaurant and ordered a few one-litre Escudo beers to go along with our huge plate of chicken and potatoes. It had been a long day of travel but I had made it, after dinner I asked them to help me home as I was in no condition to drive the chair back. They continued on to hit some other bars, but I needed to finally get a good night's sleep.

The next day in the afternoon, I met an Italian couple Stefano and Elize, who were spending their honeymoon money on a trip around the world. We went out to dinner that evening with Richard, one of the guys from the night before, and headed to a posh steakhouse only one block from the hostel. The meal, a huge steak fillet, was fantastic and the price including beverages came to only $7. At the end of the meal the restaurant even gave us complementary after dinner drinks. We meandered out of the restaurant back to the hostel as they were having a slide show of Chile offered by the hostel tour company.

We were a bit late getting to the slide show but it had wonderful pictures of some of the magnificent Chilean countryside and Pacific coast to the south of the capital. They also were offering free samples of the national drink of Chile, pisco sour. After my dinner drinking and a few of these potent samples, the tour guide, Jorge, a friendly guy with long hair and a beard, asked me if I was going on the trip to the south with him tomorrow? I gave him a puzzled look and said that bus companies never want a guy in a chair to go with them, due to all the bother of lifting me on and off the bus. He shook his head, waved his hand and smiled that it would be no problem and that he and the bus driver could get me in and out of the van and up the stairs at the hostels we visited. I didn't need any convincing and so I quickly decided to head south the next day with the guys from Pachamama Tours.

We were meant to drive off at 9:00 am. however, as with most S. American appointments, times are very flexible. We ultimately departed an hour late, but it gave me a chance to meet some of the other travelers that would be on the seven-day trip. Sara, a Swedish girl, who had arrived recently from traveling through New Zealand and would still be backpacking for another four months until hitting Brazil, Valentina, a pretty Italian/German girl on holiday from studies and Greg, an older Aussie who was also an experienced hiker, having voyaged through South East Asia and many other parts of the world. Jorge and Jaime, the driver, struggled to lift me into the front seat of the van as I half stood out of my chair allowing Jorge to grab me under my shoulders, while Jaime pushed my legs straight up. The final goal of the whole process was to get my bum up on the seat. It was rough the first time, but we made it! With a wave goodbye to Jorge's father, who had come to see us off, we escaped Santiago's heat and polluted air for the Pacific Coast.

Pichelemu a relatively short two hour drive to the west was to be our first stop. This was my first foreign bus tour and along the way we briefly stopped in the small town of Pomaire to have breakfast and do some shopping. I nipped into a restaurant for a café con lecce (with milk) and an empanada, which is a flaky turnover filled with either cheese (queso) or meat (carne). I was soon joined by the rest of the group and we shared some of the empanadas. It was a great way to meet with the new group that would be my friends for the next week.

As we drove down to the coast through the artificially planted pine forests that resembled northern Canada, it was not long before the Pacific Ocean finally came into view. The town itself was really not much to write home about, but we stopped off at our hostel, which was only one block from the beach and were greeted by our host, Mauricio, or Maurice as he liked to be called. The hostel was not chair friendly as there was a long open air hall with a series of single steps, leading to a courtyard and our rooms. We entered the room to see four beds crammed together and barely enough room to add the blue chair and close the door. My roomies, Andy, Chris and Greg, two Englishmen and an Aussie, respectively, quickly located their beds and laughed at the fact that they all had various problems, ranging from terrible sags in the middle to mine, which was higher on one side and left me rolling into the wall at times. There were no windows for circulation and we worried about making an escape should the need arise.

Following a trip to the beach to watch some of the boys try their hand at surfing, we gathered around dusk for a trip to Punta de Lobos for the magnificent views of the ocean. It was meant to be a sunset trip, but the clouds had gathered and it was looking like rain, but it was very serene for me just the same. We boarded the bus after an hour of seaside meditation and headed back to the hostel for a Chilean BBQ and some refreshment. I had brought with me a box of cheap red wine called Gato Negro, which I was anxious to use up and not carry around anymore. After returning from the stores, Sara, the Swedish backpacker, who always had a wonderful smile on her face, showed me the box of cheap wine she had bought. We exchanged samples of our vintages and both decided that mine was the better of the two. As a result, Sara sat down beside me at dinner and proceeded to drink most of my wine, while we enjoyed huge quantities of grilled beef, pork, sausages and chicken. Along with the wonderful conversation and the friendly wife of Maurice, named Gloria, kept grabbing my chair and trying to get me to dancing. Unfortunately, I have four left wheels and I also had to politely rebuff her attempts at inviting me to the back of the hostel to smoke some of the local vegetation.

The next morning, Jorge and Jaime were quite helpful and happily lifted me out of the chair and into the narrow washroom stall to sit me on the toilet for ten minutes. My left arm and the faces of my roommates were red from the mosquito bites. Chris had an allergic reaction to them and was to be ill for the rest of the week. Sara told me that her box of wine was still almost full and asked if she should bring it along to our next stop. I told her to forget it and we would look forward to some better wines somewhere down the long road of the Pan American highway that we would be traveling on. We drove for seven hours to Pucon and along the way we stopped at Temuco to pick up two girls, Isobel from the U.K and Ana from Switzerland.

It was nearly dusk and we were all completely pooped when we finally arrived in Chile's famous Lakes Region and the Germanic looking tourist town of Pucon. Our first look at the Villarica volcano, which dominated the horizon, was magnificent. I had never seen an active volcano before and in the late evening sunshine, the height of the snowcapped peak, coupled with the smoke coming out of the volcanic cone, made for quite a sight and we were all impressed. Our hostels were all spread out for this stop. I was in the main hostel, which was over booked, and had my own room with a huge double bed. The toilet was accessible but again, there was a step up to my room and then a step up to the washroom. The guys on the trip were in a sister hostel and the girls stayed with our host's grandparents. It was quite cute because that night when the girls came home late, the grandfather was still up, waiting for them until they arrived safe and sound. We toured around the town a little, which was very much geared to the tourist trade, but the Tudor houses seemed out of step with what one would expect from South America. The others booked their trip up the mountain for the following day and then we all retired to a restaurant on the main street for some Chilean cuisine and beer. I had a pasta dish and the meal was accompanied by a duet playing some folk songs well into the evening.

The next day brought some foul weather and I really felt sorry for my companions who had left early for the volcano top. I had given my camera to Greg, the shutterbug of the group, in the hopes that he would take some nice pictures of the lava bubbling out of the peak. I probably should have given him my camcorder as well, but I had hoped to go on a lake cruise, which was all but impossible in the cool, damp weather. As I wheeled along the main street to find some coffee, I bumped into Valentina from our group. She had developed a problem with her foot and the guide suggested to her that it would likely be too difficult for her to make the trip up. Bad luck for her, but good fortune for me, as I now had someone to spend the day with and after a long search, we finally found a café for our morning drink and some croissants. On the way back to the hostel, I was almost attacked by an angry, barking dog that came within one foot of me. Valentina was very calm and tried to talk to the dog, while I froze. I knew that I couldn't get away, and being in a chair meant that I was right at biting level for a big dog. Finally, after a few minutes a shopkeeper came out and chased the still barking pooch around the corner and down the street. We took no chances and waited patiently until the canine was long gone before resuming our trip back to the hostel.

After touring the lake in the dreary weather, Jaime, Jorge, Valentina and I headed over to the hostel where the guys on our bus were staying. The atmosphere was great, and it reminded me of a wooden cabin or cottage out in the northern bush back home. We were joined by Luis, a Portuguese backpacker, who absolutely loved Canada, and had brought his guitar. We spent a pleasant afternoon listening to tunes and sipping some drinks. Quite a relaxing day really, other than the upset hound we had previously encountered. After a delicious dinner in the best vegetarian restaurant in Pucon with my companion Valentina, it was time to finally retire back at my hostel for a siesta and Jorge assured me that he would fetch me after the gang had returned from the thermal hot springs they were due to go to after their return from the volcano. I was unable to go since there was about a hundred steps down into the pool. Ultimately, nobody ever did come for me and at the time I was rather put off by it, but I later found out there was no party, since they were all so tired due to the strenuous climb earlier in the day, that on their return to the hostel, they all went directly to bed.

Another day brought another trip down the Pan American highway. Actually, for me it was quite an enjoyable experience due to the fact that in 1988, my buddy Bill and I had been on the same highway at the other end, in Alaska. This end of the highway was a tad warmer and as we continued along the way, stands by the side of the road advertised a drink called "Mote con Huesillo", which was a peach drink with corn niblets on the bottom. I never tried it but I was told that it was quite refreshing. We stopped to eat some more empanadas at Calafquen Lake, and I told Sara that it reminded me of New Zealand with the wonderful green hills nearby. There were a few Chileans swimming in the water and arriving to picnic. After another stop at Lake Panguipulli, we finally arrived at Valdivia, which Jorge, the guide, felt was one of the most beautiful cities in Chile.

The hostel, while quite beautiful, was of course up another huge flight of stairs. The one good thing was that the boys and I had our own ensuite washroom but the bad side was that I was again unable to get in to use it. Not a big problem with a little help from my friends. After dinner together at a seafood restaurant, where I inadvertently caused the waitress to drop some drinks (note to self: the next time Jorge says to move—do not backup!), we had to decide what to do with the rest of our day. My aim was to take the river cruise that went down to the Botanical Gardens. Jorge and I were able to get a ticket onto the boat, after taking time to watch some sea lions which enjoyed lazing along the side of the wharf, but when I took a look at the long, skinny walkway and the narrow metal doorway that led onto the boat, I decided to get a refund. Oh well, I had tried. But as they say, things happen for a reason, so I decided to hang around with some of the gang that wanted to go to the beach.

It was always nice to have another opportunity to view the Pacific and the little beach was sheltered inside a small bay. There were a great number of Chilean families enjoying their summer holidays and the candy floss salesman beside me was doing brisk business. It had been a long sandy wheel to a cement platform that overlooked the surf, but together Jorge and Jaime got me there. They always did, and they always did it with a smile, never making me feel like I was a bother, more like a brother. In fact I was calling the two of them my "Chileno hermados" or brothers by the end of the trip.

As the sunset fell over the waters the winds began to pick up and the cool evening breeze made us think of heading back to the hostel. As we made our way back to the van, Jorge talked to another beachcomber who told us of a local folk concert just up the road. We polled the group and everyone agreed that we should check it out.

It was a modest folk fair, but I think that is what really made it so pleasantly quaint. I took the opportunity to pay the 100 pesos required for a pee and it was a great relief. But it was also time to refresh, and so I bought Jorge and Jaime a beer as a reward for their help all day. The stage was quite large and we made our way up to the front. It wasn't long before I took the opportunity to retrieve the first bottle of a local homebrew derived from apples called "chicha'. Actually, the drink was very tasty and only mildly alcoholic. The performers were a local Chilean band and some people from the audience were encouraged to come onto the stage to perform the local dances. It was great to see all the children playing near the stage and dancing to the tunes. I was reminded of my own childhood and all the Croatian folk festivals I used to attend with my family. I asked Jaime if he wouldn't mind getting me one of the tasty looking skewers that had beef, lamb and veggies on it. Soon a band from Argentina came on stage and their brand of music was really energetic and upbeat. Both Sara and I took the opportunity to buy one of their CDs to take home. By the time Sara had bought the group's last bottle of "chicha", Valentina, Andy, Chris, Jorge, Jaime and I were feeling quite mellow while we listened to the wonderful South American rhythms as the moon glowed overhead. On reflection, I was really happy that the blue chair didn't fit onto the boat after all.

The following day it was onto Puerto Montt. Chile is one of the most seismically active countries in the world and a major earthquake in 1960 destroyed most of the port. We roamed along the shops and I took the opportunity to purchase some gifts. I don't usually buy souvenirs early on a backpacking trip as I hate lugging them around for the rest of the trip, but these were knitted wares and would be light enough to carry with me. We lunched at the wharf in a tiny restaurant that our group, and especially my chair had a hard time fitting into. I tried an oyster soup along with a salmon steak and they were both awesome. After the meal it was on to Puerto Varas and the most inaccessible hostel yet. I just told Jorge that I would only go up the steep flight of stairs in the evening on the way to bed. In the meantime I needed to find a washroom and luckily the local casino was nearby. The casino had the best washroom I had been in so far in Chile, which was really not too difficult to beat on this continent. After touring around the town, which offered a magnificent view of another volcano and going shopping with Valentina for some earrings and rings, it was time to say goodbye to Sara. Sara was headed for Ecuador and at the bar we toasted her with a whisky and walked down to the bus station to see her off. We had reached the furthest point south we were to go and were near the end of the Pan American Highway, over the bridge on the island of Chiloe. In the morning we left my buddy, Andy, the happy British geologist from Cambridge, who was remaining to tour the National Parks in Patagonia, as well as Isobel, also from the UK, and Ana from Switzerland, who was off to work at an organic farm.

One of the worst things about backpacking is leaving friends behind, or watching them go forward. But meeting other travelers is also one of the best things about roaming the world. For a brief moment they are the most important people in your life, in a way they are family when your own is so far away. You share meals, drinks, laughs, experiences, and sights with them and then in an instant, they are gone. I always try to keep in touch but sometimes the stretch of time and distance exacts a huge toll on a once important friendship.

I have often felt that if everyone in the world had an opportunity to backpack and meet people from other countries and cultures we would live in a far better world. A short time earlier we were strangers and now we were friends, I am not sure if it was Chile, the long highway drive or all the "chicha" but I knew the trip north back to Santiago would somehow feel a little longer without them.

GLOBAL WARMING IN THE YUKON AND FOLLOWING OUR WAY TO ALASKA

One of the things you have to deal with in Southern Ontario is the summer heat and humidity. To those not familiar with Canadian weather, it may sound like a strange thing to say, but by mid-July through to the start of September, the warm and humid Caribbean winds come as far north as the Great Lakes, leaving people used to more temperate climes to deal with temperatures over 30°C and 95% humidity. Most summers we're able to bear it admirably, when freshening Arctic winds from the north lead to late afternoon thunderstorms, making for a comfortable night's sleep.

The summer of 1988 was atypical. A brown, thermal-inversion haze made our little part of the world look like a smog-filled freeway in Los Angeles. You couldn't see the sun properly with all the pollution in the air. My friend Bill, a big fellow with a cane, whom I'd known for a number of years from my wheelchair basketball team, and I decided we could take no more of it. We planned an escape to the Yukon Territory in Canada's northwest. It turned out to be the first far-flung adventure of my life.

Bill was an experienced traveller. Growing up in Toronto, he decided to go out West to make his fortune, but in the end, fortune got the better of him. He was working as a logger in the interior of British Columbia, when his car rolled in a traffic accident. His back was broken and his career as a lumberjack was over, but his life in wheelchair basketball was about to begin—following a long period of convalescence back in Ontario. He had regained much of the use of his legs, but still favoured one and used a cane. Bill and I had served on the executive for disabled sports in Niagara, where he was assigned by his club to help promote wheelchair sports. Over the years, despite Bill being fifteen years my senior, we had struck up a friendship, I think because of our similar wry sense of humour and some common interests outside sports. In any event, we hastily planned a trip to Whitehorse and on the way back we would hook up with an old friend of his on a stopover in Vancouver.

The flight left Toronto and as we glided above the metropolis, I will never forget leaving the pollution bubble behind and seeing blue air and a yellow sun for the first time in three weeks. I wondered what we would find in the Yukon, and what two relatively immobile tourists would be able to do there. There was no direct flight to the Yukon, so we had to make a connection in British Columbia. As I looked out the aircraft window, the flat, featureless Prairies, with their patchwork colours of grain fields, slowly gave way to Alberta's foothills and then the spectacular Rocky Mountains. With their cragged, gray faces and snow-capped peaks, the Rockies seemed so incongruous with the northern summer. As we continued, the green valley of the Okanagan and lush temperate rainforests clothed the landscape. We had concluded the first leg of the trip.

When we disembarked in Vancouver, there was no tube to meet the door of the aircraft. Instead, we were met with a mobile flight of stairs for passengers to walk across the runway. I had no idea how they planned to get me off. As the plane emptied, Bill and I were assured that someone would help us to disembark. Shortly, airport personnel drove up in a forklift with my chair on it, and we disembarked through the back door. I'm happy to say this practice has changed and is not the procedure anymore, but it made me wonder how they would manage getting us off the plane in Whitehorse! For now, that was a small concern as a cool, pleasant breeze, with a decidedly dry moisture content, greeted us as we made our way across the tarmac and into the terminal.

The second flight was along Canada's Pacific coastline and, as we prepared to land in the Klondike, the green conifer forests made us feel we were in a remote part of the world, one that harkened back to a bygone era. Unlike our earlier ride, disembarking in Whitehorse was more traditional, and the airport seemed to be brand new and sparkling clean. We were both impressed.

Our arrangements for accommodation had been a bit sketchy from our point of departure back home. We relied on the Yukon tourist office to provide us with brochures, hoping to find something suitable for our needs and within our limited budgets. We rang some of the hotels, but most said they couldn't provide large washrooms or ground access. As our exasperation grew, we finally happened upon a small place with friendly voices that mentioned other disabled guests had stayed there in the past and were quite satisfied. "Were there stairs?" we enquired. "A few", was the reply, but we were instructed not to worry as they had staff that would be more than willing to help us up them. We were suspicious, but had no other options, so we made the booking.

On arrival, a taxi brought us to the small, weather-beaten hotel a few blocks away from the centre of town and it seemed to have chair access from the outside. Once we entered the rustic lobby, we saw the few stairs and asked about arrangements for negotiating them. In the lounge were the skulls and antlers of two moose that a pilot had witnessed standing motionless, locked together in a field one autumn afternoon. The pilot reckoned that they were stuck and the hapless pair could not extricate themselves from their deadly embrace. The next spring, he flew over the same field and retrieved the heads. They had starved to death and looking at the antlers, there was no way of separating them, unless a prong was broken. The owner called out to the dining room, and two burly Native Canadians appeared and lifted my chair onto the landing. We had made it to Whitehorse.

Our first task, after checking out the hotel, was to rent a car. We went just a few blocks and hired ourselves a four-wheel drive vehicle, which is essential in the Canadian north. The truck had a thick metal bar in front of the headlights, designed to combat animals we might strike on the road. In addition, there was a large Plexiglas shield to protect our headlights and grill from impact with stones and rocks thrown up from unpaved roads. There was also a "plug-in" extension cord for an engine block heater that had been installed to keep the oil liquid when the temperatures drop below-25°C in wintertime. Most public parking spaces in the north have poles in the ground with electrical outlets, so if you go in to shop, you can plug in the car so it won't freeze up by the time you return. Getting into the vehicle, I tried to stand up in my leg braces, but I was wobbly and have always had a dreadful feel for balance. Bill hung his cane on the car door and did his best to help lift me up the extra six inches so my bum would reach the passenger seat. We started laughing and I barely fell into the seat, before he grabbed the door to prevent himself from tumbling backwards onto the ground. We must've looked a funny sight, the two of us gimping along and struggling to board the truck. But we had succeeded and were now mobile. A beer was next on the agenda.

After touring around Whitehorse, which is actually a very small town of just under 20,000 people, and crossing over the Yukon river, we decided it was time to grab a meal and a drink. The evening was getting on towards 10 p.m., but in the land of the midnight sun, the shadows were only now starting to lengthen. The evening was cool, but not cold and we found a tavern that offered value meals with home cooking. As we sat at our table watching a baseball game, we ordered our dinner and beer. Before long, we began planning the rest of the week, and Bill thought one thing we should do was drive over the Rockies to Alaska. Since the vehicle didn't have hand controls, it was OK with me, as long as I wasn't the one doing the driving. He had always wanted to do it and assured me it would be a good time. Our trip would end up at Skagway, which is a stop for many of the cruise ships that ply the coastal waters on their way to glacier and whale watching tours. As we finished our meal, we began to smile at each other as we listened to a conversation between two old-timers at the bar. "Can't stand all this global warming!" complained the first, "Yeah, damn near never gets down to -70C anymore", agreed the second. Bill and I shook our heads at each other. We were definitely in a different world.

Following a few days of touring around the environs of greater Whitehorse (and enjoying the paved parking lot at the IGA, which a full-paged ad in the local paper, the *Star*, implored us to do) we decided it was time to head out across the mountains to the U.S.. Our route took us south of Whitehorse along the Alaska Highway, which was paved, but still had a lot of loose gravel on it. Marmots peered from their burrows along the way as we drove through a forest of fir trees. We then veered to the southwest and into Carcross, which is short for "Caribou Crossing", touted as the northernmost sand desert in the world. I must confess, I can't recall how this feature came to be at this latitude, but we did stop for a while to read the historical plaques and it was quite amazing.

Continuing along the highway, as we began to ascend into the mountains, we stopped again by the side of the road to view the magnificent Emerald Lake, the water of which is exactly the hue of emerald green, and is attributed to its clear glacial qualities. We passed Kluane National Park, which takes up the whole of the southwest of the Yukon Territory, and the highway diverts around it. As a result, upon passing the park, we entered the northern fringe of British Columbia. Unfortunately, here the road takes a turn for the worse and is unpaved due to the fact that it really only serves as a link between Alaska and the Yukon, so B.C. spends little to maintain it. As luck would have it, the area had torrential rains the week prior to our arrival and the mud was very slippery, making the truck skid dangerously close to the edge of the mountains. There were no guardrails and as we finally rose above the tree line, the fog-shrouded mountaintops looked like the moon.

We crawled along at thirty kilometers an hour and it was all Bill could do to maintain control. Amazingly, even at this snail's pace, we caught up to a small car with Québec license plates. Believing there was safety in numbers, we decided to go even slower and follow him along in a sort of makeshift convoy. As we finally made the summit and then descended out of the fog, we were pleased to finally cross the border into Alaska. Unusually, as we crossed a national frontier, there was no customs installation. We assumed that since we were rounding a mountainside and there was no place to go but over the edge, it was deemed satisfactory by the Americans to wait until the traveller was closer to Skagway. One great thing was that we were back on pavement, and our French leader had picked up speed. We reached U.S. Immigration and the man in front of us was asked to get out of his car by the customs agent. He was falling down drunk! Bill and I laughed out loud. The guy had survived certain death and so had we. Perhaps he felt he could only have made the trip while under the influence.

The guard was friendly and suggested that we pause at a rest stop ahead to view the local train that travels over a narrow gauge track across the valley. We took him up on his offer and saw a small five-car tourist train crawling along the side of the opposite hill. We observed a small ladder under the track and alongside the edge of the mountainside, and wondered what maniac would use it and for what purpose.

We had finally made it to picturesque Skagway, a small touristy town that caters to the affluent travel set. After driving through its scenic streets and enjoying the magnificent vista of the harbour, with spectacular mountains as a backdrop, we settled on an outdoor café. After enjoying a leisurely dinner and dessert we decided to have coffee with our meal. It was going to be a long drive back to Canada later that day, but this time, we knew what to expect. We decided beer wasn't in the equation.

MAKING LOVE ON THE REEF

Scientists say there is only one living thing visible from space and that is the Great Barrier Reef. On my first visit to Australia, I spent all my time along the east coast of the country. The city of Cairns in the far north of Queensland was my jumping-off point for a memorable excursion to this unique living biological resource.

I arrived on a flight from Sydney and though the weather in New South Wales had been quite nice, there's something special when I land in a tropical part of the world. Ever since my first trip to Florida as an adolescent, there's been a warm place in my heart for palm trees and flowers that seem to be in constant bloom. I was pleased that the taxi rank outside the small airport was filled with neat, small mini-vans, designed to accommodate wheelchairs as well as walking passengers. The drivers were all in clean white uniforms and upon seeing me, the first van in line made a quick move toward me with a smile and the driver quickly took my bag off my lap. I was impressed. He opened the back doors of the van and an automated lift unfolded. After wheeling me in, my chair was tied to the floor with straps and we were soon off to the hostel.

The YHA hostel was a renovated motel with two stories. I'd booked a single room, deciding to splurge a little and have a bit of privacy during my stay. The hostel was situated four blocks from the waterfront and the Esplanade, which is where all the action is. I was unable to gain access into the hostel's office, since it was in a small building in front of the motel and was up about five stairs. I simply waved at the front desk and a young girl came out to take my credit card and register me. There was a small step up from the parking lot, but a small ramp had been built near the washroom. I didn't use it, as the step was so small near my room, I could easily negotiate it on my own. The washroom was off the laundry, which they gave me a key for, and had a second, steeper wooden ramp into it. The toilet itself contained a roll-in shower and was excellent. Nearby, could be found a kitchen, some vending machines and picnic tables. In front of the kitchen was a small pool with a large wire fence around it.

After checking in and enjoying a brief rest, it was time to head into town to see what it looked like and what tours were offered. The town of Cairns is actually quite flat and if you're wheeling yourself in a blue chair, that's good news. I spent the afternoon checking out the pubs and restaurants, gliding along the main tourist thoroughfare, known as the Esplanade, and wheeling out to the large wharf that housed the tour boats, which made daily excursions out to the Great Barrier Reef. The problem I was going to have was determining which one to take. The wharf was also very popular with local and tourist fisherman. As it turned out, I ended up spending almost every evening out on the wharf, sitting under the starry Southern Cross, watching anglers try to catch anything from octopi to small sharks.

The next day, I returned to the wharf and visited the tour booking office. I informed the woman working there that I was interested in a trip out to the reef and wondered which she thought would best suit someone in a chair. I indicated that I was not a swimmer, and as such, was not interested in snorkelling. She made a few calls and then suggested a trip on the Ocean Spirit, heading out to Michealmas Cay, one of the string of islands dotted along the reef in the offshore waters. She informed me that this particular tour company used catamarans to explore the reef and that the crafts had wide spaces on deck and the smoothest ride on the Coral Sea. She said they were eager to help me on and off the boat. Since I'd already checked the weather forecast for the next day and it was expected to be sunny and fine, I booked the trip immediately. Tomorrow I would be off to visit the Great Barrier Reef!

Back at the hostel, I'd already stopped by the store to purchase some groceries and decided it was time to think about preparing supper. One of the easiest and favourite meals for me to prepare is spaghetti. The stoves at the hostel were gas and had to be lit with matchsticks. I was having a devil of a time with the darn things, but luckily for me, some lovely damsels came to my rescue and helped me get my water boiling. After making the meal, I joined the ladies at the table to talk about Cairns and our various backpacking trips so far. This is one of the best things about travelling around, meeting people and swapping travel stories. Two of the girls were Canadian. Cathy from Kingston and Chantal from Ottawa were travelling together, while the third was Paula from County Cork in Ireland. After dinner, we decided to head out into the night on a pub-crawl. We moved from bar to bar and noticed that the quality of taverns was quite varied. Some were upscale and catered only to tourists, while others were less formal and were patronized by either white locals or by Aborigines. After a few hours of this, we settled on the pub two doors down from the hostel. The place was clean and well lit and the bar itself consisted of a huge wooden carving of a crocodile. At the end of the bar was the crocodile's head with its mouth wide open. I asked one of the girls to take a photo of me with my head in its jaws. It was quite hokey, but we all had a good laugh as we drank down another pint of Queensland's "XXXX" brand lager.

The next morning was bright and sunny, a perfect day to go sailing. After eating a toasted cheese sandwich and having a coffee, I went down to the pier to find my catamaran and my place on the boat. I was the first person to arrive and I asked one of the deckhands to whom I should talk. He pointed to a young lady on the staff and she mentioned that they were still cleaning the boat and doing routine maintenance. When it was time to board, two of the crew hauled me up the steps and a third brought on my chair. I liked the boat. It seemed to be gleaming and new and, as advertised, it was very spacious on deck. If the sun got too hot, there was shade as well. The only problem was going to be going to the washroom, so I would try to limit my fluid intake during the day. If I drank some water or juice that would be OK as my body would use it to rehydrate. The two things I had to stay away from were beer and coffee. If I drank either of those, it would mean big trouble later in the voyage.

As the deck began to fill, I settled on a spot along the rail where I could watch the sea drift by. Before long, we were off to the Reef. It was to take about two hours to get out there, even at top speed. During the voyage we were offered fresh fruit and drinks and asked what activities we wanted to do. Those interested in scuba diving and who had their licenses were grouped together for a briefing on safety and what to do and not to do on the reef. The Great Barrier Reef is a national park in Australia and it's strictly prohibited to touch or take any of the coral. The reef is a living thing and it's important to respect that. Others were going to go snorkelling once we arrived at the Cay, so they were handed their gear and everyone was busy putting on their SPF 30 sunscreen, which is very important at this latitude.

One of the crew asked me what I wanted to do and I told him I couldn't swim so I'd just watch the reef and the fish. He suggested that they could get me out onto the semi-submersible boat so I could go down into its hull and look at the fish and coral for myself. I was enthusiastic and if they thought that they could get me on it, I was game. The semi-submersible was popular with the older crowd and those of us who are not water babies.

As we sailed out on the Coral Sea, I imagined what Captain Cook must have felt when he became one of the first Europeans to see these waters so long ago. The turquoise waves shimmered and sparkled like diamonds as we finally sighted the sandy outcropping that was Michaelmas Cay. The island was barren and had very little vegetation, but was home to numerous species of birds and waterfowl. Apparently it was of huge interest to scientists studying how bird droppings contribute to the introduction of plant species to virgin lands. We stopped the catamaran a short distance from the island and a smaller boat was used to ferry passengers to the semi-submersible or to various locations for scuba diving, snorkelling or just lounging on the beach.

I was again hoisted by two crewmates out of my chair and down the stairs onto the little boat. I was a bit concerned about boarding the semi-submersible, but they were able to straddle alongside and pass me over. It was a steep descent into the hull, and I was placed on a bench before a very large window. After the ship was filled, we headed out onto the reef to dive to a lower depth. The top of the boat remained above the waterline, but as we slowly propelled through the depths, a whole new world of aquatic wildlife opened up. A crewmate was able to identify most of the species we saw. There were various types of coral of course: staghorn coral, brain coral that looked like its namesake, as well as plate coral and more. I was surprised to learn that the coral is protected because it's easily damaged and one inch of coral can take up to a century to grow in some species. We were told this was an interesting time to be on the reef because it was a full moon and the time was right, so many of the coral species were spawning and there was a lot of coral lovemaking going on.

The colours of the fish we saw were amazing. There was a wide variety of species including parrotfish, angelfish, butterfly fish, and an assortment of groupers. The crowd favourite was a huge fish that looked like it could easily make a meal out of all the others. It was called a Maori Wrasse and seemed to be a gentle giant amongst the legion of dwarfs. The animal seemed to have a bulbous forehead and each centimeter of his body appeared to be a slightly different colour. For me, it offered a taste of what divers and snorkellers are able to see underwater, and it was quite thrilling.

At the conclusion of our fantastic voyage, I was escorted onto the shore of the Cay and left to enjoy the afternoon sunshine on our exotic oasis in the middle of the Sea. I relaxed and sank my toes into the hot, white sand while little children played in shallow pools and snorkellers continued their search for even more exotic types of fish and coral a few yards offshore.

As the afternoon wore on, we were inevitably reminded that our time here was growing to a close. We gathered our effects and were asked to ensure the area was left in as pristine a state as it had been when we arrived. We gathered again on the deck of the catamaran for snacks and champagne. We slowly picked up speed and left our little paradise far behind. The sun slowly drifted to the horizon ahead of us as we headed back to Cairns. The crew entertained us with comedy skits and impromptu music. As we finally approached land and got our first sight of town, a Rod Stewart tune about sailing lilted over the music system on board.

It'd been a wonderful day and now it was sadly coming to a close. I hoped that someday I would return and once again explore the mysterious world of the Great Barrier Reef now that I'd seen it in person after all those years of dreaming about it.

STUCK IN THE GRAVEL BY THE SIDE OF THE ROAD

As a Canadian kid growing up in a family with parents who were Croatian immigrants, it was a dream of mine to someday visit that country to see some of the places I'd spent a lifetime hearing about and meet my relatives to put faces and personalities with the names in family stories.

While travelling on a Eurail pass in 1996, I told my mom I was thinking about visiting Croatia, since I'd be in Central Europe anyway. I have to admit that I was apprehensive, since I knew that Western Europe would be fine for my chair, but Eastern Europe would be an entirely different matter. I was thrilled to hear, three months before leaving, that my mom was going to spend six weeks in Croatia visiting her relatives in the tiny village where she was born. That clinched it. With her to show me around, help with my broken Croatian and introduce me to my relatives and her friends, I'd be crazy not to go. I decided that I was headed for Croatia.

Looking at the map, I determined that a train ride from Vienna to Zagreb would be the best fit for my itinerary. My rail pass entitled me to unlimited travel within a certain zone for one month. I knew I could get to the border of what used to be Yugoslavia, and that I would have to buy a ticket for travel over Slovenia and in Croatia. As I toured the beautiful city of Vienna, wheeled past magnificent palaces and buildings of the former capital of the Hapsburg empire, indulged in what I felt was the best ice cream I'd ever tasted, a terrible thought came to me.

During my planning for the trip back in Canada, I thought I'd anticipated everything. I'd checked to see if my passport would be valid for all the countries I planned to visit. At the time, I required a visa to get into Croatia, so I had gone to the Croatian consulate to get one, but I'd overlooked one thing. Since I had to go through Slovenia by rail to get to Croatia, I hadn't even thought to find out if I needed a visa to get into that country. Because it wasn't really a destination, just a country I was travelling through, I'd completely forgotten to check. On the eve of my morning train ride from Vienna, I made a frantic phone call to the Canadian embassy to find out what the travel requirements were. I was relieved to learn that Slovenia only required a valid passport, and unlike Croatia, no visa was needed. Thank God! I could enjoy my final dinner of wiener schnitzel without worry.

The next morning, I arrived at the train station after phoning my brother Butch in Canada and asking him to call ahead to my mom to inform her that I would be in Zagreb by 2 p.m. and would get to her village a few hours after that. The train was due to leave at 8 a.m. and I made sure to get there well ahead of time to locate the correct platform and find some help to lift me, my chair and bags onto the railcar. My German is virtually nonexistent, but I'd learned that the word "zug" meant train. I asked someone "Ist der helpen fur me on der Zug?" I have no idea what I really said, or how grammatically horrible it was, but it did the trick and two burly guys lifted me onto the padded seat and brought my chair and baggage along as well. The downside was that with all my stuff just inside the car door, there was no room for other travellers to enter my car, so I'd have to travel alone. Many backpackers would welcome this as a chance to sleep or spend some time in solitude, but I enjoy meeting new people and trying to communicate. This time, the scenery out the window would be my only companion.

We pulled out of the station and slowly Vienna gave way to countryside as we made our way south to the Balkans. After sleeping for a few hours and being awoken by the train conductor to check my ticket and passport, I looked out the window to see the beautiful Austrian Alps.

The evergreen trees reminded me of northern Ontario, and the forests were green and thick. But it was the mountains that really captivated me. I'd never travelled by train through mountains before and it was very scary and exciting. We slowly moved along the sides of the mountains and through narrow valleys, while the snow-capped peaks appeared and then drifted by. I had never seen anything so beautiful in my life. As we approached each little town, the train would slow, the whistle would blow and we'd travel along train crossings, while drivers waited for us to pass. This went on for hours and I captured as much of it on my camcorder as I could, making sure to spend some time away from the viewfinder, enjoying it in real time for myself.

As lunch approached, the conductor asked me if I wanted anything from the dining car, but I'd brought some fruit, sandwiches and drinks with me. The train was slowing again and we were getting ready to cross into Slovenia.

My rail pass was valid as far as Graz in southern Austria, but as we made our way to Maribor, I knew the new conductor would ask me to pay for a ticket to Zagreb. When he appeared looking for tickets, I told him I needed a ticket, but the only money I had was Austrian. He took it and shortly returned with my new ticket. After the border guard stamped my passport, I was all set for the last leg of the train journey.

Slovenia was definitely poorer than Austria. The houses were well kept, but were smaller and lacked the amenities of their Austrian neighbours. I was intrigued that every house had a satellite dish bolted to the roof to catch western TV signals. I wondered if this was a new innovation since independence in the early 1990s or whether they'd had them while still under the influence of communism.

The trip to Croatia didn't last long because Slovenia is a small country, and soon another border guard was stamping my passport. I'd finally made it to my parents' homeland. As that thought sifted into my brain, I heard some men singing in the next railcar. The language was definitely Croatian and I guessed it was the soccer team, which I'd seen walking past my window in their distinctive checkerboard uniforms. The houses in Croatia were even poorer than in Slovenia, and I figured that Slovenia had benefited from its location and common border with the west. That was something Croatia didn't have.

The countryside was completely flat and uneventful, which was unexpected. My parents had always talked about the hills of home. I was a bit disappointed, but glad to be getting near the capital. My next problem was going to be finding a way to the little town of Lukovdol near Karlovac. Finally, as mid-afternoon approached, we arrived in Zagreb. The train slowed to a stop and I waited. I waited and waited, assuming that the conductor would find help to get me off the train. I was wrong and became really worried when the next wave of people boarded, preparing to head back to Austria. I asked the lady who was mopping the train if she could find someone to assist me. Luckily, I'd just received assistance from the train and was back into my blue chair when the train started to pull away. It was a close call, but I was in Zagreb!

My mom had told me there were two ways to get to her village. I could either take a train to Vrbovsko, which would leave me ten kilometers away, or I could wheel down the road to the bus station and take a bus, which would drop me off at a road leading downhill into her town. Since I didn't know what to do if I only got to Vrbovsko, I decided to take my chances with the bus. Busses are a transport of last resort for me. Getting on trains isn't too bad since there are generally lots of employees to help me get on and off. With busses, there's usually only the driver, and I've had some bad luck getting them to help. Since I was headed to a bus station, which I figured would be a hub of activity, I anticipated lots of people to help.

After exchanging currency for some Croatian kunas, I wheeled down the road to the bus terminal. Zagreb was very sunny that day and the town was neat and tidy. Electric trams rattled along their lines over wide boulevards. As I wheeled along, another traveller, not a backpacker, but obviously someone who'd been on the train, and was also heading to the bus terminal, gave me a push in the right direction.

I asked the lady at the wicket for a ticket or "kartu" for the route to the coastal town of Rijecka, but only as far as Lukovol. I misunderstood the cost of the ticket and she laughed when I offered her only 20 kuna for the trip. I finally just opened my wallet and let her take out the right amount of money. She directed me to the bus bay and I asked the driver if he could help me. I was very happy to find a man from New York headed in my direction, so he and the driver helped me on and I had someone to talk to on the ride into the hinterland.

As we made our way out of Zagreb, the superhighway gave way to a two-lane road and the hills I'd always heard about started to appear. Traffic was light, and I enjoyed seeing the white houses with their red roofs as we passed. I'd forgotten how hungry I was until we passed several roadside restaurants with rotating spits at the side of the road roasting the day's pigs and lambs. The aroma was unbelievably good.

After an hour or so, we stopped at a restaurant in Severin na Kupi, which served as a rest stop. The driver could have a smoke and passengers could stretch out and get a drink. I stayed on board and the friendly New Yorker bought me a Coke. He informed me that my village was just down the road. I was surprised that he knew of the town but he said he was from this area originally and knew Lukovdol well.

Ten minutes after starting out again, the bus pulled over and the man and driver retrieved my chair and bags. One grabbed me under the shoulders, while the other held onto my legs as they helped me off and into my chair. They asked if I'd be OK and I assured them that I would.

As the bus drove off, I looked around and realized that this was very remote country. I had a new problem. They'd left my chair in deep gravel on the shoulder of the roadway and I was stuck. Only the birds were listening as I muttered some choice expletives under my breath. I finally had to throw both my backpack and bag onto the road to lighten the weight of my chair and try to get out of the trap. It took about ten minutes of spinning my wheels, hoping not to get a flat tire, before I was able to scramble out and load my bags back on. The country road ahead was steep, but it was downhill, so it was necessary to slalom from side to side to avoid building up speed and tipping into the ditch, or hitting a bump and getting knocked out of the chair. As I approached the village, I could see little houses. I took a break and watched a rooster keeping his chickens in line, while a cat woke briefly, looked at me and yawned before returning to sleep.

As I made my way to the centre of town, I asked someone if he knew where house number 61 was and if he knew my uncle Josip. The man, Veco, knew me by name (apparently, my mom had spread the word to keep an eye out for me). He guided my chair to my uncle's house and on arrival, I yelled up the stairs for him in

Croatian. I had finally made it to my mother's little village and was excited to see her brother Joe, whom I'd met in Canada once before. He had a full head of white hair and a deep voice. We celebrated with homemade wine and thin slices of cured ham, known as "shunka".

It turned out that my mom and my cousin's girlfriend had driven to the train station in Vrbovsko to meet me, thinking I would arrive there. We got slowly drunk, while Veco went to phone the police station to let them know where I was. When mom and my cousin's girlfriend finally arrived, they both laughed and cursed me for not going by train. They'd just given up on me and were heading back to the village, when a policeman pulled over their car to inform them of my whereabouts. The car they were driving was a broken, old jalopy and they were convinced that he was pulling them over to take the car off the road.

We had a long, hard laugh about that over the next week or so.

NO SEATBELTS, BRAKES, OR BRAINS BUT WHAT A VIEW!

At the beginning of 2002, I decided to go off backpacking for four months. Most of the trip was spent visiting places in Australia that I hadn't been to yet. However, I also like to use Australia as a jumping-off point for more exotic side-trips into Southeast Asia. I always get strange looks from the Australian customs agents on my return (this last time they kept checking my bags for drugs), as most backpackers leave the country and don't return again in one or two weeks. For me, since I travel alone in my blue chair, there is only so much third world that I can comfortably handle for a long length of time, and at some point I need to return to a western, first world country, to regain my strength and enjoy a proper shower.

I arrived in Denpasar, Indonesia on the island of Bali in the Java Sea, at around 10 p.m. The Tour East agency had stated that I'd find an accessible ride to my northern destination however, as I emerged from the airport to a hot, muggy tropical evening I was met by two agents driving a large van. It was all I could do to stand and I needed assistance up into the passenger seat. We started out on a three-hour ride to Lovina Beach on the north shore to find the "wheelchair friendly" resort that I'd booked through Qantas. I was extremely thirsty after not drinking during the long flight from Melbourne, and since I was flush with 100,000 rupiah notes from the airport moneychanger, I asked if I could spring for a round of soft drinks before we left the city. A cool bottle of pop never tasted so good.

The three-hour drive up and over the mountains in the middle of the night was scarier than a thrill ride at an amusement park. Winding along, with turns every two minutes and then straight down once we got past the peak. It was too bad that it was dark and I couldn't see much. I did observe some of the towns though, as we drove through in the middle of the night. They were still quite active and the Hindu influence on the island was quite evident from the small shrines we passed. Bali is a bit of an anomaly in Indonesia. It's one of the last islands to have joined the country and is the only non-Moslem island. Just after I returned from my holiday, there was a terrible bombing that killed many Australian and other tourists. It was a horrible tragedy and I think the economic ramifications are still being felt.

The arrival at 1:30 a.m. was down a long driveway to a beautiful hotel. We parked the van and I finally disembarked, hoping for a quick registration and a nice shower before bed. The problem was that when I wheeled up to the entrance, the lobby was up nine stairs! At this point, I wasn't the most gracious of tourists as I'd been assured by the travel agent in Hobart that the facility was completely accessible. I was not happy. The manager escorted me around the back, past garbage dumpsters, and I struggled over all kinds of metal debris on the ground to my room. The resort actually looked quite nice and each of the rooms in my area were bungalow-styled townhouse units, but I noticed another problem that I hoped wouldn't be evident in my unit. It was. In order to gain entry, I would have to negotiate another three stairs! The two agents and the manager helped me up the stairs and I gave the Qantas boys a good piece of my mind. What was great was the way they took my fury with smiles and assurances that everything would be fixed to my liking. I was too tired to spend much time arguing and decided to go in and go to sleep. I'd worry about it in the morning.

The next day was spent instructing local workers on ways to build some half-baked ramps out of flimsy plywood, the only material available. Unfortunately, I still couldn't use it independently, due to the steepness of the ramp, but it was better than nothing. To cap off a perfect welcome to Bali, the guests had a party the night I arrived and had put up decorations. In their hurry to clean up after the guests, staff had left tacks on the ground near the dining area, and of course, my chair found one. I had my trusty extra tube that I'd bought in Noosa Beach, Queensland and had it fixed. Eventually, after days of complaints, someone from Qantas came out midweek to see what I was talking about and agreed the stairs were a problem. You think?!

Anyway, besides those problems, the place was desolate except for a few older Dutch and Swedish tourists. Lovina Beach, located near Singaraja, is not very busy because of the long drive necessary to get there and since they have black sand, which is not the favourite of tourists. It seemed that most of the tourists only stayed for a day or two as part of an organized tour. I didn't mind the remoteness one bit because it provided the silence and relaxation I sought.

The resort offered a buffet breakfast each day, included with my package. There were some wonderfully weird Asian fruits to try, including rambutan, a red hairy fruit the size of a chestnut that you open to reveal a white grape-like fruit with a nut inside. You only eat the white fruit. And also snake fruit, which has skin like a snake, but inside is white and firm, a bit like eating a sour apple. I liked it a lot. Being so close to the island of Java, of course, the coffee was the best I'd had since my days in Kenya. I ordered a cheese omelette one morning and got an omelette with the cheese on the side!

The Qantas brochure indicated that I could rent a driver and car for a day. However, when I enquired, I was informed that they don't go up to the north coast. As a way of placating another disappointment on this trip, my guide asked his buddies to drive me. When they arrived, I wasn't sure it was a good decision. The old beat-up van had no seat belts, no air conditioning and not much in the way of brakes. But the two of them seemed enthusiastic and confident that they could do the job.

As we left the resort, I finally got a chance to see a bit of the local countryside. There were plenty of motorcycles, as well as cars, and the blue smoke coming from everyone's exhaust pipes was a testament to the terrible pollution in Asia. The cities were quite rustic, but were very well kept. Each little town or village had a sign welcoming you there and then another as you left bidding farewell. The vegetation was very thick with trees and ferns, and as we entered the rural areas in the hills, the foliage became lush. Our destination was Mt. Batur and the magnificent volcanic lake below it, home of Bali's rice goddess. From a distance, we could see the mountain coming into view and as we drew nearer, the scenery became even more spectacular. My two hosts drove to a special lookout where I could point my camera for some great shots. As is usual in such places, the vendors came out of the woodwork to ask if I needed to buy something to remember the moment. Actually it was a bit annoying, but I did need a T-shirt and some postcards, so I got them there and we were finally left alone to enjoy the beautiful natural landmark.

My drivers, one of whom spoke excellent English, also had another destination in mind. I mentioned that I wanted to see some of the famous terraced rice paddies that are reputed to rival those in Japan for beauty. We started to head back down the mountains to the Three Lakes Region and Gobleg. Yes, that is the real name of the place, Gobleg! I loved the road signs and had no idea what was in store there. As we crossed over the top of the mountain range, a sudden thunderstorm hit us. We were just at the end of the rainy season. I'm not kidding when I tell you that with these two guys going sixty kilometers an hour, down the hill, with all the rainwater from above us, floating down the road under a van with minimal braking power, it was a thrill a second! I didn't think we'd make it and avoid all the pedestrians and bikes on the road too.

After a half hour's deluge, we finally emerged from the rain to puffy, white clouds and the sun shining against a blue sky. We stopped briefly for petrol and a drink. I was shocked when I did the math to realize that the Indonesians were paying only ten cents a liter for gas. We also stopped briefly in a wonderful valley that was the home of one of my escorts. He needed water for his radiator and decided it would be a good time to stop in and see his mother. We paused along a wharf and viewed some young fishermen with long poles trying to catch their dinner. One of the anglers was my driver's cousin and he proudly showed us his modest catch. I thought about what an idyllic place this would be to live and grow up in.

The mountain terrain became a bit rough as we moved back up and away from the lowlands. I finally saw the sign indicating we were arriving at Gobleg. Our shabby van moved slowly along the road and finally we were treated to one of the most wondrous sights I'd ever been witness to. We sat on the shores taking in the two lakes, side by side, and the magnificent tropical scenery as the remaining clouds from the finishing storm drifted by. Gobleg reminded me of Interlaken in Switzerland; two lakes, with the town in the middle, except that on the sides of the valleys were the beautiful rice terraces I'd been longing to view.

I decided it had been worth the death-defying trip. At the end of the day, the guides invited me to dine with them on local Balinese fare at a roadside stand. They were impressed that I could stand the spicy food and we shared some very potent beer. I knew that I'd made some new friends and seen a piece of an island paradise that I would remember for a long time.

STORMY TIMES IN THE CANOE ON TEA LAKE

Being a Canadian, one of my favourite things to do in the summer is enjoying the great outdoors. I've been very fortunate because when I first started working, many of the people I worked with, who ultimately became my friends, were the same age and shared my affection for camping and canoeing. Even though I'm in a blue chair, I've played first base on the softball team we all formed back in the '80s. When we'd go on tournaments, instead of staying at hotels, we'd rent group campsites and all bring our tents. We never won much at softball, and nowadays most of the team are occupied with partners and children, but some of the camping experiences were great. I owe a lot to that bunch, because prior to meeting them, I'd never camped before, other than at Easter Seals camp when I was a kid. It isn't easy having a buddy in a blue chair with no tent or skills to offer, but they always made me feel like a welcome camper and said that it wouldn't be the same without me.

One of the friends I made during those years was Paul, a very smart technical guru at our company. We played softball together for many years, but actually met during one of the few earthquakes that hit Ontario. We were working late one night just after he'd started with the company and both of us emerged simultaneously from our offices in the basement after the building began trembling and shaking. It was certainly an interesting way to make a new friend.

As the years have gone by, Paul and I have shared some memorable experiences both camping and at the cottage. One of these was an excursion to Algonquin Park, one of the largest parks in Ontario. We'd been planning the late summer trip for a few months and Paul had taught himself to be quite a good outdoorsman, especially for a city boy growing up in a small neighbourhood near downtown Toronto. The provincial parks have excellent facilities for the disabled. In fact, they offer special campsites for the disabled that are flat, near the accessible washrooms and have picnic tables with the end of the seat cut out so you can easily get your chair in and don't have to sit at the end. Paul was making the arrangements and I warned him that if he was going to book the site, I didn't want a site that was painted blue. Even though I'm in a blue chair, the whole point of camping is to rough it a bit.

We started out on a Friday afternoon, since both of us had a half-day off. We met at his place and after ensuring that all the equipment was present, we loaded up his station wagon and made our way onto the highway for the three-hour drive north to the park's southern gate. As we left the cities of the south, the highway wound through lake country and slowly, the traffic began to dissipate. Maple trees gave way to conifers, and fertile agricultural farms yielded to the rocks of the Canadian Shield. We stopped at a coffee shop and then went to a hardware store to buy some extra canisters of propane for the stove. Paul is a great cook and even today, with his wife and two kids, I always look forward to an invitation to visit for dinner.

Algonquin is quite large and, unlike many provincial parks, there are many areas at which camping is available. It's not uncommon, in April, to see moose at the side of the highway licking the remaining road salt from the shoulders of the route. In addition wolves, bears, foxes, coyotes, porcupines, skunks and multitudes of cute, but annoying, raccoons, make these wilds their home. This was summer, so we registered and found our campsite, after having driven fifteen kilometers inside the park. Thankfully, the site was not next to the comfort station. One of the reasons I don't like being too close is that if the wind blows your way, the fragrance from the septic system is enough to make you want to roll over and die. We were close enough for convenience, but distant enough to hear the sound of the birds and animals, not other campers.

Paul set about putting up the tent, all the while trying to involve me as much as he could. I held up a tent pole for him, then promptly dropped it on my head and finally decided my best talents lay in coordinating the project. When a tool or small part was needed, I would try to find it. My big job occurred when the dwelling was complete. I took it upon myself to move all the sleeping gear into the tent. When I was finished, there was no room for my blue chair, and Paul had to throw some of the equipment back into the wagon. We now had a home and Paul decided it was time for dinner.

Camping in a provincial park isn't really as rough as it sounds. There are fire pits at each site and if you run out of wood, you can buy some at the camp store. Paul was using a camp stove for our pasta with fish and it was excellent. As the long summer day finally drifted to dusk and the evening star made its first appearance, we searched for our jackets and mosquito repellant. We sat out beside the campfire and Paul played his guitar. Three fellows from the next campsite were also budding musicians and before long we joined them to form the interim group "The Travelling Wildberries". Paul thought of that. It wasn't long before we heard the distant howling of a pack of wolves, who served as the perfect accompaniment before we finally drifted off to sleep.

Next morning, after a very restful sleep and a breakfast of eggs and bacon along with some much needed coffee, we prepared for the day's activity. We decided to drive around the park for a while, looking for a trail to walk. We drove around Tea Lake where the majority of campers were set up and tried to spy some animals. We did see a few deer, but other than that, we were a bit disappointed. We finally came to a trail that looked quite good. The path was partially wheelchair friendly, but we were warned that the wooden path ended at a point furthest away from where we parked our car. Near a valley, the path would reappear again at the other end before coming back to the parking lot. Neither one of us could figure that one out. Undaunted, we proceeded into the vast interior of Northern Canada, much as the explorers and Native Indians did in centuries gone by. The only difference was the wooden sidewalk and the numbered signposts identifying the flora found in each area.

The initial thirty minutes of walking went without a hitch. There were interesting plants and animal droppings we couldn't identify, although we pretended they were from something out of Jurassic Park. As the forest closed in on us, the daylight seemed to fade and we entered an eerie world of bird music and twilight. At the same time, the smooth man-made path ended and we were left with irregular dirt, brush and tree roots to navigate. I advised Paul that it was probably a good place to turn around, since I didn't want him to hurt himself trying to push me over this type of rough terrain. Also, if he got hurt, we'd both be in trouble. Paul wouldn't take no for an answer. According to the map, this part of the path wasn't supposed to last for long and soon we'd be back on the wooden trail.

Actually, we didn't have as many problems as I thought we would and we were making our way through in record time, but we soon ran into a huge problem. We finally came upon the valley that had been advertised earlier. Just as the path opened up, it also turned sharply to the left and there was a monster tree root about four inches high to climb. If Paul and I, in my chair, took a huge run at it to make the speed needed to get over the root, there was a very good chance the momentum would carry me over the edge of a small cliff. I would surely end up in a wheelchair for the rest of my life—again!

Paul peered over the edge and then looked at me. I wanted to turn back, but he said he could do it with no problem. I had to defer to him and so we took a huge run at the root. I still don't know how we did it, but as he propelled us over, my job was to grab the left wheel and lean to the same side to try and veer the chair away from oblivion. It worked and we both laughed and shook our heads at how stupid we were. Just then, a couple hiking from the opposite direction passed us with some happy greetings. We quickly found the path, completed the walk and decided to head back to camp.

As we drove along the highway, we noticed a group of cars pulled over onto the opposite shoulder. Paul slowed down the car to try to see what they were observing. It turned out that not far from the road, the campers had spotted a black bear that had climbed halfway up a tree. The huge animal seemed perplexed at all the attention and after pausing for a long while to give us a look, he continued his trip into the crown of the tree and disappeared from view. It had been a wonderful experience and we got back to our site to celebrate with a cold beverage.

The final day, we planned to get out on the water for a canoe trip. Paul didn't have a canoe, so we had to go to the camp store to rent a metal one. Poor Paul struggled with the canoe, trying to mount it on top of his roof rack and simultaneously bind it with some thin rope. It took a while, but he finally got it done and we moved onto the road to travel to Tea Lake for a paddle. We hadn't driven for more than a kilometer, when there was a bend in the road. All of a sudden, we heard a thud and looked in the rear-view mirror to find our canoe had tumbled across the highway onto the opposite shoulder. Thank goodness there was no one in the other lane! We turned around and Paul had to go through all the bother again, but this time we made it to the lake with our canoe.

We parked near a small sandy beach and Paul dragged the craft onto the sand and tried to keep it steady while I threw my legs in. He then grabbed me under the shoulder and swung me onto the floor of the canoe. I sat on the seat cushion from my chair and balanced myself against one of the seats, looking forward. We put on our life vests and Paul dragged us into the water, pushing off with his foot.

I'm not a swimmer and used to be terrified in canoes, but I have so many friends who are excellent paddlers, that I now have no problems with them. I'm also a useless paddler, but my companions normally more than make up for it. Paul was behind me so I couldn't see him, but as we moved out onto the water, I started to enjoy the calmness of the motion of the canoe and its solitude. Eventually, voices from the shore drifted out of range and the distant land seemed to move, while the point at the front of the canoe remained still, as a reference. We canoed for about a half hour and floated quite far out, making it to the other side of the bay. Paul was getting tired, but had brought along some trail mix. We stopped near some rocks and Paul pulled the canoe half out of the water while he went into the woods to commune with nature.

By the time he returned, the late afternoon sky was beginning to darken. Another of the famous Ontario thunderstorms was brewing and the waves were starting to rise. Paul and I made a beeline back to our starting point before the weather hit. Even I was paddling with all the effort I could muster and finally we approached my chair and the car. As the first crack of thunder and flash of lightning occurred, we passed a woman with a child in another canoe heading out for the first time, in the opposite direction onto the lake. They didn't seem interested in our warnings and continued on. We finally arrived at the shore and by the time I was back in my chair, the rain was really starting to fall. Paul got the canoe up on the roof in record time and it was driving rain by the time we got back to camp.

We spent the rest of the day in the tent and found it wasn't really as waterproof as we thought. We enjoyed some quality time together and finished off the beer we'd brought.

I've always wondered what happened to that woman sailing into the storm.

TARRED AND SOAKED WITH FRIENDS IN CORDOBA

Most of the time the airlines make it very easy to travel when you are in a blue chair and for most of my trip Aerolineas Argentina had done a great job, but I couldn't blame them for my treatment in the airport on arrival in Cordoba, the second largest city in the country. Instead of having my chair meet me at the door of the plane, I was transported around the halls and lobby of the airport while still strapped into the narrow, aisle chair used to get me off the plane. Ultimately we made it down to the baggage claim area despite my protests and I was made to sit in the uncomfortable contraption for fifteen minutes while we waited for my chair to arrive on the carousel. I was not impressed.

After finally extricating myself from the airport it was time to find some transport to the city. The personnel outside of the airport tried to usher me into the expensive limousine service but I spotted the taxi stand which for some reason was inconveniently located about 20 meters away from the front entrance. I made my way over to the first cab and was greeted by a young hippie driver who actually spoke quite good English. He mistook me for an American despite the Canadian flag on my backpack and began to talk about his love for Jamaican music. I noticed a strong smell in the car and I couldn't figure out why we were driving only 30 kph in the fast lane and were getting passed by almost everyone on the road into Cordoba. Finally, when he opened up the glove compartment to retrieve a fresh supply of leaves to chew from a huge plastic bag he had, I made the connection to the fact that the smell I had noticed was the fragrance of coca leaves that he had been chewing all along. Coca is legal in the northern parts of Argentina but not in the rest of the country. I don't think it troubled him one bit. After a journey that took much longer than it should have and an extra trip around the block after he passed my hostel the first time, I departed with a copy of a business card he handed me in the hope I would call him again for a repeat trip. He was definitely an optimist.

The hostel I had booked into had told me that the accommodation was on the first floor and that the entrance had no stairs. They were correct on both counts but I was the one who made the mistake this time. In Europe and most of the world the floors are counted up from the ground starting at zero, so the first floor would be the second floor in Canada. I had forgotten this and what a big problem I created. The ancient elevator was long broken and I could not get up to the rooms. Luckily for me the front desk attendant Fernando and the other front desk guy Frederico assured me that they would have no problems getting some help to lift me up the steps. I decided to stay at least one night to see how it went and then try to figure out something in the morning. Upstairs in the dorm room, which was supposed to have four and six bed dorms, the room was actually two rooms with no door between them making for what was really a ten bed dorm. In addition, the attached washroom had a step up, but once inside the toilet was at least useable, though the shower was not. Once again this was not what I had bargained for but when backpacking these are some of the interesting things that come up.

Cordoba was much bigger than I had thought it would be and my research into the town had been terrible. I was expecting a small-ish relaxing town but it was quite the opposite as it bustled with university students. As I explored the vicinity I did like the fact that we were near a huge park, the only problem was the lack of beveled curbs and the level of difficulty I would have to endure in traversing the sidewalks to get there. The university was nearby and a main shopping street was only one block from the hostel. Around the opposite corner were some small shops and a wonderful Italian bakery that I ended up going to each morning to enjoy a cappuccino and pastry. In the hostel, the first person I met was a friendly outgoing American chap from Arizona, named John. He had been at the hostel for a week or so and was waiting for a replacement credit card from the States to catch up with him. As it turned out John was also a roommate of mine, so it was good to know someone right off the bat. It had been a tiring day of travel from Iguazu Falls and I decided to call it an early night.

The next morning I woke early after struggling up the single step into the washroom, I sat out on the balcony of our room, while my roommates snored away. Unfortunately, I had caught up with the rain from the south and I realized that there wasn't going to be much to do on this wet day. After washing and dressing I yelled down the stairs to Fernando who happily helped me down the winding stairs, with the assistance of another backpacker. Actually, our first attempt at descending the stairs was less than a complete success as Fernando let go of the back of my chair prematurely and I ended up with the back of the chair on the floor and a smack to the back of my head. Oh well, nothing in there to be harmed at least! Most of the rainy day was spent outside the front of the hostel watching life go by whilst drinking a cup of tea or talking to some other hostellers in the lobby of the hostel where the TV was located. I had also received an email from the two German students that I had met in Iguazu directing me to the flat they shared about ten blocks away for a party they had invited me to. When you are backpacking your social calendar can fill up in a hurry. I also wanted to go to the hostel BBQ that Fernando and Frederico were hosting tonight. The BBQ was normally held on the roof and that is still where they were planning to do the cooking, but the actual feast would have to be moved indoors. This was a good thing for me since rooftop parties are not generally wheelchair friendly.

In the meantime, three weary backpackers arriving from the north of Argentina had made it to the hostel on one of the long bus trips that South America is famous for. I can't tell you how many of these hardy souls I have met who spend up to 40 hours on busses moving around the continent. Actually it is quite a cost effective way of getting around and if you purchase the first class ticket or "executivo" class as it is known they have a chair that folds out flat for a good night's rest, while meals and alcoholic drinks are included. Of course all this doesn't help much if you are subjected to 40 hours of a crying baby on the trip. Anyway the trio consisted of Florian, a German student who was doing volunteer work in La Paz, Bolivia, Andi, a budding Swiss musician in a "ska" band and a pretty Belgian girl by the name of Kathleen. Kathleen was in the process of opening a bottle of red wine when I arrived, and after greeting me with the customary three cheek kisses, she offered me a glass. So there we sat in the lobby of a hostel on a rainy night in Cordoba listening to the guys try to play tunes on an acoustic guitar. As the evening passed, we eventually made it to the kitchen where the table had been set for the BBQ. By now it was just before midnight which is normal suppertime in Argentina, and I had long ago given up hopes of joining the German girls at their party. The meat had been grilled to perfection and along with various cuts of beef there were some different varieties of sausages. Kathleen and I were now drinking an alcoholic beverage that a Brazilian chap had brought with him from his country. I had told the German-speaking guys about the party with the German girls and they were very interested in attending. I told them that there was no way I was going to be able to make it in my condition so I gave them the directions. In the end, they did find the place but whoever answered the bell at the party would not let them in, so they ended up going to an all night dance bar with Frederico from the hostel reception. They must have had a wonderful time because they didn't make it back to our room until eight in the morning.

The next morning I had breakfast with Kathleen in the hostel cafeteria and she mentioned that she was interested in seeing Plaza Espana the huge park nearby. The weather had cleared up and she asked me if I was interested in going with her. I mentioned that she did not know what she was getting herself into with trying to push the blue chair around for the entire afternoon, but she wasn't put off and insisted it would be no problem. After spending the morning doing some shopping, she met me in the lobby near lunchtime and then mentioned that she wanted to go back up to her room to pack her knapsack for the day and that she would be right back. I stayed downstairs in the lobby and waited for her to return. After an hour of waiting for her I finally saw one of her roommates and asked if she had seen Kathleen back in the room. I was told that Kathleen had crashed on the bed with her Walkman on and had fallen asleep while listening to the music. Her roomie asked if she should go up and wake her but I said that I would go across the street for a coffee while she was snoozing. After three hours Kathleen finally woke up. She was quite refreshed and after enjoying a cigarette outside the hostel we finally began to make a move toward the park accompanied by Mark, a fellow from the UK whom I had been talking to while waiting.

The sidewalks in Cordoba leave a lot to be desired, most have cracks, the curbs are huge and never seem to be beveled at the corners, while the streets themselves would be impossible to cross if I had been on my own. Both Kathleen and Mark took turns at the controls of my chair and frankly it was quite nice to have some friends to push me around for a change. I kept a lookout on the cement just ahead of my path to ensure that I didn't navigate over anything that could have knocked me out of my chair. After some traveling and views of the nice greenery that the city had to offer on a sunny Sunday afternoon, we happened along a small lake in the middle of the Plaza. Some of the locals were out in paddleboats or just sunning themselves. We contented ourselves with gazing at the ducks and geese on the water and Kathleen used her excellent command of Spanish to converse with a cute family sitting beside us at the water's edge. After another hour of strolling along we decided to stop at a restaurant in the middle of the park to quench our thirst. Eventually the afternoon began to wane and as we made our way back to the hostel we happened onto an outdoor venue that was constructed to resemble a Roman theater. Sadly it had fallen into a terrible state of disrepair and was now padlocked behind some huge broken fences. We took lots of pictures there and then enjoyed a tasty ice cream before finally making it home.

One of the things that I really loved about Kathleen was that there was never a dull moment or a minute wasted. By the time we returned she already had planned for us to head out to the night market in the city center later on. I wished that I could have gone upstairs to stretch out of my chair for a few hours but the deal I have made with the two guys at reception was that I would only go up and down once a day. It made for some long days in the chair but generally it worked out to be a good arrangement. That evening the three of us were joined by John, Florian and Andi and our group headed into the city on foot in search of the markets. Initially we were a tad uncertain as to where to go but we asked some of the residents and they pointed us in the right direction. It was quite a nice atmosphere and there certainly was an abundance of kiosks selling souvenirs. I took the opportunity to buy some cups and other trinkets, along with a small necklace for Kathleen in thanks for pushing me around all day. After a few hours of shopping and wonderful conversation we decided to head into a nearby pub to get something to eat. When we entered the premises we were told that food was served upstairs and that the pub was downstairs, but they made an allowance for me and brought our food down. I don't think that I'll ever get used to eating so late in the day, but it had really been a fabulous day.

The next morning John and I headed out to the university to see what was happening there, while Kathleen and her roommate ventured out to see some museums. We had the terrible luck to run out of paved road on the way and John and I ended up going through some hot tar that we had overlooked. Well, when you are in a blue chair, having tar on your wheels is second only to dog poop in what not to wheel through. John was annoyed that he had tar on his shoes, while I had it on my tires, my pants, my hands and just about everywhere else. We did muddle into the middle of university registration for the upcoming semester before finally throwing in the towel and heading back. That night after getting cleaned up (or at least as clean as you can get when you can't get into the shower and have tar all over) John and Kathleen joined me for my final dinner in Cordoba. Kathleen had wanted to stay inside and eat as I think she was a bit down after saying goodbye to Florian and Andi a few hours earlier on their way to Buenos Aires. But we convinced her to come and she and I shared a pizza made with pungent Roquefort cheese, while John dug into a huge lomito steak. Just as we finished eating in a restaurant with tables outside on the sidewalk, someone on a balcony above the street decided it was time to throw out the day's water over the rail. You can guess whom all the water landed on. Thanks to my Tilley hat most of my head was dry but my back was wet from the sudden water bomb. I was totally upset at this point but Kathleen thought the whole thing to be hilarious and eventually I saw the absurdity of it too. It was the perfect complement to the tarring I had endured earlier on.

The next morning I awoke very early to take a taxi to the airport on my way to Mendoza. I was really touched when Kathleen got up early to see me off. In fact, she carried the front of my chair down the stairs that morning and also gave me a homemade hair ornament as a going away gift. Sometimes the people you meet along the way are the most memorable part of the places you visit. For me that is the way I felt about Cordoba.

A FEW PINTS AND A PUSH TO THE M.C.G. FROM A FRIENDLY VEGETARIAN

Sometimes in your travels, you run into someone who is a kindred spirit, that you like right off the bat. I was at my hostel in North Melbourne after arriving on an early morning flight. The office wouldn't register me until 11 a.m. so I was in a queue waiting my turn for a terminal at the Internet café situated in the lobby. A British gentleman a few years older than me was in the same situation and we struck up a conversation. He'd just arrived from Byron Bay and we exchanged a few stories from our travels. Tony was spending a few months in Australia and had already seen quite a lot. He'd left his wife and dog at home in wintry England and would ultimately hook up with his son in Western Australia. It was nice to make a new friend so easily and after we checked in (following an unsuccessful attempt at trying to book into the same dorm room), we made arrangements to meet in the cafeteria for lunch.

Tony liked to walk, and by that I mean he walked a lot. He said he didn't mind giving me a push around town and although I usually like wheeling about on my own, because I can go at a slower pace and see a bit more in depth, I'm not averse to grabbing a free lift if the opportunity presents itself. It was in that spirit that we ventured out into a warm and sunny Melbourne afternoon to see what the city was all about.

From our location just above the Queen Victoria Market, we moved past the site of the old Melbourne Gaol to parkland, the site of the Royal Exhibition Grounds. We lingered at the colourful flowers and trees and I thought about how much I missed the squirrels we have at home. In Australia, squirrels would probably be considered pests because the ecosystem is dominated by marsupials, although I've always found their antics humorous and entertaining. We continued on to Fitzroy St., one of the trendy parts of Melbourne where outdoor cafés and art shops abound. As a fresh southerly change of wind blew in from the Antarctic and it began to rain, we decided to get out of the weather by taking refuge in one of the small pubs that also punctuated each block in the area. It gave us a chance to dry out and get to know each other. Tony was on a journey of self-discovery and he knew how to talk. What was unusual was that he was one of those rare people who make every observation about human nature seem relevant. Additionally, he was able to start a conversation about anything with anyone. I'd always wanted to be like that.

As our beer started to wane, so did the showers and we decided to cut the trip short and head back to the hostel for dinner. We stopped at a grocery store to pick up a few items and then went to prepare our meals. I stuck with the simple spaghetti dinner that was one of my homemade staples. Tony was a better cook and being a vegetarian, had only bought veggies to cook up into a healthy dish. His nose was still red from remaining out in the sun on the beaches of Queensland and I warned him to take care of it or he might end up with some serious problems. He seemed unconcerned, but I suggested he start wearing a hat as protection from the strong Australian sun.

One of my roommates on that trip was another Englishman named Martin from Wigan, who was a soft-spoken fellow about ten years younger than I, but with shoulder-length hair which he kept in a ponytail. He was quite an intelligent guy and it seemed like every night when I arrived back in the dorm room to crash for the evening, he'd have his nightlight on and would quietly be reading a book. Not usual behavior for a young backpacker. He was also quite a sports fan and followed the Rugby League, which made a lot of sense coming from Wigan where they have a famous team.

Tony and I had made arrangements to go down to Melbourne's sports precinct, along the Yarra River, not far from downtown. From our hostel in North Melbourne, it was downhill to Flinders Station, which is the commuter hub for the city. Tony asked me if I wanted a push, but I pointed out that since I was going with gravity, I could manage until we reached the river. Tony moves at a very rapid pace and it was all I could do to keep up with him. He seemed especially interested that even though the curbs at the end of each block were bevelled, many of them were in a state of disrepair or had cobblestones leading up to the curb, so the irregular surface made it difficult for my blue chair to navigate. Sometimes, when I'd really built up a head of steam, I'd have to slow down suddenly to make sure that the small wheels at the front of the chair didn't become stuck and cause me to topple head over heels onto the footpath, not that it hadn't happened before!

As we proceeded down Elizabeth St. and passed the Victoria Market, the pedestrian traffic became more intense and I had to watch my route to ensure that I didn't crash into the ankles of some unsuspecting person waiting for the light to turn green. Outdoor cafés and numerous small shops lined our path on either side of the wide street. It seems that downtown Melbourne has more travel agencies per square foot than any other city I've ever visited. It definitely has the most pubs. In the middle of the street, on either side of a median, ran the tracks for the famous green and yellow trams that are a primary mode of transportation in town. I was quite used to them in Toronto, where the tram doors have a small stop sign on them. If a tram stops to let riders on or off, cars must stop behind the doors to let them do so, and you can drive on the rails in front of the tram. In Melbourne, they employ a "hook turn" which is unique even in Australia, as far as I'm aware. You drive on the left in Australia and to make a right turn in Melbourne on some intersections of Elizabeth St., you must move to the far left, turn your right blinker on, and let through traffic pass you by to your right. You then look to your right at the street light for the road that you want to turn onto. When that light changes to green, you can proceed to complete your turn and all through traffic for that road must also let you clear the intersection. I can tell you from what I saw there was plenty of confusion for people who were driving rental cars from outside the state and other countries.

We turned the corner as we reached Flinders Station and Tony took over control of my vehicle. We crossed the street and walked through some parkland until the magnificent Oval finally came into view. We could see for the first time the huge artificial light poles and massive stadium that is named the Melbourne Cricket Ground or MCG. The MCG is to cricket in Australia what Yankee Stadium is to baseball in the U.S. Many of the most historic cricket Tests in Australian sports history down through the years have been played on this pitch. For me, not being much of a cricket fan, I was more interested in it as the facility that the Grand Final of the Australian Rules Football League is played in each year. That game was usually shown on TV back home and I'd stay up into the night to see it.

We passed the finely trimmed lawns and lovely flowerbeds into the lobby to purchase our tickets. We still had a few minutes before the tour started, so we entered the Australian Rules Football Hall of Fame to the side of the lobby. It was interesting to see all the old uniforms and even some of the names and plaques of players, whom I remembered from when the league used to be called the Victoria Football League. It turns out that the sport was invented as a means to keep cricket players fit during cool, rainy winters, since Victoria doesn't have the year-round warmth that much of the rest of the country enjoys. I found it totally ironic, as no two sports could be more completely opposite.

Those of us booked on the tour congregated in the lobby at the time indicated and were met by an elderly gentleman who was a member of the MCG. The MCG is a club, and it's so popular that fathers put their kids on the waiting list as soon as they're born, so they can become members later in life when older members have died, creating a vacancy. Our guide asked us in turn what country we were from and I told him that I was from Canada. At the end of the introductions, he mentioned that Canada and the U.S. played the first international cricket match in history and many historians believe that may be the earliest meeting of two countries in any sport. We went outside and then into the MCG itself. The back halls and rooms were quite old and small and I was left behind when they went downstairs to see the cricket training area, but there was an elevator up to the member's lounge and the Cricket Hall of Fame.

Tony was in his glory. He was from England and you could see that as someone who'd played the sport as a boy and had loved it all his life, he was thrilled to see the old photos, hats and memorabilia from this elegant game of endurance and sportsmanship. Even I got caught up in the history of it and imagined myself out on the wicket hitting a six over the boundary. We went back down to the main level and our old fellow led us into the dressing room the AFL players used in winning the Grand Final the previous year. Apparently Brisbane had been losing at the half and off the main training area is a little room with benches and a blackboard. The coach drew up a plan on the board, fired up the team with a rousing and emotional speech and they came back to take the title away to Queensland, much to the annoyance of Victorians who'd invented the game. We made the same walk and were allowed to go out onto a small patch of grass, marked out with orange pylons. As I looked around the great stadium, I couldn't help but think of those players and what they might have been feeling or thinking. I wondered what it would be like to play for all the fans surrounding you. This was sports history and we were on the field to enjoy a small piece of it.

After the tour, Tony and I didn't want to leave, so we stayed in the coffee shop for a cappuccino and a biscuit to enjoy the moment a while longer. It was time to head back, so we stopped at a pub near the hostel that offered a meal of vegetarian pasta and a beer for $5. You can't go wrong with that. We finished off with a walk and then stopped into another livelier bar to end the night. Between us we split three pitchers of ale and I was quite polluted by the time we got home. Thankfully, Tony was there to guide me back safely. I had to wake up twice that night to relieve all the stress on my bladder, but it was one of the best days I had on my visit to Melbourne.

Sadly, Tony passed away prior to the completion of this book, but he loved to travel as much as I do. For a brief moment in both of our lives, we were able to share some smiles, a few pints and his love of cricket. He will be greatly missed.

I think he hit a six!

MY FRIENDS AT THE ARK IN THE ABERDARE MOUNTAINS

If I could recommend one part of the world to every traveller, it would be Africa. Unfortunately for me, I've only been there once and it was only to Kenya in East Africa, but for one month in February about ten years ago, I had the time of my life.

My old university buddy Wayne, had been posted to Nakuru, Kenya in the early '90s in his capacity as a Quality Control Manager for a battery company. I met him in his hometown over the Christmas holidays at his parents' house. I'd been visiting a friend from my wheelchair basketball team, who lived around the corner. Wayne and I had lost touch over the years, but I thought I'd see if he was home and renew the friendship. As luck would have it, he'd just returned from overseas with his wife, Brenda and his two little girls, Jessica and Lindsay. Political tensions in Kenya were rising in the run up to elections and he'd brought them home five months early, but he was headed back to complete his assignment. As his little girls softly sang the Kenyan national anthem to me in Swahili, he mentioned that if I wanted to come and visit him, he'd be happy to host me, as he had the use of a house and staff. Truthfully, it was an opportunity I never thought I'd have, and I told him that if I could arrange for the time off from work, I'd make the trek to Africa.

After a few weeks in Kenya with Wayne, he decided it was time to travel north to visit a tourist lodge that offered the chance to see wildlife in its natural habitat. The Ark, located high in the Aberdare mountains, had a salted mud pit and floodlights, so guests could stay up all night and observe different animals that come to either feed or take advantage of the mineral-rich soil that they eat to maintain their health. Princess Elizabeth was in the vicinity when she learned that her father King George had died and left her the throne.

As we left Nakuru and headed north along the narrow two-lane highway, the altitude slowly rose and the warmth of the lowlands, with their magnificent purple jacarandas and ever-blooming bougainvilleas, gave way to cooler winds and tea and coffee plantations. Each morning, workers went out to remove the topmost leaves from the tea bushes, the ones that have the most flavour and caffeine. Passing broken-down trucks along the way, each stranded driver would alert the oncoming traffic with broken branches laid out along the road as a poor man's warning device. The clean mountain air was constantly interrupted with the odour of diesel that the long line of motorists bellowed out.

After about an hour, we stopped at Nyahururu, which in colonial times was known as Thompson's Falls. The falls drop down the opposite side of a deep gorge and, like all falls, the thunder it provided was deafening. Of course, I grew up near Niagara Falls, so I know a bit about waterfalls, but what made this wonderful for me, was the African scenery that surrounded it. Nearby, was a market where we spent some time purchasing gifts for people back home and men in tribal dress would pose with you for a photograph for a small fee.

Continuing on, we left the car to pose for a picture beside a sign of Africa with a horizontal line depicting our navigation across the Equator. I took the opportunity to mention to Wayne that it was cold now that we'd crossed back into winter in the northern hemisphere. I'm sure he'd heard that one before, but he laughed anyway. As we climbed higher, we passed a small bamboo forest of a variety that only grows in a few, rare climates throughout the world. We'd arrived at the home of Mark and Tina, two young missionaries originally from North Carolina, but who'd spent the years prior to coming to Africa, in Virginia. Wayne and Brenda had met the couple during their time here and it was obvious that the ex-patriot community was very close. The young pair accompanied us on our trip to the Ark for the next two days and one night. They welcomed us with a refreshing Coke and invited us in, but Wayne declined and we loaded up to continue our travels with my new friends.

It wasn't long after we'd got back on the road that Wayne pulled the car over and stopped. As we looked across to the right, the twin peaks of Mt. Kenya were visible between puffy clouds against the blue sky. "That's amazing!" he exclaimed, as we recorded the moment on the camcorder and took in the view with our eyes. He mentioned that he'd driven the route many times and had never seen it so clear. He said that his wife, Brenda, had never been by on a clear day to get a look. He immediately dubbed it the "Walt Factor" and from then on, anything that went well on the trip was due to my presence. We arrived for lunch at the Aberdare Country Club, some 8000 feet above sea level. Too bad for Wayne, he had to drag me up fifteen stairs from the car park onto the patio. Naturally, he was out of breath, but I grinned and offered no sympathy, while taking the opportunity to mock him for being out of shape. We had a great laugh about that.

After a pleasant lunch, a pint of Tusker beer and a conversation that helped us get to know each other better, the four of us headed down the steps, into the car and off to the Ark for our evening of animal gazing. On arrival and after a long narrow, unpaved road through the wilderness, the forest opened to reveal a large, three-level A-frame lodge.

As we moved our gear into our respective double-bed rooms, we looked out the windows to see the one thing that had eluded me on the trip so far. There were elephants and plenty of them! We moved up to the observation deck after having a cup of tea. It was by now mid-afternoon and the elephants, about fifteen of them, were milling about, groaning and interacting with each other. Some of them seemed solitary, while others were obviously part of the maternal hierarchy common among these animals. A baby could be seen with an older sibling, but the smallest was never far from its mother and the other elephants were huddled close as well. After watching the elephants for the better part of two hours, it was time for dinner and a bit of rest. The lodge provided free tea and coffee all night and the aim was to try to stay up for as long as you could throughout the night to see what animals came by. We were a determined bunch with a plan, eat and rest now, then stay awake later.

Following our chicken dinner, we retreated briefly to our rooms to rest for a short while and dress warmly for the night ahead. We were up high now, so the cool African evenings would be even more so. Mark, who by now I was referring to as "my father", was continually nagging me to put on a coat, incredulous that I wasn't cold. When you're from North Carolina and have just met a Canadian who had left a minus 15°C winter behind, you can lose a bit of perspective regarding the definition of cold. After our respite, we returned to the observation lounge with the other guests. We were fortunate to have a zookeeper from Florida, named Lex, in our midst. He was leading a group from the U.S. and was able to easily identify each animal as it made its appearance. There were quite a few. Bongos, bushbucks, Jennet cats (a small lynx-like animal), mongooses, and countless antelopes took advantage of the salt on offer for them.

As the hours drifted away and a new day began, many of the older tourists slipped away to their accommodations, but we hung in there. At 12:30 a.m., two young elephants emerged from the forest and had the mud hole all to themselves. I watched in amazement as one grabbed a clump of grass with its trunk and then swept its front foot along the base of the clump to shear it from the ground before eating it. They remained only briefly and before long the Ark was again devoid of wildlife.

Mark couldn't stay awake any longer and bid us good evening, as we implored him to try to stay awake. Tina, Wayne and I were left, with a handful of others, to see if anything else would venture out of the still, African night. Half an hour later, our diligence was rewarded. To gasps of delight from the diehard observers, a mother rhinoceros and her baby cautiously ventured out of a thicket into the floodlights. The baby was very cute, but very big and seemed more interested in the new smells and sounds coming from our area, than digesting mud. Wayne and Tina went down the stairs where at animal level and only hidden behind blinds, they could get a better look and hear the sounds without glass muffling them. The mother grunted her disapproval at junior's movements, but the boisterous youngster even took a few steps on the buffering gravel to get up to the blinds and have a good sniff around.

Before long, a young elephant approached the pair and the baby quickly moved behind its mother. There seemed to be a standoff in the making. The elephant made some strange low sounds and spread its ears wide to make it appear even bigger to the rhino. After five minutes of standing and grunting at each other, the mother rhino decided that discretion was the better part of valour and withdrew with her offspring. It was now almost 2 a.m. and the last thing

I saw that evening was that lone elephant, standing in our midst under the Kenyan moon.

We were too tired and too happy to stay awake any longer. The next morning we filled Mark in on what he'd missed. It had been a trip to remember and one I couldn't forget, even if I lived as long as an elephant.

A NIGHT AT THE OPERA ON CLARKE QUAY

I'd heard good things about Singapore and the fact that it was a cosmopolitan mix of Asian cultures made it seem even more exotic to me. The real reason I wanted to visit was that it had formerly been a British colony and so they spoke English. After my earlier visit to Japan, I was looking forward to being able to talk to some of the locals.

Changi is not what you'd expect from an airport in this part of the world. I think it may be one of the most modern anywhere. On arriving at customs you're duly warned that the import of any drugs into the country is punishable by death. It couldn't be simpler or more ominous than that and it said a lot about what Singaporeans value the most—order. There are rules against spitting, chewing gum is prohibited and a Canadian who crossed the law recently was given a number of lashes as punishment. I'm a very law abiding fellow, but all these rules made me feel very self-conscious. A good friend of mine from my baseball team was from Singapore. Her late dad was Indian and her mother is Chinese. Tina can cook up a fabulous hot and spicy Singaporean noodle dish and I was looking forward to trying out some of the local fare. In fact, Tina's mother still lived here as did many of her siblings and they were instrumental in finding me a place to stay on my visit.

I left the airport to find the taxi rank and head into town. I know that Singapore is located very near the equator, but as the doors opened, it was a shock to feel the humid heat and it struck me like a brick. In addition to the muggy air, the atmosphere was made all the more uncomfortable by a series of forest fires burning to the south in Indonesia during the time I visited. No worry. I was comforted by the fact that I was back in a tropical climate and there were lots of palm trees around. I had heard that Singapore was an expensive place to live. Apparently obtaining a car is a big hassle and so I was surprised that the taxi trip into the city was so affordable. My friend's mom had booked me into the YMCA when I was unable to find any wheelchair friendly hostels in the travel guides I'd purchased. She'd made the first night's deposit for me and I was to give her a call to arrange a meeting when I arrived. The "Y" was quite a way from the centre of town, but with the cheap cost of travel I knew there'd be no problem. I also knew that with the 100% humidity, coupled with the sun being directly overhead, I wouldn't be spending much time wheeling around in my blue chair.

The hotel was quite nice, but when I checked in and they showed me the suite, I was unable to get through the narrow door into the washroom. They quickly found me another that was more acceptable and I was all set. It was time for a cool shower. As I left to go down the elevator later on in the day, I noticed a picture of a fruit that looked similar to a pineapple. The fruit had a red circle around it and a diagonal slash through it, indicating that is was prohibited. I thought that these rules in Singapore were getting a bit over the top. I later found out that the fruit in question is known as a durian, and that it's the smelliest fruit on Earth, but that it's also among the sweetest. The odour is so pungent that the hotel was concerned that if someone brought the delicacy into a room, it would foul up the whole floor!

The next day, I hopped into a cab and asked the driver to take me to the waterfront. Driving down the road into the Central Business District, I was struck by the cleanliness of Singapore and the beauty of the skyline. I was dropped off at Clarke Quay, which is the hub of tourist activity on the island state. I wheeled along the pedestrian mall looking for T-shirts, trinkets and postcards. As I was browsing in a shop, the owner asked me whom I was with. I informed him that I was travelling around the world on my own and that I had come from Canada. He was incredulous.

I'm surprised sometimes that more people don't have that type of a reaction, but I guess I should be glad. Sometimes people talk about air travel as though they had to flap their arms all the way to get there. Instead, you're in a comfortable seat with a television and radio to entertain you and they feed you wonderful food and drink. It's an expensive venture, but it's not that difficult either. I've loved to travel since first doing it when flying all over North America with the wheelchair basketball team. We used to take over ten players who were permanently disabled on flights and we never encountered any problems. That's what gave me the idea later in my life to start to travel and I've enjoyed it ever since, but I digress.

It had become so hot that I decided it was time for a beer. That's really not the proper thing to do when you're losing body fluid to perspiration, but it's what I generally do. I sat in an outdoor café looking out at the bumboats as they drifted by and ordered a Tiger beer. It was cool, refreshing and delicious. After that it was time to meet Tina's mother so that I could repay her the room deposit. I waited for her in front of the requested hotel and after a short time she and her daughter arrived in a new car. The two women helped me into the back seat. After stowing my chair in the trunk, I repaid her. They wanted to take me for a tour around Singapore and with such charming companions I would've been crazy to decline. We travelled along Raffles Avenue to the lavish Raffles Hotel, reputed to be one of the most expensive in all of Asia. We drove through the famous Chinatown and saw local merchants in action.

Singapore's population is primarily Chinese, although there are large minorities of Malays, Indians and Europeans. Each of these live in a peaceful harmony that Singapore is famous for, although to be fair, the government's tight fist certainly keeps a lid on any potential racial problems.

As we moved across Orchard Road and entered Little India, I was amazed, not by the shops, but by a particular Hindu Temple that we stopped in front of. The temple was light blue and ornate figures representing various deities were abundant. The figures were both scary and enthralling. We circled the central park and passed the Zoological Gardens. To the right was the magnificent span crossing the Strait to Malaysia. It had been a great tour and, as I thanked them, I asked if I could be dropped off where they had picked me up. It was so nice to meet people who were related to a good friend of mine, and in a country so far away. It really is a small world.

As the evening started to fall and the heat of the day began to abate somewhat, traffic on the promenade began to pick up. Tourists queued up outside outdoor restaurants for a dinner table and buskers and musicians played to appreciative audiences. I was drawn to an outdoor stage where some Chinese musicians were tuning up. I've always enjoyed Indian and Chinese instruments because their scales are out of key with western ones and so they have that exotic sound to them. It turned out that there was going to be a free performance of an ancient Chinese opera. Many people had already gathered, so my view was obstructed. It didn't take long for one of the musicians to notice and he came down off the stage to move some people out of the way so soon I had a front row seat. The performing troupe was from Mainland China and they were travelling around Asia on a brief tour. The story told of a King who went out into his kingdom disguised as a commoner in search of the fairest woman to become his bride. There were many twists and turns in the plot and it ended up as convoluted as a soap opera. The make-up and costumes were beautiful. Although I don't speak Mandarin, there was an English translation available on a movie screen, so I was able to follow along with the plot. It was a very unique type of entertainment to have stumbled upon.

The next day, I decided to remain near the YMCA and enjoy a bit of the life outside the downtown. I wheeled for a short time through the neighbourhoods and enjoyed a satay dish from a vendor with a mobile cart. While wheeling through an open, forested area, I was suddenly approached by two soldiers with machine guns. I hadn't been chewing gum or spitting, so I wondered what was going on. It turned out that I was going up the driveway leading to the Israeli embassy. They politely asked me to turn around and head back to the street.

I was happy to oblige, as I couldn't even begin to guess what the punishment might be for violating that law.

UP MT. WELLINGTON IN A YELLOW SUBMARINE

I've visited Australia many times over the years, but for some reason the one state that had always eluded my schedule was Tasmania. It wasn't because I didn't want to go there or wouldn't find it interesting. I think it was because from what I'd read and seen, it seemed like the part of the country that most resembled Canada. The climate wasn't a hot, beachy one and from what I knew, the land was very hilly and not great for wheeling around easily. But on this year's visit, I'd finally decided to get down there to see what it was all about.

It was a short plane ride from Melbourne to Hobart and as I flew over the landscape, its greenery reminded me of New Zealand. Most of Australia, at least the parts that are not tropical or coastal, is very dry and brownish, but on this island the panorama was magnificent. Rolling hills gave way to gentle valleys, cut by streams and rivers. Arriving in Hobart, my first task was to figure out how to arrange a lift to the hostel. I was informed by the attendant near the concourse, that there were no buses suitable for chairs and that I'd probably have to take a taxi. As I was registering my disappointment, an older couple, likely in the sixties, asked where I was headed. I named the street and they said they'd be happy to give me a lift. Those Aussies, they're so friendly, laid back and helpful. I accepted. The gentleman put my chair in the "boot" of the car and we were off.

I'd run into major problems trying to book accommodation at a hostel while in Hobart. Since the invention of the Internet, I book most of my hostels on personal computers at Internet cafés, while picking up e-mails and researching the next destination for things to do. The Youth Hostel Association or YHA, is the McDonald's of hostels; they're clean, helpful, well located and generally boring. For me however, most of them offer accessible rooms with shower facilities that meet my needs. So, most of the time, even though they are a bit dull and lifeless, they're a comfortable place to stay. No such luck in Tasmania. The YHA had all sorts of stairs, even though in the picture in the guide it looked as though it had a first level that would be OK. After contacting numerous places, my last chance was called Narrarra Backpackers. The owner, a man named Nigel, explained to me in his letter that he'd be happy to have me as a guest. "Just one thing, we do have a few stairs to get to the room and the toilet, but there are always lots of people around to help". He sounded confident, seemed like he wanted to have me as a guest, and I had no alternative. I decided that was where I would stay.

As the couple slowed the car, the first realization of what an effort this was going to be dawned on me. The street was very steep. I thanked the couple and asked if I could buy them a meal, but they declined and drove off. The front of the hostel was right on the sidewalk or "footpath" as they refer to it, bordered by a small cement porch, and a little step that I could negotiate easily. I opened the door, fearing the worst and was greeted by a friendly middle-aged man with a graying ponytail. It was Nigel. He knew who I was immediately and offered to show me my accommodation. The hostel's large central living room contained a TV set, some chairs, a couch and at the front, a large dining room table. Off to the side, was a kitchen and on the lower floor were the dormitories and the laundry. I was told they had computer access upstairs, but I knew I wasn't going to make it up the flight of stairs to use it. There were only three stairs leading to a landing, off of which were the washrooms. Then it was up another step to my room, which had two beds, but I had the room to myself. Opposite the bedroom were the showers and sinks. Basically, if I had to go anywhere I'd need a bit of help, but it was cozy and it was going to be my home for the next week.

I remember two people from my stay there. First, there was Dani, a young cheerful German lass. Also at the hostel was Janice, who wanted to go by the name "Bhoomi", a Sanskrit name the meaning of which I have unfortunately long forgotten. Bhoomi is a late middle-aged woman from Alice Springs in the Outback, who spends almost every waking moment knitting. To earn money, she set up stalls at flea markets or outdoor festivals to sell her knitted "beanies", what I would call toques or Americans call ski caps. I still regret not buying one from her. She was quite talented and had made one with a knitted Tasmanian devil on it. I think it was her showpiece item, but she had a photographic portfolio of all the beanies she had made over the years.

Hobart is a beautiful old city. It's hilly, but the scenic harbour and the busy, active downtown pedestrian mall leading to the waterfront and Constitution Dock at Sullivan's Cove, speak of a vibrant city that offers a wonderful lifestyle. It was mostly downhill for me to get to the centre and I quickly decided to hop on a tour boat that included lunch and a trip up the Derwent River. Departing the cove, we headed slightly south toward the casino and then up the river, passing under the span of the wonderful Tasman Bridge, that I'd crossed by car on my arrival from the airport. I've always enjoyed ferries and cruises, as they allow me to travel in my chair while enjoying outdoor breezes and the smell of the seas. The entire trip lasted about two hours and as we reached the furthest point and were turning to return, a storm started to blow in. A lightning bolt hit the top of Mt. Wellington, which overlooks the city and as the rain started to come down, I made a hasty retreat into the cabin, just in time for my lunch to arrive.

Over the course of a few days, as I was in the hostel making toasted cheese sandwiches or spaghetti for supper (both of these are easy for me), I got to know Dani, the blonde German who sometimes helped Nigel run the place if he was away on one of his tramping adventures. She had a bubbly personality and we hit it off immediately. She had a yellow station wagon and asked if I would like her to take me up Mt. Wellington. Of course, I had to dub the vehicle the "Yellow Submarine" and so, on a sunny Saturday afternoon, we headed up the slope. Dani had driven the car from Bendigo, Victoria and taken it on the overnight ferry from the mainland. It was a bit messy, but remembering the state of the Buick I'd left in the underground parking back home, I wasn't complaining. The trip up the mountain wasn't too steep and all along the way, Dani kept waving to people she knew from the hostel as they rode their bikes to the summit. It didn't take long to reach the top and after getting back into my blue chair in the gravel car park, we looked out over a magnificent view of the city and water.

On the trip back down, we decided to go to a Jazz Festival that Dani had heard of and while there, we bumped into some other young travellers who were staying at the hostel. We spent a very pleasant afternoon, talking, laughing, drinking and listening to some outdoor music. It was a simple afternoon, but it was very enjoyable.

We arrived back at the hostel and Dani suggested that we attend the Salamanca Market, where Bhoomi was selling her beanies. It was a short, downhill stroll, but I knew that after sitting in the sun all day, we were getting tired, and that the trip back uphill would be more of a challenge. Bhoomi was sitting in her stall, knitting away, and before long, a young Aussie came along with her boyfriend. She had purchased a beanie a few weeks before and now it was his turn. He tried them all on and settled for a brown hat with black knitting on the side, meant to look like smoke. It was Janice's bushfire hat that she'd made to represent Australia's seemingly constant battle with fires. She had sold a few of them and they were very cleverly designed. On top of her talent, she had a sarcastic wit. Bhoomi was also a mean *Scrabble* player and each evening, she tried to win games with obscure Aussie slang words, that I wouldn't allow her to use.

After Dani struggled to get me uphill and back to the hostel, I felt it had been a long day and decided to have a late shower before going to bed. After asking for some help up the stairs, and getting my wash gear from my bag, I scrambled out of my chair to sit on the floor of the shower stall. This would be great, I thought, a nice hot shower and then a beer and a long snooze. I turned on the water and then to my horror, I realized that whoever had showered before me, had pushed the showerhead off to the side! The water was going down the side of the stall. I sighed and put my facecloth against the wall to get it wet. My refreshing shower was not going to happen that night.

During my time in Tasmania, the Winter Olympics were being held. I got up early one morning to watch the final hockey game between Canada and the U.S. The game started at 7a.m. and the Australian network was picking up the Canadian broadcaster's feed. I felt like I was at home listening to the crew from "Hockey Night in Canada" describe the 5-2 victory that would give Canada its first men's gold medal in fifty years, and this after the women had beaten the U.S. for the gold a day earlier. By the time the game was ending, the whole hostel was awake and cheering for the Canadians, even an American from Minnesota, who said he felt the U.S. had won enough gold for one Olympics.

That afternoon, I decided to go back to the waterfront to pick up some postcards and get caught up on correspondence. It wasn't long before I wheeled by a café and three youngsters yelled me over to have a beer with them. They'd spotted the Canadian flag on my backpack and were on a pub-crawl to celebrate the morning's gold medal victory. The two lads were from Vancouver and the girl was from Saskatchewan. We spent the next four hours shouting each other rounds and crawling to different taverns, all the while making a loud nuisance of ourselves. I got quite drunk by the early evening, and before I lost consciousness, I asked them to wheel me home. I'm glad they were lucid enough to find it, because I wasn't.

I had a horrible hangover the next morning, but I did it for my country.

THE EXCITEMENT OF A TIDAL BORE WHILE LOOKING FOR MOOSE AND WHALE

One of the constants in my life is my friend Wayne, with whom I went to university. Ever since, our lives have been inextricably linked through both good times and tough ones, as with any long relationships. Wayne has been both blessed and cursed with work assignments over the years that have taken him to many different destinations, most of which I have always taken advantage of by visiting. A few years ago his company in Ontario transferred him to Nova Scotia on Canada's eastern maritime coast.

I had never been to Nova Scotia so I was really happy to fly out to Halifax on the east coast. Wayne happily picked me up at the airport and we headed back to the west coast town of Truro, at the top of the Bay of Fundy, which is famous for the fact that it has the highest tides in the world. As we zipped along the highway toward where he lived he pointed to a high pole with a flat platform on top, by the side of the road, where a pair of nesting ospreys were raising their chicks. Wayne said that every time he drove by he would try to monitor the progress of their growth. Unfortunately, the baby birds were not visible on this occasion.

Wayne had rented a large house on a rural road and luckily the basement of the house was accessible from the driveway and the washroom was completely wheelchair friendly, and there was a small bedroom down there too! Wayne immediately took me out to where he worked, which was an aerospace company that made wing flaps for small commuter jets. Wayne was the plant manager so he had the keys and after a trip to the store on the way, he wheeled the barbecue outside to the back of the plant and we proceeded to cook up some steak, salmon and Digby scallops. As we drank our east coast beer and enjoyed the meal, we gazed at the sunset whilst watching small planes take off and land at the adjacent landing strip. We talked and laughed well into the evening getting caught up on each other's lives. It had been a great start to what promised to be a wonderful visit.

We decided to head south and travel right around the bottom loop of the province. We rose early, ate a nice breakfast of eggs and toast that Wayne was famous for and then piled into his rented car and began our trip to Digby. My friend Sue, from back in Ontario, has told us to look up her mother if ever we were near that town, so I made a point of calling her on the phone the night before and asked if it would be OK for us to drop by. She seemed to have heard of me from Sue and was happy to have us drop by. The pine forests of Nova Scotia were quite amazing and the seascapes that we glimpsed from time to time as we buzzed down the highway never failed to disappoint. We arrived in Digby after a few hours and with our map that we had printed off the computer, we were not too long in finding the proper street and house. Wayne got out first to ring the doorbell and a small, friendly, white haired lady welcomed us into her home. She introduced herself as Hazel and we reciprocated.

Hazel had prepared a wonderful meal of fishcakes and a salad, which each of us enjoyed, while I got caught up on Hazel's daughter and her life as a child. For dessert, she had made a berry crumble which, like the meal was delicious. We were treated to a tour of her immaculately kept little house on top of a hill, from which you could see the water and Hazel was proud to tell us that the mayor was her next door neighbour. Wayne and I decided to take her out for a ride in the late afternoon sunshine and so we made our way out to Sandy Cove to enjoy the views of the Bay of Fundy and also a tasty ice cream cone. After an hour or so we dropped Hazel off at her home and waved goodbye as we proceeded south along the west coast of the province.

Wayne and I decided to go down to Yarmouth on the southwestern part of Nova Scotia. Yarmouth is a small town and we were both quite amazed at how pretty it was. We headed for the pier to see where the ferry, known as "The Cat", left to take passengers and cars to Maine and back. As you can imagine the pier was quite busy but we enjoyed stopping and having a beer in one of the local pubs and watching the tourists as they went about their business. We still needed to find a motel, so I was getting worried due to all the traffic around, so we went in search of a place to rest up. Luckily, the first reasonably wheelchair friendly motel had a vacancy and so we decided to relax with a pizza and then get a good night's rest.

The next morning, after a breakfast that was included in the price of the room, we started out on the road again. It was another perfectly sunny day and Wayne always laughed and commented on the "Walt factor" of how we always had great weather whenever we were travelling together. After seeing the road sign for the most southerly point in Nova Scotia, known as "The Hawk", we decided to go off the highway and try to find it. We did get lost for a short time, but ultimately we did find it on Cape Sable Island and we took the opportunity to take a badly needed pee.

The forests were deep green and each of us kept our eyes peeled looking for moose, but to no avail. We lunched in Liverpool and then on through Bridgewater, north along Highway 103. We stopped again in the late afternoon in Lunenburg, which most Canadians have a soft spot for. It is a cute little fishing town and the famous racing ship "The Bluenose", was built here and raced undefeated during its existence. The craft is depicted on the Canadian ten-cent coin and if you are originally from Nova Scotia, then you would proudly refer to yourself as a "Bluenoser"!! After an hour or so of walking around and enjoying the stark but somewhat weathered architecture of the canneries and boat building houses, we continued on toward Halifax.

Wayne wanted to make one more stop before we hit the capital city and so we again got out of the car in the cute little village of Mahone Bay. Wayne mentioned that this was his wife Brenda's favourite place in the province and it definitely was made for postcards. There were numerous churches around and one could tell that tourism was the big industry here. On the waterfront, there was a large park with a gleaming white gazebo that we used to take photographs from. We found a small restaurant on the waterfront to have our supper. We couldn't resist the opportunity to stop off at Peggy's Cove to see the lighthouse and as we sat beside the rocks and heard the Atlantic waves crash against the shore, a playful weasel cavorted in front of us. It was a perfect way to top off the weekend's travels. In the evening we finally made it to Halifax, where my plane had landed originally. The waterfront was a hive of activity and we even hopped on board the small ferry for the brief ride across the bay to Dartmouth. Back in Halifax, the buskers and shops along the wharf were still quite busy, but after a beer in one of the numerous pubs there, we finally decided to leave for Truro, after all, Wayne had to work in the morning!

During a week of Wayne working and I either hanging around the factory or relaxing at the house in the little village of Lower Onslow, there really wasn't much to do. Wayne's cousin Stephen from England, and his wife Karen were also staying with us and Wayne mentioned that it was time to see the world's largest tidal bore that came up from the Bay of Fundy to a nearby river. Wayne was always getting excited about things like this, so the four of us went out to see the Schubenacadie River. The tidal bore is basically the back flow from Cobequid Bay, and the seawater actually reverses the flow of the river at high tide. We sat around with various other tourists and slowly a sea wave could be seen coming from the Bay. Wayne was thrilled, the other three of us really weren't, but it certainly was a "Bore", there was no doubt about that!!

On the weekend Wayne thought it would be a great idea to head up to the northern part of the province and so we decided to drive along the beautiful Cabot Trail which circled the western half of the large island known as Cape Breton. It was another sunny day and we rose early to beat any traffic, although this was the Maritimes and there never really was any traffic to speak of. In about an hour or so we finally crossed the Canso Causeway at Port Hastings which welcomed us to the island of Cape Breton. The first part of the trail along Highway 105 followed an inland route, where thick pine forests sometimes gave way to open farmland. Along the way we kept our eyes above the treeline to enjoy the soaring flights of hungry hawks. Our first view of water came near Whycocomaugh and we weren't sure if we were looking at fresh or seawater in Bras d'Or Lake. After lunch at a friendly waterside cafe called the Red Barn, where hummingbirds entertained us throughout the meal, we decided to continue on up the coast to Baddeck. It was getting late and Wayne was tiring from the drive so we found a motel just across the road from the water. On the waterfront was a small park and Wayne had fun trying to push the blue chair through all the brambles to get as close to the shore as possible. As the sun dropped both of us suddenly got thirsty. It was time to finish the day off at the pub.

Rising early, we were headed to Ingonish at the southeastern gate of Cape Breton Highlands National Park. It didn't take long for us to be startled just after entering the park, right in front of us was a young moose and in the middle of the road! We had come around a turn and thankfully Wayne was going slowly to view some of the magnificent cliffs along the seaside. We were the only car around and the moose didn't seem to know what to do. I was just about to reach into my bag for the camera when suddenly the beast lifted his head, looked at us briefly and then bounded into the woods. We couldn't believe it. What was even more amazing was that only ten minutes down the road, a number of cars had stopped beside the road and people were pointing and taking pictures. Wayne looked halfway up the hill and there by the shoulder of the road was another male moose, this time a huge bull. He was on a ledge overhanging the road and so was a safe distance up. He had his head bent down and was busy munching on the top of a large bush that was further below, seemingly oblivious to our presence. Wayne and I got out and took some rather amazing photos and then just enjoyed the view until the moose had his fill and spurted away over the hill. What a morning for moose viewing!

The breathtaking scenery along the Cabot Trail is what draws visitors from all over the world to travel around it. Wayne and I stopped in places with wonderful names like Wreck Cove, Cape Smokey and even saw some seals at Green Cove. In the afternoon, we stopped near Pleasant Bay for lunch and I noticed that down on the wharf there was a sign for a whale watching tour. Wayne hates the water almost as much as he hates flying but since he had some Gravol with him in his bag, we decided to go for it. We were now on the top western edge of the island and we were about to sail onto the mouth of the St. Lawrence River. It was a small craft and only about fifteen tourists were coming with us. We moved slowly at first and I glanced at Wayne to see how he was doing. He was pensive, waiting to see if he would throw up, but gradually a smile came over his face as he grew confident that the medication was doing its job. We bumped around a bit on the tiny boat and I had to hang on to the rail to ensure that my chair didn't go flying around the deck, as the brakes had worn down over the years and were generally useless. As we headed out further into the wide river, we spotted some more seals and then finally we could see the backs of the minke whales. I was surprised at how many there were in the pod, well over ten of them and the whales really weren't that big, slightly larger than a dolphin, but it was absolutely thrilling to watch the minke whales as they raced along, jumping out of the water alternatively. Even Wayne was enjoying himself and had a huge smile on his face.

We were on the last leg home and it was late afternoon, but there was still one unplanned event to enjoy. Residing on the west coast of Cape Breton is a large population of Acadians, descendants of some of the original French settlers in Canada. Many of the Acadians were deported by the British once they won control of the province and many settled in then French controlled Louisiana and became known as "Cajuns". We were in the small town of Cheticamp and suddenly we were in a traffic jam! It turned out to be a parade and festival marking the 400th year of Acadian culture, so we simply got out of the car and enjoyed the parade since there wasn't much else to do until the road opened to traffic later on.

It had been a wonderful visit to Nova Scotia with Wayne and we spent the rest of the drive enjoying the sights of the end of the Cabot Trail and laughing at all the wonderful sights we had enjoyed during my visit. It wasn't Africa, but it was almost as fun!

CRUISING BETWEEN THE LAKES IN THE ALPS

I'd always wanted to visit Switzerland, but I'm not really sure why. I knew it was very expensive, but I didn't have a lot of money, it was also very mountainous, and those places aren't generally too Walt-friendly. It may have something to do with the *Sound of Music*, or all the clean air and cowbells, but whatever the reason, it was to be the last stop of my month-long backpacking tour of Europe and it was going to be a long day of travel on the rails.

There was a trip from Zagreb to Zurich, but according to the timetables, I'd only have five minutes to make a train change. Realistically, that wasn't going to happen and so I was forced to go back from whence I came. I'd take the morning train to Vienna and then hang around there for about six hours, before boarding the sleeper to Zurich. I'd spent the previous evening with some of my Dad's relatives who lived in the Croatian capital. They lived out of town, in a house with lots of stairs, so my mother and I had shared a room at a youth hostel near the centre of town. It was her first hostel experience and she was pleasantly surprised. My aunt met us in the morning for breakfast and brought with her a huge bunch of bananas, numbering over ten. I like bananas, but not that much and they don't keep well, so not wanting to offend her I took about half-a-dozen and thanked her. The two elderly ladies accompanied me to the platform and we looked around for assistance in boarding the train.

Croatia had just completed over a half century of communist government and old habits die hard. Unlike the rest of Europe, where getting help was no problem, these government employees turned up their noses at helping us and waved us away saying that it was someone else's job. Just as the train was preparing to pull out and my two companions were preparing to drag my blue chair up the small steps into a car, two young workers finally relented and helped me on, even as they were berated by the ladies. I kissed my mom goodbye and headed back to Vienna.

In the haste to get onto the train, I'd inadvertently boarded a first-class car. My ticket was only valid for a second-class fare, and I'd purchased a ticket to Maribor, the last Slovenian town before I'd be able to use my Eurail pass again in Austria. When we'd crossed out of Croatia and into Slovenia, the conductor finally came through and asked me for my ticket. He scrutinized it and began to admonish me for not having one that was valid for first-class and said in Slovenian that my ticket should go to Graz, Austria, beyond Maribor. I protested as best I could in my terrible Croatian, but he started to fill out all sorts of forms, and I thought it was going to cost me a fortune. He asked me for 400 tolars, a currency I didn't have and was unaccustomed to. I gave him 50 Austrian schillings, as all my Croatian money had been left with relatives there. He didn't want to take it, but I showed him my empty wallet and he left in a huff. I knew I had some change coming, but I didn't think I'd ever see him again. To my surprise, he returned just before the Austrian border and with my change in Austrian money. Later, when I did the conversion, I'd only paid an extra $4. It hadn't been too expensive after all and I'd received my money's worth in entertainment as well.

After spending the better part of a day in Vienna and enjoying some more of my favourite Austrian ice cream, it was time to head back to the nearby train station to arrange for my couchette sleeper. Normally the extra fee for such accommodation is under $15, but for some reason, on this train they wanted upwards of $150! Needless to say, that didn't fit into my budget. It looked like I'd have to be satisfied with a second-class seat on the train. Unlike most trains, this one was quite new and fancy, possibly because it catered to a pricier crowd, but whatever the reason, instead of the usual bench seating that I could stretch out on, this car had airplane-style seating. The seats were upright in groups of three on either side of the aisle. I'd have to be seated for ten hours and it wasn't the most comfortable chair to be in. It had been a long day and the night was going to be sleepless.

After a terrible night of trying to find a good position to snatch at least a few winks of sleep, we finally pulled into Zurich on a sunny morning. I was never so happy to get back into my blue chair and though I was bleary eyed, I had to arrange somewhere to stay. The tourist office directed me not to a hostel, but to an inexpensive (for Switzerland) student accommodation that cost 40 Swiss francs per night. That was above my budget, but I was heading back to Canada in a few days and I could afford it.

I checked in and decided to look around the town. I knew it would be an early night for me so that I could get caught up on some sleep. Zurich is on a sort of river delta between the Sihl River and the Limmat River. Just south of the city, the Limmat empties into Lake Geneva, known to the locals as the "Zurichsee", which I always thought was a funny name for a lake. I wheeled around the clean city streets and was impressed by the lack of graffiti. It was interesting that there were quite a few drug and heroin addicts in the park across the way, but I was told that they tended to stay in a certain part of the park and generally left people alone. After wheeling around for a short time and generally doing some people watching, I found myself in the financial district. The bankers were all very sharply dressed and seemed very serious. I'd always wanted to open a Swiss bank account, just to say I had one. I thought about it for a while and even entered the lobby of one bank, but the guards and sterility of the interior freaked me out and I decided to leave. I still sometimes regret that, but I'm not sure why.

The next day, I decided to take a brief boat trip on the Zurichsee and enjoy the local scenery. The small tourist boat pulled away from the wharf and we slowly left behind the children playing in their paddleboats. The area around the northern fringe of the lake seemed to be a huge green space. Small, well-kept houses lined the top of the shore and below, picnickers and families strolled along in the afternoon sunshine. The impressive skyline of the city was dominated by architecture harkening back to its medieval past. In the distance to the south, historic buildings could be seen atop the high banks of the lake. I was getting too tired to stay awake and upon returning to shore, I made a quick retreat to the residence for a good long sleep.

The following day, I was bright-eyed and bushy-tailed, ready for a day trip to the beautiful town of Interlaken in the middle of Switzerland. My train trip took me through the Swiss capital of Bern, but from what I could see from the train, it didn't look too impressive. Most administrative towns are quite boring, but generally, since all the bureaucrats are in town, they have the best amenities and a fine lifestyle. As we continued south, the train slowly began to make inroads into the wonderful Alps. Each turn brought a new feast for the eyes. Green alpine conifers were so thick that I couldn't see the ground underneath them. Then, they magically opened up to reveal lush lowland meadows with the obligatory herd of cows that have made this country famous. Small villages of a few houses and a church were evident in each new valley we traversed, and it seemed that in only a few hours I'd been completely removed from the hustle and bustle of urban Europe. As we crept along the tracks over the next mountain, I could feel the stress of the entire month of backpacking melt away.

We pulled into the small station at Interlaken and I was instantly struck by the magnificent natural beauty surrounding me. The town itself was very cute, consisting of one main street, mostly catering to the tourist crowd. Interlaken is a resort town situated between two lakes, the Brienzersee and the Thunersee. In addition to wheeling around looking for postcards and drinking a cappuccino in a café, I decided to seek out an excursion. For me, the first choice is always a boat ride. Interlaken offered a boat cruise on the Brienzersee to the town of Brienz on the far side of the lake. The boat I booked was a magnificent historical monument on water. It boasted a classic steam engine and those sailing aboard, who were able to navigate the stairs, were welcome to go down and have a closer look at it. I had to content myself with the view down the hatch to watch it run. I'm definitely not a very mechanically inclined person, but even I was impressed and it seemed the perfect way to set sail for the short trip to Brienz. As we wafted along the calm waters, I peered out at the hills along the lakeside. Even here in a resort town, there were cows on the hillside and as a backdrop, the magnificent Swiss Alps rose in cascading order up to the clear sky.

The town of Brienz, where we stopped for a few hours, was a bit bigger than Interlaken, but it was even more idyllic, slower paced and with fewer pedestrians. I was getting hungry and began to look for a place to have lunch. The menus on display at some of the restaurants were outrageously expensive, even by Swiss standards, so I decided to pass on the idea. I began to wander away from the lake, which wasn't easy for me as it's uphill away from the water. I happened upon a grocery store and went inside to buy a roll and some meat, but I noticed that they had a deli with hot food. The prices were still high, but they were much better than on the main road. I bought a cooked chicken leg and some coleslaw for 7 francs. That was over $10, but it was quite good and it fit my budget. I was running out of Swiss currency since it was my last day in Europe and the next day I'd be heading back to Canada.

I knew that for a long time to come I'd be dreaming about the beauty of this country and I hoped that someday I'd be able to afford to return.

DUSKY LODGE WITH THE WHALES AT KAIKOURA

It was New Year's Day. It wasn't just a new year, it was a new century and I was determined to do something memorable. I'd head down to one of the best places in New Zealand to go whale watching, Kaikoura, on the east coast of the South Island, north of Christchurch.

The first day of 2000 was a sunny one in Wellington, but after all the partying the night before, I had to wake up at 5:30 a.m. and try to sneak out of my hostel without disturbing any of my roommates. Most of them were dead to the world anyway and lying motionless in their bunks from the revelry the night before. I moved through the early daylight down to the wharf to catch my ferry to Picton, the port city that would be my gateway to the south. As usual, I was one of the first to arrive. I should've known better; even those who worked on the ship were moving a little slowly. I like to get to my rides early to scout out the surroundings and determine what position is best for me to see all the sights. I'd never taken the ferry to the other island before and I was really looking forward to it.

We finally pulled away from Wellington Harbour and I felt as though I was pulling away from the previous century as well. The new century held all the same fresh, new possibilities that each day brings but, for some reason, I chose to reflect on all the places in the world I'd been lucky enough to see, and I hoped there'd be some new and interesting ones in the future. We hit the open waves and made our way into the Cook Strait, separating the island from the "mainland", as the southerners called their island. After a long while, we sighted land in the distance. I moved onto the deck to observe our approach and was amazed at the panorama that came into view. Rolling hills seemed to flow out of the water, and as we slowed down, the now sheltered waters calmed and green mountains rose impressively above us. Flocks of hungry, fluffy sheep clipped the paddocks in the gentle meadows punctuating the valleys. I can honestly say that I'd never seen a more pleasing view in my life. It wasn't that the hills were high (they weren't) or that the flora was unique (it wasn't) it was the whole placid picture that warmed my heart. I thought of my Dad, who'd just passed away and had been a shepherd in the old country. He would've loved to see the flock that I was looking at now.

We entered the picturesque harbour at Picton to disembark. I had a few hours, so I explored the waterfront and tried to find the train station for the next leg of the journey to Kaikoura. The station was only a short distance away, so I headed back to the tourist information building to catch up on e-mail and correspondence. I've always enjoyed train travel and when the train finally prepared to depart, I made sure I had a seat facing the ocean. The trip to the southern part of Marlborough was not a long one, and slowly the green, lush hills of the northern part of the island gave way to a brownish semi-arid landscape to the lee of the western mountains. The train offered a menu including a chicken curry. I gave the attendant some money and ordered one. Shortly, I was enjoying a fabulous hot curry. Who would've thought that you could get such an affordable and tasty meal on a TraNZ Rail trip? As we moved south along the coast, parallel to a highway, I enjoyed watching families driving by on their own holidays.

We pulled into the small station at Kaikoura, which was actually very plain, but did have a nice patio and lounge for ocean-side viewing. This was also the place my whale watching tour would depart from, but I didn't want to purchase a ticket right away, as I needed to examine the weather forecast before making the $95 commitment. I needed to get my bearings. I'd booked myself into a hostel, but was unsure where it was located. I knew the town was small, so it must be nearby. I made the mistake of asking a taxi driver if it was far and he said it was, so I used his services. I should've known better than to ask him, as two minutes, five dollars and less than one kilometer later, I was at my hostel, Dusky Lodge. It was the first time I'd ever been taken advantage of in New Zealand, but in all fairness, he may not have been aware of my ability to wheel over short distances.

I'd spoken with the owner of the Dusky Lodge over the phone, inquiring about access for someone backpacking in a chair. He'd mentioned that there was a washroom on the main floor, but that the shower facilities were "around at the back". I wasn't really sure what that meant, but he said it was great for wheelchairs and I'd be fine. I arrived around lunchtime and when I checked in, there was a girl at the desk. She gave me a key and showed me to the four-bed dormitory that was the first room down the hall from the foyer. The lobby was the entertainment centre where the TV and stereo were located and past the back hall, was the kitchen. It was still New Year's Day, and so many backpackers were still just rolling out of bed and having their first "cuppa" of the new century.

The washroom the owner had spoken of was indeed around back. The driveway to the rear of the building fell off steeply from the road and as a result, when I was at the bottom of the hill, I was level with the hostel's basement, which served as the ten-bunk dorm for those who were really watching their pennies. There was a glass patio door at the entrance and I was to use their showers, since this was the one that was accessible. It was a bit of a bother, but it was possible. Back upstairs where I was staying, there was an outside balcony with a barbeque and from all the empty beer bottles, it looked to me that this was the place most of the partying had occurred the previous night. Someone asked if I'd like a coffee, so I accepted and sat out enjoying the great view of green fields behind the Lodge and mountains in the distance beyond the paddock.

The owner finally appeared on the back patio. His eyes were squinting and he was terribly stooped over. I was wondering what had happened to the poor soul, when I finally realized he was either still plastered from the night before or he was suffering from one of the worst hangovers I'd ever seen. He looked at me in my blue chair and some vague memory sparked in his still sobering brain. "Willy?" he asked. "No", I replied. "Warren? Wilf?" I laughed and told him he was getting closer, then I finally stopped teasing him and introduced myself. One of the girls mercifully made him a coffee and he told me he'd hosted quite a bash at the Lodge and that it hadn't broken up until 4 a.m. The next day when I saw him again, he was actually feeling human and was in much better shape.

I decided this was going to be the day to go whale watching. As far as I could tell, it was nice enough to risk the money, but when I arrived at the booking agency adjacent to the train station, they were unsure if they were going out due to expected inclement weather in the afternoon. I stopped for a cappuccino and decided to wait and see if they'd go out at all. After an hour or so, with buses of people who'd previously booked arriving and wondering whether they'd see any whales today, the pressure was on them to make a decision. They finally relented and we were on our way.

The staff carried me onto a huge machine that resembled the largest dune buggy I'd ever seen. It was quite steep and I was scared they were going to drop me on the way up. Once we'd navigated a distance out to meet the tour boat, I was manually transferred into the lounge inside the deck, where I'd remain during the voyage. I was a tad disappointed, since I like to stay outdoors when boating, but they told me it was too steep to get me onto the upper deck and since I have a bad sense of balance anyway, it was probably best to remain indoors.

We chugged out into the Pacific to try to find some whales, hoping it wouldn't take too long. Kaikoura is located on the edge of a relatively shallow shelf that drops off into the depths of the ocean. The little animals whales love to eat called "krill", congregate in these warm waters and as a result, the whales follow them here. The company conducting the sighting, owned by the Maori, was very ecologically conscious and endeavoured to disturb the whales as little as possible. They restricted their trips to certain times of the year and generally left the aquatic mammals alone when breeding. In the cabin, one of the gentlemen who worked on board was like a walking encyclopedia and droned on and on in a dry, rehearsed soliloquy about the history of the area and all the whale facts you'd ever want to know. It was informative, but he never stopped and it got to be a bit much after a while.

One of the interesting things we saw was an albatross. They have a huge wingspan and spend almost all their lives at sea, except during the breeding season. Our guides were having a hard time finding whales, even while in radio communication with other boats and the weather had deteriorated to the point that some guests were becoming seasick.

Just as the crew decided to pack it up for the day, we got word of a sighting of some sperm whales. We motored over to a small flotilla of boats and the spouting spray that was certain evidence of a whale. It was thrilling. As we approached, the small black spot in the water became very large and I was surprised at how close we were to it.

Even though I was still sitting on the bench and most of the others were standing in front of me, there were enough gaps that I could get a good look at the whale. It lounged around, just floating there. We watched for about five minutes and then the large tail came out of the water. We knew that when its fluke emerges, it's generally the last time you'll see the whale, as it's readying to dive down to the depths.

It'd been a long and bumpy day's travel on the Pacific, but the boat was buzzing with excitement at the magnificent animal we'd witnessed. They say that the best experience is an experience shared and today I knew that was true.

A RAINY AUTUMN WEEKEND IN THE BIG APPLE

With all my travels around the world over the years, I've overlooked travel to interesting destinations closer to home. A number of years ago, my brother John and I, along with our two friends Phil and Rob (who were John's co-best men at his wedding) planned a hasty trip to New York City. It turned out to be just as memorable for me as it was for them.

We decided to avoid the long drive and ride the rails with Amtrak from Niagara Falls, Ontario. I love trains and they're especially great if you're in a wheelchair because I don't even have to leave my chair. Unlike many train services in the world, Amtrak doesn't have a car specially designed for the disabled. Instead, I was left in the dining car where the only extra wide washroom was. I was a bit disappointed, but my travelling companions were quite happy with the arrangement. Because of the lack of bench seats on the left side of the car, Phil decided to stretch out on the floor and use his knapsack as a pillow. Rob and John sat on the opposite side. As you might expect with old friends, most of the trip was spent reliving old tales of fame and glory from younger days. Actually, I was the odd man out. They'd all gone to secondary school together, while I attended another school that had fewer stairs. The three of them had also lived together in Toronto, so had common experiences from that time to draw on for stories to exchange. I didn't mind because many of the stories were new to me and were very entertaining.

The trip across the border, toward the Atlantic Ocean, is almost due east. I looked out the window and admired the rolling hills of upstate New York. For Canadians, the U.S. is still a bit of an enigma. We like to think that we're at the centre of the universe sometimes, but many Americans barely give us a second thought. We chuckle at their accents with their flat "a" sounds that seem to come from their noses. Yanks mock us for our Scottish sounds in words like "house" or "about", they swear we're saying "hoose" or "aboot", but it's all in good fun. As we drew closer to NYC, the countryside was slowly replaced by a familiar urban landscape. At each stop, there was more graffiti at the stations and the vicinities seemed to be in a greater state of disrepair. By the time we finally pulled into Penn Station, we'd been in the dining car for well over ten hours. All the coffee and junk food had taken its toll. We were hyped up for our visit. It was my first time here and I wanted to see as much as possible. The only problem that remained was finding a place to sleep.

I'm a person who likes to do a bit of planning prior to a trip. That's not to say I want to have a rigid schedule, but at least it's good to know where you're going to spend the first night, so you can drop off your stuff, refresh yourself and then head out to see some sights. My brother and our buddies had assured me that there'd be lots of places of quality to choose from once we arrived. I'm an experienced traveller, but I deferred to their expertise since they'd been here before and I hadn't. When I had suggested booking the YHA hostel, I was mocked and told that half the fun was arriving and then bargaining for a cheap room. Of course, I had many preconceived notions about the cleanliness of what we'd find in our search, but I knew it couldn't be as bad as I imagined.

As it turned out, the United Nations was celebrating its fiftieth anniversary, the same weekend we'd chosen for our visit. My worst fears had come true and we were left scrambling for accommodation. Turnabout is fair play and I took great delight in teasing my companions at how surprisingly easy it was to find a hotel. As we walked the streets in the damp evening air, we'd stop by any reasonable looking place offering accommodation to see if something was available. Mostly, we were met by staff who shook their heads even before the question was out of our mouths. The closest we came was a place off of Times Square, whose name I will not mention. We entered the shabby lobby and Rob and my brother went to the front desk to enquire. Phil and I waited near the front door, contemplating staying out for the night and just walking around. Phil decided to make a call to his brother who lived in the city, and as he did, the other two arrived back, saying the place did have a room for us. We were still weighing our options, wondering whether there'd be any rats or bugs, when Phil quickly came back, walked right by us and tersely barked "C'mon guys, let go". We looked at each other with perplexed stares and followed him out onto the sidewalk. It turned out that the phone box Phil had found was crawling with cockroaches and he said if the lobby was that bad, he didn't want to spend the night.

We continued our search and my teasing was beginning to wear a bit thin. None of us was too worried. We knew from experience that even a night spent in NYC coffee shops would be an interesting time and we could look for something else later on, or failing that, we could crash with Phil's brother, even though it would mean dragging both me and my blue chair up a few flights of stairs.

After exploring Times Square thoroughly and admiring the lights and all the activity, we found ourselves in front of a Howard Johnson's. Phil, the intrepid searcher, popped into the lobby and told one of the staff our dilemma, also providing a small bribe. He came out to tell us to grab our things and get inside as he'd found us a room. We were quite happy and headed up the elevator. It was actually a suite, with one large room containing two beds and a small room with a single bed. Since my brother had done all sorts of complaining about the sorry state of his back since we'd arrived, we gave him the small room to enjoy in solitude. Rob and Phil would share one of the beds in the large room and I'd have the other. Just one small problem: the washroom door was very narrow and the facility was totally inaccessible. If I intended to do any business in there, someone would have to carry me.

We woke early to a dark, gloomy New York morning. Light rain was falling and the streets took on a clean, shiny appearance. In the days before the tragic collapse of the World Trade Center, it was a major point of interest for tourists, like us, to go to the top and view Manhattan and the surrounding boroughs and waterways from the highest observation deck in town. That was out of the question. Even our planned trip on the Staten Island ferry to see the Statue of Liberty didn't look too promising. Unless the weather cleared, which was not in the forecast, we'd have to content ourselves with prowling the streets and avenues of the island and seeing as many sights and districts as we could on the hoof.

We sat in a local diner out of the rain for an hour eating a large, cheap breakfast of bacon and eggs that I'm sure didn't do any of us much good, but we needed the caffeine fix to help us on our way. Initially, my brother John was in charge of pushing me along the sidewalks. He wasn't very good at it. The bevelled curbs had a bit of a lip as they rose from the street and John wasn't very adept at tilting the chair prior to moving up onto the pavement. When the front wheels of the blue chair hit, the chair stopped and I kept going. It happened twice, almost tossing me head first, before I took matters into my own hands and started popping small wheelies each time we moved onto another block.

Some of NYC life can be a bit sad for tourists to see, but I suppose that's one of the attractions of big cities and not unique to NYC. We passed many poor or mentally ill people rooting around in public trash containers searching for bottles or cans to recycle for cash. Some of the unemployed sat on the street with cups begging for handouts of small change and cardboard signs spelling out their plight. What puzzled me was that many of them still had enough money to own large dogs. On the other hand, New York is a bustling city and, for people willing or able to work, there are many opportunities and that's one of the reasons it's such a magnet for people from all over the world.

We walked toward Central Park, but the gloomy weather changed our minds about going for a stroll inside. Instead, we went to Rockefeller Center to see if we could get onto the morning TV show through the window. Unfortunately the morning show was over, but we peeked inside to see the sets and then decided on a walk down Broadway. I was thrilled to see the theatres I'd heard so much about over the years, as well as the magnificent billboards advertising current plays or musicals. None of us actually wanted to attend a performance without the company of a lady, but it was fun to look around and ask about the availability of tickets for the evening's performances.

Phil and I wanted to visit Wall St., so we all made our way toward Lower Manhattan. Phil was now in control of my vehicle, as I'd finally let John off the hook due to sore his back was from stooping over to reach the low handles. In all fairness, that's a common complaint I've heard from many of my friends over the years. When we arrived, I was surprised at how small Wall St. is. The New York Stock Exchange building is quite impressive, but it was a Saturday and so we were unable to go in and see the centre of capitalism in action.

As the rain started to fall harder, we sought sanctuary in the entrance of a small church. It was early afternoon and people began to arrive for a wedding that was about to get underway. Phil, John and Rob decided to use their umbrellas to keep the young ladies dry as they made their way in from their cars. It became a game for us and we laughed as everyone thanked us and thought what a nice service the celebrants had employed. The smokers stayed hovering near the entrance with us and by the time the wedding was about to begin, we'd been invited to stay for the marriage and reception. The offer was tempting and we thanked them, but the weather had let up and we wanted to see a bit more of the city.

After stopping for another cup of coffee, we walked towards Canal St. where shops sell exotic foreign goods. My brother was looking for a gift to make up for the weekend away from his wife and ended up buying a purse, after stopping at what seemed like every stall on the road. We were hungry and since Little Italy was in the vicinity and both Rob and Phil were of Italian descent, it seemed like a good place to dine. We enjoyed a long meal with some great antipasto and main courses, but the restaurant we chose was almost empty. The food was excellent and the conversation was animated. Rob is a funny guy and seemed to know all the trivia and interesting facts about NYC. He's also pretty good at doing impersonations of famous personalities and we were cracked up when the coffee and dessert came. By the time we left, we'd met the owner and he'd given each of us his business card and asked us to tell our friends about the place when we returned home.

It was a long walk back to our hotel and now it was Rob's turn to guide me along the mean streets. He's shorter in stature and didn't mind at all, so I enjoyed his push the most of the three. The relentless rain was beginning to take its toll and I was starting to lose feeling in my legs, something that's not good for my disposition. I was feeling a bit like a drowned rat, but my companions seemed to have regained their energy. As we walked along, we saw Jerry Stiller, the man who played George's father on the TV show, *Seinfeld*. He was talking to someone and we didn't want to bother him, but he did wave to us. That was our first brush with fame that weekend.

There was a crowd in front of the Planet Hollywood restaurant and we stopped to ask what was going on. It was the anniversary of the opening and some famous stars were going to attend. My brother John scurried up some scaffolding in front of the building to get a bird's eye view of the celebrities. Both Rob and Phil wandered off into the crowd to see what was going on and I was left alone for a while. Since I'm in a chair and couldn't see over the crowd, I decided to wheel to the corner to look at Carnegie Hall, while they were occupied in their star search. My brother saw me heading away from the crowd, came down and ran after me. When he caught up at the corner, he yelled at me, "Walt, this is NYC! You can't just go off by yourself!" I looked at him with a long stare and replied, "John, I've travelled all over the world by myself. I think I can handle one block in this town". I guess he was just being my older brother, but he ultimately relented and returned to his perch atop the metal grids. Eventually, Bruce Willis arrived at the party and the crowd went wild. My brother waited until the crowd noise died down, then yelled out "Bruuuuuuuce". Apparently Mr. Willis heard him, pointed at John and waved. It made John's weekend.

I was too cold and wet to continue and decided to give the guys a break from pushing me around in the wretched weather. I told them I wanted to head back, so we grabbed a cab to the hotel. My legs were frozen and I had to hit the can. Phil was enlisted to lift me into the washroom. He grabbed me under the arms and dragged me awkwardly onto the seat. Rob and John had a good laugh and I received some relief. When I got to my bed, I crawled under the sheets to warm up and dry out. The three of them headed back out into the New York City night for some more coffee and another long, wet walk.

We had a great time that weekend, but I've decided to visit again in the summer when the weather is drier and hopefully the UN is not in session. That's my UN resolution.

THREE HIGH FLIERS IN THE WILD, BLUE YONDER

One of my favourite stories is about two friends of mine, Rex, a native Kiwi, whom I met on my first trip down under back in the mid '90s, and Tom, a smiling, blonde Aussie, with a typical outgoing personality, who lived on Queensland's Sunshine Coast. Rex was trying to decide whether to move to Australia on a permanent basis, and decided to spend a year there. He purchased a car and caravan to live in, and went about the country investigating its nooks and crannies, while looking up old friends along the way.

All three of us belonged to an old BBS for people interested in discussing the Asian-Pacific region of the world. BBS was the forerunner of what is now the Internet. Rex was on his travels and would sign off his e-mails "Rex, currently in Noosa Heads, QLD" or wherever he was. As it turned out, that's exactly where he was, and Tom, who ran a small I.T. consulting business in the same town, posted a message asking to meet him for a pint because he wanted to discuss something. Tom was looking for someone to work with him fielding questions on publishing software, and the two struck up a friendship and became workmates.

I'd visited Rex in Noosa two years earlier, before this had happened, and was introduced to Tom, whom I liked immediately. He had a great outlook on life and a terrific sense of humour. Now, I was planning on visiting Noosa again, but Rex was back home in New Zealand acting as best man at a wedding and Tom was up in Cairns installing an Internet café. I was going to be on my own trying to figure out how to get to Noosa. I'd been there on my last visit, so at least I had a rough idea of where it was.

My flight from Sydney to Brisbane was a short one. One of the great things about that airport is that the trains run a connection through the terminal. I knew from experience that I had to buy a ticket on the "Queenslander", which runs north from Brisbane all the way to Rockhampton. My stop was at Nambour, inland from Noosa on the coast, where my hostel was. The train staff placed my blue chair in the first-class section, even though my ticket was for economy. I was told it was the only place they had the proper restraints for the disabled, but I wondered what would've happened had I been travelling with someone with the same ticket I had. Would they be required to go back into the other section? The car was great and as I looked out the window to watch the passing tropical scenery, there was also the option of watching a TV screen mounted onto the ceiling, showing a view down the track. That was excellent.

I arrived at Nambour just as darkness fell and was told that if I wheeled just a few block to the bus station, there'd be a Sunshine Bus headed for the coast in about thirty minutes. I found the bus stop and waited. I was concerned since I remembered that these were not full-sized busses, but small ones, more suited to schoolchildren. I was also alone, and that meant there was no one to help me get on. As the minutes dragged on, three others assembled and though they looked like the cast from *Deliverance*, I asked the one who appeared to be the youngest, if he could help me onto the bus. He said it was no problem and the other two, one an older man with a beard and the other an Aborigine, piped up and said they'd make sure I got on. When the bus arrived, two of them assisted me onto the bus, while the third took care of my bags and the bus driver folded my chair and stowed it beside me. He asked where I was headed and I told him Noosa. He asked more specifically where I was staying in Noosa and I told him the name of the backpackers hostel. "Oh, I know that one, mate. I'll swing by and drop you off, if that's OK with everyone?" My fellow passengers nodded in agreement and when we arrived, they all pitched in and helped me get out and up the curb to the hostel. I don't think you'd get that type of help in North America. Here, most drivers worry about insurance regulations and none would deviate from the bus route to take someone directly to where they were headed. That was what I loved about Oz!

After spending most of a 41°C day by the river sitting under a tree, reacquainting myself with Noosa, my friend, Rex, finally pulled up in his new Land Rover Discovery and greeted me with a throaty "G'day". Even though we'd only met on two occasions and then only for probably ten days at the most, we'd become good friends. He's a robust guy, slightly rounded at the edges, in his fifties and with closely cropped, but annoyingly grayless, hair. We'd kept in touch through the years via e-mail and this time, I was going to spend the week with him in his caravan. The last time I'd visited, his caravan park was down the street from the hostel that he'd just picked me up from, so I stayed there, and wheeled down to the park to hang out with him in the evenings. Now he was a few kilometers out of town in Tewantin, so I'd try to crawl into his trailer and crash there. We were both worried about getting me in, but as a back-up, I mentioned that I could sleep in his 4x4 or camp out in a tent. I remembered that his trailer was rather small.

When we arrived, I was quite impressed by the quality of the facilities. They had a restaurant, games room, disabled showers and toilets, TV area and a swimming pool. Campgrounds in Australia are far better than those in North America and don't have the same stigma attached. Due to the climate, caravanning is quite popular with all generations and you can move about the country from one ground to another, all belonging to the same national chains. We got caught up over dinner and a few beers and then it was time to figure out if I could fit into the caravan.

As you entered, the table was folded down into a cushioned bed, which was where I was going to sleep. Down a narrow hall, the sink and kitchen were on the right and closet space on the left, while at the far end on the left was Rex's bed. I crawled in successfully and told Rex that he was going to have to heave me up the last two feet onto the bed. "One, two, three", we counted in unison (I have no idea why I counted, as I was just dead weight), then he lifted and I was on the bed. I asked him to stow my chair in his car, as the morning dew and bugs would've left it in a dreadful state by sunrise. Together, we'd overcome the challenges of the sleeping arrangements and I was asleep quickly.

One of the weirdest things about Queensland, is that they don't push the clocks forward to observe summer time. As a result, I was awakened at about 4:30 a.m. by a roost of noisy kookaburras sitting in a gum tree about fifty yards away, screaming at each other like there was no tomorrow. Rex was used to it and I could hear him snoring away. The next night, I remembered to put in my earplugs.

After a few days relaxing at Noosa Beach, where Rex dropped me off on his way to work, it was time to do some exploring. On the weekend, Rex and I had decided to head out on a bit of a drive that would take us to Eumundi, the home of a wonderful market and a very Australian rural setting. As we drove up and down the slight hills on narrow two-lane roads, I was pleased to see a mob of kangaroos munching on grass in a farmer's paddock. Actually, despite how cute they seem to tourists, kangaroos and wallabies are widely regarded as pests in the remote areas and are often legally culled to keep their numbers in check. The market was a typical assortment of stalls selling local handicrafts, some of which were quite good. Rex was interested in some quality, handcrafted furniture, as his belongings back in NZ had been lost in a fire at a storage facility and he was expecting the insurance settlement soon. As the day passed into mid-afternoon and the crowd became larger, Rex and I decided to meet up with Tom in town. Tom's friends were opening a "chop shop", which is Aussie slang for a bargain, second-hand store.

It was a short drive and after finding suitable parking, we were greeted by Tom's smiling face pointing us toward the top of a small hill overlooking one of the major intersections in town. The friends, who were to be the proprietors of this establishment, were an interesting assortment of pleasant, hippy-type throwbacks, one of whom stood out with his huge closely cropped sideburns. There were assorted finger foods and wine to celebrate the opening and I purchased an interesting key fob of a pig. If you squeezed the pig, some gelatin poop would come from its backside. We stayed for less than an hour, before Tom decided it was a nice day and asked if I was up for a flight in his light plane. I sure was. Two years ago, we'd tried to go up and were unable to when the small hangar was blocked by a car and trailer. Tom had been hopping mad about that.

We transferred into Tom's silver coloured four-wheel drive vehicle for the short trip to Gympie, Queensland, where the Mooney aircraft was housed. At Easter, my two friends had travelled from here over the Outback to Alice Springs and above Uluru on a great adventure. This time, there were no vehicles blocking our access to the hanger and after manually removing a small plane that was parked in front, Rex and Tom rolled out the four-seater. It was reddish, looked to be in fine shape and was something that Tom was extremely proud of. In his earlier days, Tom had been a pilot for the famous Australian Royal Flying Doctor's Service, which provides medical rescue and emergency treatment for people who live in rural areas, remote Aboriginal communities and on far flung sheep and cattle stations. I decided to remove my heavy shoes and leg braces to help get into the plane more easily. Tom and Rex lifted me onto the right wing and with Tom reaching out from the passenger seat and Rex on the ground, we were able to drag me into the cockpit. My blue chair looked quite lonely as it sat empty beside the grassy runway. Rex climbed into the back seat. We closed the cockpit, revved up the engine and taxied out to the runway. As Tom radioed his intention to take off, I could feel the excitement build up in me. I was very confident in Tom with his flying experience and even Rex had obtained his flying license in his younger days. We bumped along the ground, built up speed and suddenly we were airborne.

We had escaped gravity, my old enemy, and I looked out the window to a lush scene below. As we gained altitude and banked into a left turn, some mountains in the distance became evident and the cars and buildings shrank below us. The noise from the engine and wind rushing through the cracks in the seal between the plane and the plastic dome of the cockpit, made conversation all but impossible, but it didn't stop us from trying. I looked back at Rex and handed him my camcorder to record the scene as it unfolded. He had a big smile on his face and was trying to show me a point of interest, but I couldn't understand what he was saying. After about fifteen minutes, Tom asked if I wanted to drive for a while. Of course I did, but I warned him that I had a terrible sense of balance and wasn't sure if it was possible. "Don't worry. I'll hold you up and keep you straight", he offered, telling me to grab the steering wheel on my side of the cockpit. I took the reigns. Tom showed me how to increase altitude, bank to the left and right and then flatten out. I was terrified and thrilled at the same time, but hey, it was something I'd always wanted to do. In Canada, there's a famous disabled ultralight pilot who's travelled across North America, so I knew I should give it a go. After five or six minutes, I asked Tom to take back the controls. I sat back and enjoyed the view of the subtropical landscape that the Sunshine Coast and interior of Southern Queensland had to offer. As the end of the flight neared, we soared over our friends at the bargain shop and Tom used the mobile phone to alert them to our presence overhead. We banked and then headed back to Gympie. After touching down and moving back into the blue chair, I reflected on what had been a truly wonderful experience. What was even better was being able to share it with two good friends. It was important to me, because when I travel alone, my experiences are usually not shared. I suggested that it was time for a beer and that it would be my shout.

We headed out to the town of Boreen Point and a typical old Australian pub. As a cricket match played on the TV inside, the three of us, an Aussie, a Kiwi and a Canuck, sat alone with our frosty beverages on the patio, reflecting on what had been a great day.

Tragically, it was one of the last beers I would ever share with Tom. I did catch up with him once more in Melbourne, when he visited his hometown for his sister's wedding and prepared to move his I.T. firm back to Victoria. But upon my return to Canada, I learned of his untimely death three months later, after collapsing following a hiking trip in Germany with his girlfriend, Laila. He'd fallen ill, collapsed and died. He was still shy of his forty-first birthday. What a terrible loss to his family and friends.

Even though I knew him for only a short while, I was glad that he seemed to count me as one of his friends as he would always introduce me as "Walt, my friend from Canada". He was a wonderful bloke and all his friends and family miss him greatly.

"AR MATEY, COME AN' SPEND THE NIGHT W' ME"

The train pulled into Antwerp from my visit to Nice on the Riviera, and I wondered what the heck I was doing back in the northern part of Europe. Belgium wasn't really on my list of destinations, despite the fact that I worked for a Belgian pharmaceutical company, and it was too far north for my liking since that summer of 1996 was a rather cool one on the continent. I was in town to rendezvous with my buddy Lenny, whom I had hooked up with earlier in Amsterdam and a girl who was also on the baseball team back home. Trudy was travelling with her friend and had given me a phone number and a date when she'd be in town. They were two friends I really liked, and after ten days in Europe, it would be nice to speak English with some people from home.

    The problem of arriving at the train station and finding the tourist office was becoming old hat. I located it and asked for assistance in finding a hostel that would be manageable for my blue chair. The lady at the desk looked a bit perplexed. Usually, the attendants smile and quickly have a place in mind, at least as a starting point. This woman gave me a vacant stare and I was not getting a good feeling. She asked me to sit (which is one of my best things) and wait while she went to talk to someone in the back office. I waited for about five minutes and she held her finger up, asking me to wait for a second while she made a phone call. I turned to look out the window at the dull low clouds as they rapidly floated by. The darkness and the light rain made me long for the sunshine and warmth of southern France. In time, she displayed the optimistic smile I was looking for. She got out a map, drew a line on it marking the route to my accommodation and informed me that there were no youth hostels in Antwerp that were suitable for chairs, because the town is so old. She'd booked me into a residence for retired sailors called "The International Seaman's House". Oh, I thought, this is just what I need, a few nights in a rat-infested building with a bunch of smelly, toothless old sailors, swapping stories about their pirating days. I was not happy, but I had no choice and set off into the dreary weather to check it out.

As I wheeled along the narrow streets, I began to notice the beauty of the city. Ancient buildings were crammed together in an effort to restrict the space between them, and people carrying their umbrellas, seemed to take no notice of the horrid weather. After about thirty minutes of wheeling through the streets, I finally came upon the Seaman's House, and it was a pleasant surprise. It was a modern facility with automatic sliding doors at the entrance, leading to an open and welcoming atrium lobby. The people at the front desk had been expecting me since the call from the tourist office and they knew who I was immediately. I checked in and was taken up to my room on the third floor. I was later told that all Seamen in Belgium pay into a fund for their retirement and that if they become too old or infirm to take care of themselves, they are entitled to trade in their pension cheques for room and board here. It also served as a conference and convention centre for business related to the seafaring industry, so they always had accommodation available. The room had an ensuite bath and, although there was no TV and the bed was a bit small, I was happy that I'd made it. I decided to take a shower and then stretch out for a while. Because the weather didn't look like clearing up and my friends weren't due in town until tomorrow, I couldn't think of any other productive activities.

I woke up at about 2:30 p.m. and to my great delight, the skies had largely cleared. I decided to head out into the afternoon to explore for a while and find an activity for the day. The streets were drying up, but there was still a thin layer of grime that seemed to cover everything. When I wheel, I don't use gloves. I'm not sure why, as it would probably be better in the long run, my hands would be cleaner, and I'd have fewer calluses than I currently do. However, for me gloves have never felt right and I've always worried about sweat building up inside them and getting some terrible skin condition. Anyway, after only a few minutes, my hands were their usual shade of black and the sleeves of my jacket weren't much better. I have some dysfunction in my right shoulder, making me a semi-quadriplegic, meaning that I'm not one of those young guys with muscular upper bodies who zip along the sidewalks. I plod along, but I go at a steady pace and have developed enough stamina over the years from playing competitive sports, to keep going for up to ten hours at a time. Even going slowly, you can cover a lot of ground in a day, and it's also good for your health as the cardiovascular exercise keeps the weight down. When you're in a chair, weight is a constant battle, and if you're like me and enjoy a tasty Stella Artois with your meal, then all the more so.

I found a section of the city called "the Meir", which is basically a pedestrian mall for shoppers and tourists. As the weather had improved enormously, the cafés had opened and people were enjoying sunshine and conversation. The buildings reflect the best that the Renaissance had to offer and the road led back to the central train station where I'd arrived. I wheeled though the Grote Markt, which is the town centre and watched buskers entertaining the townsfolk and visitors alike. The guide stated that this area was the old focal point for business and the trading of wares from different unions of craftsmen in times past. I stopped briefly into a free museum that displayed historical artifacts of Antwerp. Today, Antwerp is a centre for the diamond industry and has a large Orthodox Jewish population. In the middle of the square, Brabo Fountain, named after a mythic figure in Flemish lore, loudly sounds its presence with its waters. I've always been drawn to fountains and I sat mesmerized by its Baroque beauty.

I finally decided to go on a river tour, so I headed down to the Wharf to see if there were any available for the evening. I found one and boarded the vessel for a trip down the Scheldt River. I like to take these tours as they're very laid back and I can sit in my chair and watch the scenery slowly drift by. Perhaps it was due to the weather earlier in the day, but there weren't many of us on the boat. We left the wharf and began to drift among small waves. It wasn't long before the poor weather began to set in again and the warmth of the sun disappeared. I couldn't believe the number and beauty of old castles we saw on the voyage. For me, this is about the best way to go looking at castles—from the outside. As you can imagine, they're a horror as far as disabled access is concerned. But here, gliding along, I felt like a pawn on a chess set weaving through a column of rooks. The castles were absolutely magnificent and spoke of a history that seemed so distant from today's fast-paced modern lifestyle.

Upon disembarking, I was quite hungry and decided to scout out a place to eat and drink. I wheeled back towards the Seaman's House and although they had a conventional dining room there, I wanted to spend my first dinner in a proper restaurant. In Europe, it's conventional to post your menu outside so that prospective customers can discuss the food without making a commitment. I was evaluating a restaurant that had lamb on the menu and was trying to convert the Belgian franc, which was worth about five cents, into dollars in my head. The owner, who looked to be of Arabic or Mediterranean descent, was standing outside having a cigarette and took a look at me. After wheeling around for a number of hours, and with a mess of windswept hair and black hands, I must've looked like quite a sight. Generously, he smiled, waved me inside and said "Gratis", which I took to mean that he thought I was poor and was offering me a free meal. I did decide to eat there, but I paid the bill and the lamb was delicious. Prior to eating, I showed him my dirty hands and arms and asked if I could wash up. He called out to the kitchen and before long, a young woman came out with some water in bowl, a rag and some soap. It is always nicer to eat bread with your hands when they're clean.

The next day, I phoned the number Trudy had provided, but it just rang and rang, as it did the following day. I found out when I got back to Canada that she'd switched accommodation on me. We must have just missed each other for the next two days. They told me they'd been to all the pubs and got drunk in most of them. To top it off, I finally ran into Lenny as he walked past me in the train station in Brussels as we were both heading out of town. He had his head down, looking a bit tired, and walked past, but I yelled out his name to draw his attention. He said he had a great time with Trudy and her friend and it was too bad I didn't hook up with them. We talked a little longer and then parted ways. He was headed to Prague via Cologne. I was headed south to find some sunshine.

THE BAHT IN MY HAT

It had been a long flight from Melbourne to Thailand, not that I wasn't in good company. Many of the people I saw heading up into first class were players I'd recently seen on TV at the Australian Open tennis tournament. For them, Thailand was simply a stop on the long flight back to Europe, but for me it was a destination. I'd always wanted to visit this country for the exotic landscape, the people, the architecture and, of course, the food. It was approaching darkness as the plane began to circle Bangkok and as I caught my first glimpse of mainland Asia, I was surprised at what I saw.

As expected, the city was a huge metropolis, but the condition of the atmosphere above the town was a shock. There was a blackish-brown pall that seemed to hang over it like a cloud that wouldn't move. I'd heard stories about polluted cities like Bangkok and Mexico City, but had never experienced it first-hand before. I had no time to worry about it now. I had to get off the plane and to my hotel. The first problem occurred as I was still sitting on the plane waiting for the staff to bring my chair up to the cabin—they informed me that it had been lost! That was not good. Happily it turned out that my blue prop had only been misplaced and after about twenty minutes they apologetically returned my chair to me and it was none the worse for wear. I next had to get some currency exchanged into Thai "baht". I was assigned a man to help guide me through the airport and the first task, as usual after long flights, is to enjoy a moment of great relief. The washrooms were totally accessible, so that little dilemma was accomplished without a hitch. On the concourse of the airport's main floor, my guide directed me to the "money changers" as they're called. All the fellows behind the desks seemed to be offering the exact same rate, so I signed over a traveller's cheque and received my money. My Tilley hat has a secret money pocket in its top, so I put the fee I'd need to get out of the country in it (hence the catchy title of this story, with apologies to Dr. Seuss). I mentioned to my companion that I needed a taxi to get into Bangkok, so we made our way outside into the thick, humid Asian air. One of the huge advantages of being in a blue chair is that you often get preferential treatment when it counts the most. I sometimes feel a bit sheepish about taking advantage of the situation, but when you're faced with throngs of newly arrived visitors from all over the world and you quickly get to the front of the line for the next taxi, you try not to worry too much about it. I tipped my helper and got into the next taxi in line.

I had booked a hotel that I'd found on the Internet. Again, from what I'd read and heard from other backpackers, the famous Khao San Road, which is the centre of action for budget travellers, was not a place I'd be likely to find accommodation to fit my needs. The YHA in Bangkok had e-mailed me and politely suggested that I look elsewhere for a place to stay. The Baan Sabai hotel was what I'd found. They advertised first-floor accommodation with air conditioning and a main floor restaurant, all of which sounded good to me. My cabbie had informed me, in broken English, that I had to pay extra to go on the toll road to get into the city. I was a dumb newcomer so I told him to go ahead. It cost me an extra 50B, which isn't much, but I noticed that since it was so late in the day, there was hardly any traffic on the roads. We struggled to find the hotel and finally the driver had to break down and ask someone in the vicinity exactly where it was. We pulled up, and I quickly realized that the hotel wasn't what it had advertised.

I was staring up from the street at six steps into the building. The only good thing about the steps was that they were relatively shallow and very wide, resembling a terrace, so my entire chair could fit on one of them. I was very disappointed though. It meant that during my stay, I'd have to ask for help whenever I wanted to get in or out. After receiving assistance into the hotel, I received more bad news. The room with air conditioning that I'd booked, was unavailable until the next day. I was tired and tried to make the best of a bad situation. At this point, I just wanted to get the key to my room and crash out on the bed.

The room I was first given was not much to write home about; there were two single beds pushed together to look like one and it was hellishly hot. There was an overhead fan, but it was quite a high ceiling so it offered little relief. Outside, I was to use a public washroom that had one step up to it. I asked someone for a boost and was able to make it close enough to a urinal to do my stuff, but I hoped that after a night's sleep, things would look better in the morning.

After a restless night's tossing and turning in the sauna of a room they'd given me, I woke up and managed to get up the step again into the washroom and used a facecloth to refresh myself as best I could. I asked the attendant at the front desk about switching to the room with A/C and they assured me there would be no problem.

I was starting to gain my bearings and actually the hotel was quite nice, aside from all the bother I'd come up against so far. The fact that those six wide and annoying stairs were there meant the hotel was recessed away from the street and so we were subjected to quite a bit less noise than had it been located nearer the traffic. The floors and walls were a unique, polished marbled brown and the lobby was wide and inviting with complimentary newspapers. Offset to the right of the lobby, was the restaurant in a wooden, almost western Canadian motif. I sat at the edge of the window looking out over a patio and ordered a breakfast of bacon and eggs. The coffee was just what my brain needed to kick into gear. Following breakfast, I asked for help down the stairs and decided to head out onto the street to gain a bit of perspective on Bangkok.

The street wasn't very wide and neither were the sidewalks, so they were unsuitable for my chair. I wheeled down the middle of the street, as many other pedestrians were doing. In fact, most of the stalls on the little street seemed aimed at shoppers on the road, rather than the footpath. Dogs, that looked like they were battling the mange, and losing, either walked very slowly or just rolled over into the gutter by the side of the road. I'd read that it was not unusual for dogs to appear in restaurants as part of the fare. I'd heard of it in Korea, but apparently in Bangkok it appears as "urban deer" beside the wine list. The dogs I'd seen didn't look like they'd put up much of a fight with a chef.

There were stalls selling the usual Coke and different types of food. A couple across the street from the hotel offered cheap laundry service, their price based on the weight of laundry, rather than the number of pieces. There were a number of other hostels and cheap hotels, but none of them seemed to be level with the road. There were several restaurants as well and most of them seemed to be doing a brisk morning trade. Most of the backpackers I saw were young and I knew from experience that when you're out on a world tour for months or years on end, it can really help your budget to spend long periods of time in countries like Turkey or Thailand where the living is cheap, people are friendly and the weather is warm.

I left our little street and was now on a much busier one. It immediately reminded me of Nairobi with all the diesel smoke and smell rising up from the mufflers. It wasn't too hard to figure out where all the pollution hanging over the ground came from. I was quite surprised that Bangkok had bevelled curbs for the disabled at every street corner. It was great for me, but I was trying to cross the street to get a look at the river, and the traffic was almost unbearable. It seemed that vehicles spent the green light clearing the intersections from turns, until the light changed again.

Another problem were the famous "tuk tuks", a cheap method of manual transportation in Bangkok. These vehicles are like oversized tricycles, on which the back has been modified with a compartment for people to sit on a covered bench out of the sun and rain. But I couldn't hear the darned things coming and I was practically run over by a few. The city employed a uniformed man at all major intersections to regulate traffic flow. He must've seen the difficulty I was in, because he scrambled from his position, stopped traffic and helped me across the busy street. I was very grateful and finally got over to the quiet river on the other side.

I'd wanted to ride one of the boats that offer waterway tours of the city. When I made my way to the dock, there was only one that was suitable for a wheelchair. There were quite a few narrow, shallow boats that I always avoided like the plague. On top of the fact that they were an uncomfortable ride, they were so low in the water, that I was fearful of being splashed by the polluted river and coming home with some type of skin affliction or worse. The man on the large boat told me it had been hired out for a special occasion later in the day and wouldn't be running as a ferry or sightseeing boat at all. I was out of luck, but at least I'd given it a go. I ran the gauntlet of vendors at the dock trying to sell me all sorts of trinkets and decided to wheel parallel to the river to see as much of the city as I could from my chair.

As I rolled along, I noticed that behind some office buildings were Buddhist shrines with incense burning. I sat and watched for a while and saw people coming out on their lunch hours and praying in front of them. I thought that was very pragmatic and since there was no separation of church and state here, it wasn't unusual. The river, once you overlooked the pollution, was quite an artery of traffic, as ferries and commercial craft plied their way along. I came upon a large park and thought it would be as good a place as any to rest and do some people watching. A group of adolescents had gathered at the foot of a tropical tree and one of them had a guitar. As he strummed a tune, the rest of the crowd crooned a nice song to accompany it. A young couple walked along arm-in-arm, which was surprising, because I was under the impression that public displays of affection were discouraged. In any event, the woman had a bagged drink with a straw in her hand. In Thailand, when you buy a soft drink or juice from a vendor, you have the option of paying extra and taking the bottle with you, or saving the deposit and having the drink poured into a small plastic bag with handles and then drinking it with a straw. It was well thought out and a bit unusual, but reminded me of when my cousins from Nebraska visited Ontario a long time ago and were shocked to see that we buy our milk in plastic bags to save on waste. It's one of the neat things about travel—noticing the many ways different cultures respond to the same problems.

The park was quite large and a number of people were lounging around in the sunshine or playing games. In the middle, but toward the river, was a covered pavilion in the shape of a "Wat" or Temple. The walls were white and the roof was a distinctive red with curved and ornate carvings. It was a very striking focal point in this refuge from the busy noise and bustle of the rest of the city. I was getting a bit tired in the heat and grime of Bangkok and decided to make my way back. When I arrived at the hotel, I asked a couple of American backpackers to help me up the steps and then I enquired at the desk about the availability of my room with air conditioning. It was ready for me to move into. I hadn't unpacked, so I gathered my bags and leg braces and moved down the corridor into a spacious room with A/C and a window that looked out onto a beautiful courtyard with lots of plants and flowers, as well as a babbling fountain. There were also wooden tables, so anyone who was cooking their own food could eat outside or just take a time out and get caught up on postcards. I had the use of my own toilet and shower and although it was up a small step, I couldn't see it being a problem. In fact, I decided to get undressed and have a shower right away. The travel of the last day needed to be washed away and I definitely needed a cool splash.

After a long nap in comfort, I nipped back to the restaurant. I'd noticed in the morning that they had an extensive list of Thai dishes and I wanted to take advantage on my first visit to the country. I hoped to taste as much as I could in the short time I was there. I had quite an appetite and made a bit of a pig of myself. I ordered both a hot curried chicken and Pad Thai. While I was enjoying my meal, I spent some time watching life go by on the street below. Across the way, at one of the roadside stalls, a truck had stopped and the driver and a merchant were examining a number of handguns. They discussed the transaction as if they were bargaining for a bag of carrots or rice. I was freaked out, as I'd never seen anything like that before.

I finished what had been a great meal, but the weapon episode had left a bad taste in my mouth. The next afternoon I was headed back to the airport and to a lovely tropical island in the south of the country, but I knew now, if I hadn't before, that this was definitely not Canada.

A WALK WITH A COYOTE IN STANLEY PARK

Vancouver has to be one of my favourite cities in the world, at least when it's sunny. One of the attractions for me, being in a chair, is that it's one of the few parts of Canada that receives very little snow. That, coupled with its location near the Coastal Mountains and nestled against the sea, makes it very picturesque.

Following my drive across North America, I stayed at the youth hostel in the downtown area. There's another YHA hostel located close to the university, but that one isn't accessible. The hostel I stayed at was on the West Side, local slang for the downtown area near Stanley Park. Much of Vancouver is on a small peninsula, bounded by suburbs that stretch in all directions (except to the west) as they do in most large cities. The hostel is very modern and the disabled room has an ensuite washroom and bunk beds, which I could never figure out. What if you had two guys in chairs travelling together for a sports event? Anyway, the only problem was that the payphones were in the hall just outside my room and at around 2 a.m. it was common to be awakened by backpackers from Down Under, phoning home hoping for mom and dad to send them a bit of money. Another small problem was that the exit was a steep cement slope up to the sidewalk that I couldn't negotiate on my own. It wasn't much of a problem though, since usually people were outside smoking cigarettes and willing to lend a hand.

The transit system in Vancouver is completely friendly for the disabled and drivers don't seem to mind seeing me at bus stops, as they do in other places I've visited. I could easily travel downhill to the shopping areas near Canada Place and the business district by putting that aggravating force called gravity to work gliding at my own pace. Later, I would take the bus home on the uphill leg. There are connections to the SkyTrain, the rail line out to the suburbs, or if you're interested in hopping a ferry, that's a nice alternative too. Canada Place is the centre of the waterfront, where cruise liners begin or end many of their journeys. The billowed white sails atop the structure reminded me a tad of Sydney and let the tourists know they were in a town with an intimate historical relationship to the ocean. As you move through the downtown area, there are many large buildings, but unlike most U.S. cities, many of them are condominiums, because Canadians prefer to live in the downtown areas near their work. This in turn seems to encourage shops and restaurants to remain open late, contributing to a vibrant nightlife in the downtown core.

I met a friend of mine, Joe, who played on my softball team back in Ontario. He was working in BC for a week, tuning up the computers for his firm. It was his first time out west and he was really enjoying it. We took the opportunity to wheel all around Vancouver. We crossed the seedy East Side with its derelict buildings, drug addicts and prostitutes. The local Chinatown wasn't much compared to the one in Toronto, which surprised me, since there's such a large Asian population. Many people from Hong Kong came over before the return of the former British colony back to China, worried that they would lose their capitalist economy and rights of freedom. Many have since returned, but an equal number have remained, making Vancouver a city with one of the highest Asian populations outside Asia. We ended up having lunch on the patio of a restaurant in Gastown, a trendy part of the city with nice shops and cafés. We were enjoying our lunch when we noticed a commotion across the street, through the window of an upper floor of a large building. It turned out to be a domestic dispute, and though emergency personnel were called, everyone was safe, except for the man who'd caused it, as he'd driven both his arms though the hotel window in anger. It was a lunch to remember.

We proceeded down Robson St., which is Vancouver's answer to Rodeo Boulevard in Los Angeles. All the finest shops and dining are located here and if you're going to spend money, make sure you bring lots of it with you. Many stores that catered to tourists had Japanese-speaking employees. In addition, almost all the stores had signs in Japanese. The few Canadian things I saw for sale were maple syrup and smoked Pacific salmon. I wondered if they'd go well together. After moving up and down both sides of the street and keeping a tight fist on our money, we decided to stop into a sports pub to share a pint of draught ale and watch some of the games on their multitude of TVs.

On this trip, I also took the opportunity to renew my friendship with my buddy George, whom I'd met a number of years earlier in Hawaii. He was a bit older, as was I, but he was just as sharp and funny. He'd retired, giving his business to the kids, so his time was his own. We met at a Chinese restaurant on the same street that the hostel was on and even though it was quite popular and had a lineup outside, that didn't bother us. The food and conversation were great.

I was also able to hook up with a couple who'd moved out to BC from Ontario when Paul was transferred. I'd previously worked with Gerri and she'd also played on the softball team with her two sisters, until they all got married and started having children. Luckily, their apartment was only a few blocks away as well. Downtown

Vancouver is quite compact, so even a slow fellow in a blue chair, such as I, could make my way around in a relatively short time. They invited me over to dinner and it was a great meal and wonderful to see them both. Paul was working hard and out on the road a lot, but Gerri had only started to work at the hospital part-time and still had some time on her hands to enjoy the city. She told me she was into running and walking, now that she was living near a park, and invited me to go walking with her the next day. We spent the evening talking and snacking on Pokey sticks, a long chocolate-covered biscuit from Japan, designed to be dunked in coffee or tea. I ate mine all by itself and enjoyed it immensely.

The next day, the famous Vancouver rain and drizzle finally made an appearance, but Gerri told me that she still went out everyday, rain or shine, and asked me if I still wanted to go. I had my rainproof jacket, so I said I was up for it, if she was willing to push. We rolled down the street to Stanley Park. The park is a huge green space in the city with an aquarium in the middle. It's where Terry Fox, a great Canadian amputee athlete who was running across Canada to raise money for cancer research, had hoped to finish his run. Sadly, his cancer returned after only half the trip and he died before completing the journey. Later, Rick Hansen, a wheelchair athlete, made his own journey across Canada and the world and did end it here. I thought about both of them as we entered the park.

We first made our way to the middle of the park and had a look at the totem poles that had been given to Vancouver by bands of the Pacific First Nations. They were huge and each one was hand-carved from a single tree. We began to walk along the seawall, which rings the park that borders the water. The yacht club at Coal Harbour is quite nice and has many expensive condominiums with spectacular views that we both enjoyed for free. Gerri did most of the work. I was quite impressed with the speed of our pace and she seemed quite comfortable with the wheelchair as well. As I looked toward the ocean, I could see red starfish in the water. This really shocked me. I knew we were looking into the Pacific, but I was unaware that this species was found so far north. A mother duck and her duckling paced us from the water below, until we finally headed away from the wall as the path veered inland around some construction on the seawall.

Gerri bent down and whispered in my ear, "Walt, do you see that?" I had no idea what she was talking about and began to look around. She pointed out an animal in a clearing to our left, about seventy-five feet from where we were walking and it seemed to be following us. Gerri identified it as a coyote. Apparently there had been a few reports recently about sightings of coyotes in the park and authorities were concerned about whether they were sick or might attack a hapless jogger. It looked like a big dog, but had a very bushy tail and seemed more alert than your average dog. I urged Gerri to pick up the pace and warned her that if it got too close, she should run for her life and I would remain as a tasty dog treat. I joked that the animal would probably spit me out or break its jaw on my chair. We began to hurry and before long, we'd left the coyote in our wake or it had finally moved on to a find a raccoon or squirrel. It had been quite exciting while it lasted.

We ended our excursion at Granville Island, which has a farmer's market and some fresh food shops. Again, there were plenty of types of smoked salmon and fresh fish available. Gerri took the opportunity to do some grocery shopping and we both enjoyed an ice cream to top off the day, as the sun finally decided to squeeze out from behind the clouds.

I hope to make my home in Vancouver someday and was even considering it during the drive out to BC recently. The clear air, the lack of snow, the mild climate, the mountains and the lifestyle are all reasons to want to stay there permanently, but I have to wonder if somewhere out there, there's coyote with my name on it.

DOWN ON ST. PATRICK'S DAY AND UP TO THE ANDES

I must confess that after backpacking through South America for five weeks, it was great to spend my last week in the beautiful town of Mendoza in the foothills of the Andes. The hostel was wheelchair friendly for the most part, although many of the small ramps in the building were too steep to navigate on my own. I had access to an ensuite washroom that included a shower and for a short while I was alone in my six-bed dorm, so I didn't have to worry about waking in the middle of the night due to inconsiderate roommates! It was quite a change from the ten-bed dorm in Cordoba, where two of my nine roommates included a pair of young Spanish speaking students who thought nothing of turning on the lights at three in the morning to make their beds. They then proceeded to stay up for another hour or so while make farting sounds with their armpits and laughing hilariously at their juvenile humour.

Mendoza was perfect for me. It was laid back, relatively quiet and most importantly, it was flat. It was great to be in a place where I would be able to wheel into the downtown area with little problem. The hostel was a bit distant from the middle of things, about six or seven blocks away, but for the most part it was a pleasant wheel, which included a wonderfully green plaza with a beautiful fresco depicting the settlement of the Spaniards in the area and the treaty they had made with the native peoples in the area. Nearby was the large Plaza Independencia, which was the focal point of activity in the town and adjacent were three or four blocks of a pedestrian mall with a wide variety of shops and restaurants to choose from. I spent many afternoons sitting at a table in the courtyard sipping a coffee or a cerveza and watching life go by.

On my first night in Mendoza the hostel was hosting another of the famous late night barbeques that I had come to love about South America. The fellow who was in charge of the grill was Carlos, a friendly young Argentinean-Italian fellow, who refused to call me by my name and instead would always point at me with a big smile and yell out "Canadian"! As luck would have it one of the other hostellers named Karsten, from Holland, recognized me from the hostel in Ushuaia and offered me an Andes beer. At first I hadn't noticed him but after a short while I did remember his happy countenance. The dinner, which only cost three dollars included a variety of salads, a house wine and an unlimited choice of delicious cuts of prime Argentinean beef or pork, as well as about four various types of sausages. Each one of them had been grilled to perfection. Adjacent to the patio was a bar with a dance club, although it being mid-week there wasn't much going on, but I was assured that by the weekend the place would really be rocking. It was already very late and the combination of a belly stuffed with protein and all the wine and beer would ensure a long and restful night's sleep.

The main reason that I wanted to go to Mendoza was due to its access to the Andes. I asked at the front desk if they knew of a tour company that might be capable of taking on a fellow in a blue chair and they were optimistic that they did. I mentioned to them that I would need a company that had a small van or bus so that it would be easier to be helped on and off. The lady behind the desk said that my best chance would be if one of the companies was not fully booked for the day and then they would be riding out in a smaller vehicle. So at least I had started the ball rolling.

Like most good travelers, we all claim to have at least a dram of Irish blood on St. Patrick's Day and it being that day I was really looking forward to going out for a party later in the evening. It turned out that Mark, the fellow who had helped push me though Cordoba on my last stop, had now caught up with me after his ride in on the bus. I had hoped he would stay at my hostel, but he had been accosted by one of the many paid touts that frequent the bus terminals, trying to entice weary travelers to their residences. After getting cleaned up and a snooze, he showed up at my hostel to pick me up and we made our way to an Irish pub in Mendoza. Just as we entered the bar, one of the other patrons came over and sat beside us at our table. It was Jane, a red haired girl from Yorkshire in the U.K. with whom I'd had a conversation at breakfast. At that time she was with her sister, but her sibling had just left to head back home and she was now on her own. Who better to be having a drink with on St. Patrick's Day than a girl with red hair? Actually, it was quite a disappointment because despite all the signs around us advertising various Irish beers, there was not a drop of the authentic stuff to be found in the place. I had to content myself with a dark version of the local Quilmes beer. After a short while, we decided to head back out to Mark's hostel for another of the many hostel barbeques on offer. We invited Jane, but she decided to remain at the pub, despite its lack of Guinness. We vowed to drop by again after the barbecue.

I don't know whether it was the fact that I had started drinking on an empty stomach or that the sidewalks were not in the best state of repair, but we were out of the pub for only about ten minutes before my chair hit a rut, stopped dead in its tracks and I continued forward, hurtling out of my seat and onto the cement. I barely had time to think or take inventory of my limbs before about five or six locals, who had been smoking outside of another bar all raced forward to assist me back into my chair. I thanked them profusely in my lousy Spanish and Mark was quite apologetic, but for no reason at all. I always blame myself when I fall out of my chair since I am the one who is supposed to be looking down at the area in front of the wheels to see if there are any obstacles. By the time we made it to Mark's barbecue my foot was really throbbing and when I removed my sock I could see a bit of blood. I kept squeezing my foot to see if anything was broken, but as near as I could tell (with all my experience of being on the receiving end of medical treatment during the first fifteen years of my life) I was still all in one piece and nothing seemed to be broken. We enjoyed another great meal and loads of sangria but when it was time to take me home, Mark and I decided to wheel along the side of the road instead of up on the sidewalk, just to be safe. We did stop by the pub again on the way to see Jane, but the place was so unbelievably crammed with Irish wannabes that we just kept going. It had definitely been a memorable day!

The next day was one of relaxation and another barbeque at my hostel. I had acquired a roommate from Montana named Achai. The hostel kept girls and guys separated so his girlfriend Liz was staying in another room. We ended up playing hearts with a Kiwi girls and I enjoyed loads of meat that had been superbly grilled. For some reason the others had not joined the feast, but I shared mine with them and we ultimately adjourned to the bar beside the patio that was now rocking to a live band. I found out the next day that Achai must have had a good time because he told me that he had woken up sometime during the night sitting on the floor next to the toilet! Even I had never done that.

I finally received some good news from the front desk, one of the tour companies had rang the hostel to let us know that they would be around the next morning at seven to pick me up. I asked if they would be in a van and I was assured they would. Next morning I woke up very early and tried to skulk out of the room very quietly, so as to not disturb my now full complement of bunkmates. The only people awake were the kitchen staff just arriving to prepare the morning's breakfast that was included in the price. I was able to have a piece of bread and jam and a quick coffee, before I had to head back to the room to hit the washroom before the trip. As I sat on the can, a loud knock cracked on the door, the van had arrived. So much for my attempt at not waking the other backpackers!

I knew that I had forgotten something as soon as I saw the guide staff for the trip up into the Andes. I had neglected to mention that I would need some young and fit people to be working this day so as to help me in and out of the van. The driver was a friendly but ageing fellow named Bruno and the guide was a young waif named Carla who spoke very little English. So in lieu of any help from them for the rest of the day, we enlisted the help of the evening front desk guy who was still at the hostel and he was able to push my legs up a foot or so thus enabling my bum to get up to the level of the front seat of the van from my half standing position. I was all set and the blue chair was tossed into the back of the van. After wandering around Mendoza for about a half an hour to pick up some other backpackers at various hostels, we were off to the mountains.

It was not long before we had finally left the city and the van moved out onto the highway that I began to notice that something was terribly wrong with the van. Fumes were somehow coming up through the floorboards and getting into the cab where I was sitting. What puzzled me was that I seemed to be the only one noticing that anything was wrong. I asked the driver and guide if they could turn on the ventilation, but they didn't seem to comprehend what I wanted. I had to satisfy my oxygen needs by periodically sticking my head out the window. It wasn't until we had our first stop that I found out that some other passengers could smell the fumes in the back of the van as well.

Despite these minor tribulations the scenery as we made our way west toward the Andes was quite amazing. Initially we drove through some wonderful vineyards that reminded me of my home in wine country back in Canada, and finally as we began a slow ascent through the foothills, the vegetation became sparse in the now semi-arid climate as only shrubs and small grasslands could be seen on the gray landscape. After some time traveling we stopped at a babbling brook that was sheltered in a valley between two small mountains. Apparently this had been the site of a small Spanish outpost in the days of colonization by the Spanish. The native peoples had attacked the fort and a famous shootout ensued. I couldn't really understand most of the story due to my rudimentary knowledge of the language, but I assume the Spanish ended up winning the battle.

I couldn't believe the magnificence of the scenery as we sped along the highway and began to move up and past mountain after mountain. I have been into the Rockies many times but unlike those hills, the Andes were impressive due to the strange colours of the minerals that each was composed of. We would move past an orange mountain and then the next would be green, followed by black, red and brown. I must say it was absolutely fascinating and breathtaking at the same time, made even more brilliant as the sun glistened against the rocks seeming to magnify the effect of the colours. Our second stop was a viewpoint of Mt. Aconcagua, which at almost 7000 meters is the highest peak in South America. Many of the backpackers I had met on my trip had made the excursion up the side of it to the base camp, which is the jumping off point for all the really serious mountain climbers in their assault on the apex. Unfortunately for us, the top of Aconcagua was obscured by cloud but we could still see many of the glaciers that looked like a sweet topping dripping down an ice cream cone. We continued up the road to our destination which was the border between Chile and

Argentina, by now I was starting to feel a bit ill from all the fumes, but at least with these stops I was able to regain my breath and fight off any feelings of wanting to throw up.

We had been on the road for quite a while and lunchtime was approaching. We entered a small road that turned off the highway and everyone began to disembark at a restaurant for lunch. I told the driver that I would stay in the van since it would be much easier to not have to bother with worrying about getting back into the vehicle. I gave Bruno some money and after a short while he returned with some bread and a bowl of thick soup consisting of ham, potatoes and pumpkin. It was quite good and I must confess it was strange sitting there all by myself as the wind blew through the cab, while the local dog sat quietly outside my door, sniffing my lunch and hoping a share of it. In the end, he got his wish as I threw out a bunch of pork bones that I almost broke my teeth on.

I had thought that this had only been a meal stop, but once everyone had returned we continued past the restaurant toward a gate that marked the start of our climb up Mt. Helena. I took the opportunity to look up to the top toward our destination and I was shocked at how steep the mountain was. The road was unpaved and weaved back and forth in an effort to mitigate the effect of the slope and ease our ascent. Slowly Bruno guided the little white vehicle back and forth following other busses in the climb. By the time we had risen halfway up, I could look back down into the valley that we had only just been in. The sunbeams accented each of the hills to reveal a veritable Van Gogh of colours all the way down the valley. I can honestly say that it is a sight that will remain with me for the rest of my life. Slowly and surely, we finally edged our way past small patches of snow to the top of Mt. Helena. The temperature had dropped markedly and dark clouds covered the sky as snow flurries wafted by. At the top was an impressive statue of Christ and on either side were more restaurants and outdoor gift shops, one on the Argentinean side, the other under the flag of Chile. Of course, this is the time when my bladder finally decided to get full from all the water and soup. I finally had to ask Bruno to retrieve my chair and then I flopped into it to wheel off to find an inconspicuous place to attend to the call of nature, since the washrooms were up a huge flight of stairs. So there I sat, behind a building in a quiet corner of the mountaintop that marked both an international border and the continental divide, in shirtsleeves as the wind howled and snow fell, while trying to make sure the angle of my pee would take it away from my chair. This moment was what backpacking to me was all about. With the help of another guy on the trip I was able to get up into the cab of the van and finally warm up a bit.

On our return trip back to Mendoza we stopped at Puente del Inca an old Incan bridge that archeologists had uncovered. As the group disembarked to go and see a small Spanish church behind the bridge, Bruno drove me over to the souvenir stands where I purchased a wonderfully soft llama sweater to take home. After enjoying more magnificent Andean vistas on the trip home we stopped one last time, at the Lake of Horses for a coffee break. Carla informed us that this was once an area where wild horses roamed free along the countryside.

As we left the mountains behind us and the moon suspended over what remained of the hills to the west, I was happy that I had finally been able to see the Andes, which was one of my big objectives in coming to the continent. It had been most impressive and I had survived 13 hours inhaling poisonous fumes. It was more than I could have ever hoped for.

A WARM CHRISTMAS WITH A GOOD FRIEND IN SYDNEY

I'd always wondered what it would be like to spend Christmas in a warm climate. It may be because I'm in a wheelchair, but I'm not fond of snow and cold. I remember going out behind the fire hall at the end of our street with my brothers on a toboggan and playing goalie for hours, sitting on ice the Smokies had flooded for us. When they finally dragged me home for supper, my hands and legs were so frozen, I'd have to sit by the heat register for half an hour just to warm up and get the sting out. Many Canadians go to the southern U.S. or the Caribbean over the holidays, but I was going to be in Australia this year and I was looking forward to my first summer Christmas.

Sydney is a beautiful city. The harbour is magnificent and the famous Opera House that sits at the edge of Circular Quay seems to herald that you're in a modern city that's vibrant and full of confidence. Sydney is also very big, owing to the countless suburbs that make it up. With the Olympics less than a year away, the city was putting the finishing touches on its new facilities and merchants were preparing to take advantage of the upcoming economic boom that the tourism and free TV publicity would bring. Even at the quietest of times, Sydney is a bustling place, but at the end of 1999, the pace was frantic.

I arrived at the airport to an orange haze hanging over the city from numerous bushfires, which have become all too frequent in New South Wales in recent years. The country had been suffering from years of drought and the lack of water in the hinterland was beginning to take its toll. Even worse, was that most of the fires were caused by idiot arsonists with no idea of the cost to property and lives. I made my way through the airport to the City Rail terminal, recently completed in advance of the Olympics, and bought a ticket to Central Station, opposite my hostel. The YHA was sparkling and modern and the room I was assigned was excellent. There were two beds, but I never had a roommate. The kitchen facilities downstairs included two separate kitchens and even tatami mats, so Japanese backpackers could sit on the floor and enjoy their meals as they are accustomed. Off to the side of the lobby was a small travel agency and on the other side, a restaurant complete with Internet facilities. The only real problem was that the elevator didn't go to the top floor where the pool was and the bar downstairs, which is affiliated with the hostel, was inaccessible. But for me, the location was perfect and the close proximity to trains made it a desirable place to be.

I'm always pleased to revisit my favourite beach at Manly and wheel down the Corso in my blue chair on the short route from the Ferry Terminal to the beach. Alternatively, I loved exploring Darling Harbour and sitting in front of all the outdoor cafés watching life go by. I did my grocery shopping at the Haymarket, and enjoyed a Chinese soup from a stall inside the mall. Wheeling up busy George Street, stopping to sip an afternoon beer and eat a pub lunch while watching a live NFL playoff game, was quite a nice way to wait out a passing shower that helped blow away the orange haze.

I phoned up a close friend of mine, named Sue. I'd known her since my earliest days of playing competitive sports in Ontario. Sue had come to Canada to follow the love of her life, but when that didn't work out, she decided to stay and make it her new home. She was a physiotherapist who worked at a rehab hospital specializing in spinal trauma. In the early '70s, a number of patients who'd broken their necks and were now quadriplegics, created the rules for a wheelchair sport called "murderball". Sue was one of those who played, refereed, organized and was generally responsible for the sport's initiation. I first met her in those days, but I was only fourteen at the time. Later, when I was older, we'd served together on the executive of the provincial wheelchair sports organization and had become good friends. When Sue finally tired of winter, she decided to move back to Sydney to be closer to her aging mum. I missed her a lot and missed attending artsy theatres, followed by the weird Bohemian restaurants that we'd inevitably find.

Sue suggested, over the phone, that we get together for a meal and I mentioned that "The Rocks" would be a good place to start searching for a place to eat. We met at Circular Quay and when I saw her smiling face and red hair, I felt like it was old times again.

We stopped at a German restaurant and, as is often the case with me, I ended up ordering the same thing as my companion. Sue had decided to order a roast pork dinner and as we sat outside on the patio, we plotted our weekend out together. I mentioned that I'd be around over Christmas, so she invited me to spend that day with her and her family, as she was having them all to her place for lunch. I was secretly hoping she'd invite me and I accepted without hesitation. Dinner finally came and Sue was quite pleased with all the "crackling" on top. Crackling was the baked crust or skin of the pork. It was deep red and flavourful, but it took me quite a time to chew through it. The beer helped wash the salty stuff down. In the meantime, Sue suggested that she'd pick me up on the weekend and we could head up to Palm Beach, where all the elite and wealthy "Sydneysiders" live.

On a bright Saturday morning, Sue gathered me up in her small, brown Holden Commodore. I still have difficulty getting into the left side passenger seat when I'm in Australia. Back home, my car has a two-door bench seat and since I'm left handed, I get in on the right side of the vehicle, use my left hand to pull the chair in behind the seat and then slide across under the steering wheel. Getting in on the other side makes me feel like a fish out of water. The city seemed to be lulled into a holiday quiet as we made our way out of the urban area and up along the shore. The houses were indeed magnificent and Sue showed me the house that business magnate Kerry Packer lived in. The foliage was brown due to the recent lack of rain, but some flowers were still in bloom and the gum trees, that were used to dry spells, were still crowned in green. We made it up to Palm Beach and Sue fretted about how much money to put into the parking machine. I told her not to put any money in, since we were not leaving sight of the car and the cliff above the beach, which was our picnic destination, was only a short wheel away. Besides, we'd just seen the council ticket officer leave the area on our way in. It was a windy view that day, but quite impressive being so high and looking down at the sunbathers on the white sand and the swimmers. Sue had brought sandwiches and drinks, so we enjoyed a delicious meal, looking out across the Tasman Sea.

It was getting to be afternoon and Sue wanted to show me the Pittwater, the head of the river nearby. I remembered a restaurant we'd been to on an earlier trip there and suggested we find it and have dinner and a beer on me. After driving through a few more suburbs and seeing more amazing properties lining the shore, we finally found the restaurant located at the back of a hotel. It was a cafeteria-style establishment, with stone tables on the patio overlooking the river. As we were eating our fish and chips, a rugby team arrived in the midst of a Christmas pub-crawl. Each of them was dressed as Santa Claus, complete with the beard. It must have been hot for them, but unlike their Canadian cousins, they'd left the padding at home. I made sure that Sue took a photo of me with them, toasting the camera. That was surely something only a warm Christmas could offer. On the way back, Sue dropped me off at Manly beach and we shared an ice cream to top off the day. I caught the ferry back to my hostel.

A few days later, it was Christmas and the weather had taken a turn for the worse. Gone were the sunny skies and now the parched land was finally receiving a much needed drink of water. The rain was fine for the forest fires, but not so good for my Christmas plans. I started out for the train, with my gift for Sue and some chocolate for the family, to make my way to Epping Station. The old gentleman working at Epping that day was quite sweet. He made a big fuss about helping me off the train and up into his station. Then he personally phoned Sue for me to tell her that I'd arrived and directed her toward the best road to take to pick me up. I thanked him and waited outside, out of the driving rain, for Sue. After getting drenched getting into her car, we arrived at her townhouse in the suburb of Marsfield.

Luckily, there was only a small single step up to her home and I detected a whiff of cat as I entered, which was fine with me as I'm a great cat lover. One of the felines remained on the stairs giving me a good look, but the other stayed out of sight upstairs. It seemed funny seeing a Christmas tree with festive trimmings against a green background through the patio door, but it was what I'd wanted. After a short while, Sue's mum, sister and three nieces joined us. After singing some carols and opening gifts, it was time for the buffet lunch that Sue had prepared. As we were getting ready to eat, the sky cleared. Sue ordered the girls outside to spark up the barbeque because she'd bought some prawns that she wanted grilled for one of the dishes. It was unique watching the girls cook the giant-sized shrimps on a now lovely Christmas afternoon. We opened some "crackers", which are popular in England, but I'd never had before. They're small tubes that you pull from either end, which make a sharp sound when opened. Inside you find a joke, a children's toy and a paper crown to wear. We each wore our crowns for the rest of the day. To finish off the meal, we participated in the traditional lighting of the Christmas pudding. It reminded me of a scene from *A Christmas Carol*. Actually, the pudding seemed more like a cake to me and Sue's mum had a devil of a time lighting it. I had to ask one of Sue's nieces to drive me to McDonald's to use their washroom, as the one in the house wasn't accessible. Other than that minor glitch, it was a wonderful day and I was especially thankful to have such a good friend allow me to share it with her family.

Sue drove me back to the hostel in the evening after her family had left. We said goodbye for a few more years. I'd enjoyed a warm Christmas, but for the first time in my life, I missed the snow and houses lit up with Christmas lights brightening the long, dark winter evenings. It was time to phone Canada to wish my relatives a Merry Christmas, since we were a day ahead and they had yet to celebrate.

ALL THE LIVING LAWN ORNAMENTS ON LAKE NAKURU

I tried to look out the window of the Alitalia plane that had finally brought me to Nairobi. It had been a long flight. The first leg took me to Rome, where I could finally breathe after a night trip in the days before smokeless flights. For some reason, Alitalia had the unusual arrangement of having one smoking section in the front of the plane and another at the rear. The rest of us hapless non-smokers were stuck in the middle, but that hadn't stopped smokers from coming to visit their friends in our section, with cigarettes in hand or mouth. We've come along way since those days.

After a brief change of planes, and a cappuccino at Leonardo DaVinci Airport, we made a refueling stop in Jeddah, Saudi Arabia. The alcohol was locked away, the plane was boarded by guards who walked up and down the aisle. I still have no idea what they were looking for, but whatever it was, they didn't find it. A look outside revealed a bright, hot desert world with unique, almost completely white structures bordering the tarmac. I would've loved to be able to get off and explore, but Jeddah is the second holiest city, next to Mecca, in the country. Since I wasn't a Moslem, a visit would likely not have been allowed.

But I was now in Africa for the first time. Unfortunately, I couldn't see very much in the darkness. There were no special narrow chairs to help get me off the flight, so three smiling Africans came to my seat and lifted me from the plane. I was placed in a chair that looked like it had been here since independence. A bright sign advertising "Kilimanjaro Spring Water" beamed at me from across the room. I was left waiting to be reunited with my blue chair.

My friend Wayne, whom I was visiting, was an old pal from university, and once I'd cleared customs, he told me he was sure I'd chicken out and not come to see him. He was almost right. I can still feel the panic that ran through me as I tried to go to sleep the night before I left snowy Ontario. But I was here and Wayne seemed quite pleased about it. He'd rented a hotel room in the capital and we were going to sleep in town over night in order to avoid driving in the dark and possibly hitting a zebra or some other large animal. It would also give us some time to get re-acquainted.

We woke at 5 a.m. for breakfast and then started out on the two-hour ride to Nakuru, west of Nairobi, in the Highlands. As we left the city, I was amazed at all the people walking on the roads. Transportation costs money that many of them didn't have, so they were left to use their feet. The smell of diesel from the traffic certainly made an impression and the general poverty reminded me that I was in a very poor country and a culture that was totally alien. We drove uphill along the Great Rift Valley, made famous as the archeological site of some of the oldest bones in human ancestry. We paused along a viewpoint to look at Mt. Longonot, while vendors attempted to sell us trinkets. As I looked below into the valley, it seemed to be a patchwork quilt of different coloured farmyards. Puffs of white cloud quickly blew past in the warming early morning air. We had to hurry back to Nakuru as Wayne had to get to work.

We arrived at Wayne's compound on the outskirts of the city. He employed a guard, known as an "askari", to protect himself and his family, when they had been here. They were all back in Canada now, and Wayne had only three months left in his contract. The house seemed eerily quiet, except for my old friend, Cujo the dog, who greeted me with a happy grunt and a wagging tail. I was shown around the house; the living room with fresh flowers that Jennifer, the maid and cook, had cut to welcome me, the kitchen and then down the hall to his daughters' room, now empty. My room was across the hall and the master bedroom was at the end. Nipper, the cat, one of the least friendly felines I'd ever met, actually let me pet her before cowering and running away. Wayne had to head to work, but he told me that Jennifer would be by to take care of me. While he worked, I decided to find my bed and get some rest. It had been an exciting, but tiring, day and a half.

When I finally woke up in the early afternoon, Jenny had arrived and wanted to prepare lunch for me. I wasn't up to it, but I did ask for a cup of tea. I sat on the back terrace, which overlooked Lake Nakuru and the town of Nakuru, with a population of over 100,000. We were a mile above sea level, and even though it was afternoon, there was a pleasant breeze in the shade. Jenny brought homemade oatmeal cookies with my tea and left to return to her chores.

I was still in awe of the fact that I was in Africa. How many people could say that they've been here? Many would love to come, but have an underlying fear of the unknown that causes them to hesitate. The winter weather in Ontario had been wretched, but I was in Eden. Oh, there were plenty of bugs that could infect you and the water could contain any number of unpleasant surprises, but it really was paradise.

Wayne's backyard had a wonderful view high above the lake, which seemed to have a pink ring around it, due to the huge concentrations of greater and lesser flamingos attracted to its brackish water. In his front yard, was a sisal plant, which is used like hemp to make fabric and rope. A poinsettia tree towered at nine feet; it didn't offer much shade, but was impressive just because it wasn't in a pot. Wayne had planted a banana tree two years previously, that was about to bear fruit. A rooster crowed from the neighbour's yard and Jenny appeared at the far end of the property to hang out the washing. I sipped my tea and pondered how lucky I was.

The next day began the weekend and Wayne had planned our first safari. Instead of going to the local game park, we were headed back to the Intercontinental in Nairobi to visit the park there. As we drove through Nakuru to get out of town, the jacarandas flaunted what was left of their purple blossoms. Apparently a few weeks prior to my arrival they'd been in their glory. I felt they were beautiful now, but I was told it was nothing compared to what they had been.

As we travelled along the highway, we spotted a herd of zebras grazing by the side of the road. I asked if we could stop to admire them. For Wayne they were a dime a dozen, but for me, everything was new and exciting. Except for their stripes, they looked like small stocky horses, but I was assured that they had a nasty disposition.

As the two of us wove toward the capital, I turned to Wayne and said, "Can you believe we're driving through Africa?" Wayne nodded and acknowledged that for him, even after almost two years, he still had to pinch himself. I was recording much of the drive on my camcorder, but each time we came to a police checkpoint, Wayne instructed me to drop it below the dashboard so the cops couldn't see it. They didn't like being recorded because the checkpoints are mostly to shake down the locals for money. Wayne never stopped for the checkpoints and he said it wasn't worth it because his car was faster than theirs, so they couldn't catch up to him. If he stopped, he'd be asked for a bribe and would lose all his money. I definitely had a lot to learn about this new culture.

We'd woken early for breakfast, but I don't think either one of us slept soundly through the night. During the previous evening, we'd experienced one of the famous East African thunderstorms. The lighting and thunder was spectacular and for a while we enjoyed the show from our balcony. The problem was that the deluge had left roads flooded and many were only mud. We arrived at the game park and Wayne was able to get both of us in for the resident fare. Normally tourists are charged much more, to extract as much hard currency as possible.

Just inside the entrance was a small zoo that housed sick or injured animals. The residents included hyenas, miniature pygmy hippos, cheetahs, a lion, a leopard, and a tiger. Tigers are not native to Africa, so I really have no idea how it got there, but it was definitely a neat thing to see. We approached the fence that separated us from the lion. The animal seemed annoyed by our presence and suddenly the great beast charged. I couldn't help but think that if he'd got me, it would've added new meaning to the phrase "meals on wheels".

The muddy roads slowed us down a bit, but Wayne had invested in a four-wheel drive vehicle and seemed confident that it would meet our needs. There was a memorial on the spot where the President of Kenya had burned twelve tons of ivory. It's a serious offence to be caught smuggling ivory out of the country and the government tries very hard to prevent poaching of elephants and rhinos.

Our first wild animals of the day were a troupe of baboons that decided to sit on the road in front of us. We waited for them to move, but we finally tired of them and honked our horn as we drove slowly past. Some herding animals were spotted in the long grass and both Thompson's gazelles and bongos were in great abundance. In the distance, reaching up into a tall acacia tree, was a pair of giraffes. We drove up to them as slowly and carefully as possible, so as not to disturb them. I loved watching the graceful animals and thought that if I were an African animal, I'd most like to be a giraffe.

It amazed me how easy it was to spot all these exotic animals by ourselves, without the benefit of a guide. Some cape buffalo began to charge our vehicle. I thought they were slowing down, but Wayne knew they had a nasty temper and decided to beg off. A band of rare wart hogs squealed as we interrupted their search for a meal in a grassy opening. Then, the highlight of the day, we spotted a rhinoceros. It was in the distance and we actually had to drive out on the grassland, away from the road (which is not recommended, in case you can't find the road again), but it was worth it to try to get a closer look. We sat there for half an hour watching it, until it finally faded into the grass. After enjoying the rhino, we returned to the road and happened upon a flock of ostriches.

Suddenly, as we were passing a shrub, we found ourselves only ten feet away from a black rhino! It wasn't easy to get a good look at its profile through the long grass, so Wayne decided to slam his hand against the truck door to try to get a response. I was only slightly terrified! If the rhino charged, we could both be dead. Wayne kept the motor running and his foot on the gas pedal, but the rhino simply looked at us and then bent its head back down to resume grazing. What a thrill that was.

We stopped for lunch under a tree overlooking a water hole, as the early afternoon sun came out. We'd picked up some tasty homemade bread and goat's cheese at a kiosk near the house back in Nakuru. I still think those were some of the tastiest sandwiches I've ever eaten in my life. I'm not sure if it was the food, the company or the environment. It was probably a combination of all three.

By the end of the day, we'd totalled fourteen rhinos and some crowned cranes as well. It was time to head back to Nakuru for dinner. Wayne took me to his favourite haunt, the Rift Valley Sports Club. Wayne had become a member since his arrival and it was where he'd stayed when he first came to decide whether to take the new job. As usual, we were the only people in attendance, although

I'm not sure why, as the food was quite good and we both have a sweet tooth that we could satisfy from the dessert cart. After dinner, we entered the male-only bar off the main lounge. The head of many a native animal had been mounted on the wall so that the locals could have something to hang their hats on. We enjoyed a pint of ale and a game of snooker. Supposedly, if a wife or girlfriend comes looking for a bloke, the barman will always say that he's not there, but then the fellow must buy the whole pub a round to compensate for the lie.

It had been quite a weekend, but I'd developed a slow leak in one of my tires and it had gone flat. Later the next day, we went into town to have it repaired. They only had twenty-six inch tires in Kenya, but my blue chair takes twenty-four inch tubes. No problem for the Indian proprietor of the petrol station. He simply cut two inches off the tube and glued the ends together again. Believe it or not, it actually held until I got off the plane back home in Canada. That tube lasted longer than some of the animals I'd seen on the wall in the bar that night in Kenya.

I TOOK MY TIME IN TAI MEI TUK

I love to visit exotic locales. To me, that's the whole point of travel. I enjoy seeing how other people live, how they've adapted in an ancient environment beside today's modern technology. Nowhere in the world is that juxtaposition more evident than in Hong Kong, and that territory, recently returned to China after decades of British rule, was to be the last stop on my most recent adventure.

Unfortunately for me, I hadn't come soon enough to fly into the old Kai Tak airport, which my friend Cyril told me provided a thrilling descent between large office buildings. The government had recently completed the spacious and bright Chek Lap Kok airport from dredged land reclaimed from the sea. This airport wasn't in the middle of Kowloon, but rather out on the western fringe of the city. I had a window seat on the Qantas flight from Australia and as dusk approached, the mountains and buildings of one of the busiest cities on earth, came into view.

I'd made prior arrangements for accommodation in Hong Kong. There were a number of YHA hostels in the city, but the only one with the international symbol of access beside it was named "Tai Mei Tuk". I'd had an enormous problem trying to complete the arrangements. For some reason, in the business capital of Asia, they were unwilling to accept my credit card number. I exchanged e-mails with Tai Mei Tuk over the period of a month and was finally instructed to wire the money electronically to their bank account. It all seemed a bit disorganized and unproductive and I wondered what I was getting myself into.

Since it was getting dark and I was travelling alone as usual, the Chinese airline representative asked if someone was picking me up. I said I was on my own looking for my hostel at Tai Mei Tuk. She suddenly had a perplexed look on her face. She, and another employee, decided to escort me down to the transit terminal and help me arrange transportation. We stood at the bus station sales wicket for what seemed like an eternity, waiting to be served. To my surprise, I was informed that the two of them were trying to determine how to get me to my destination, since it was so far out in the countryside. That came as a shock to me, because I didn't think Hong Kong had countryside. As far as I knew, the territory was so small I'd be close to everything.

It turned out that the hostel I'd chosen was in the far northeast of the province known as the New Territories and that it would be a long bus ride to the vicinity. Thankfully, these people kindly assisted me and placed me on a wheelchair friendly low-rise bus that would take me to the city of Tai Po. Once I got off there, I was to get a cab and hand the driver a piece of paper, written in Cantonese, with directions to my youth hostel. I did as instructed and the taxi driver called the hostel on his cell phone to confirm the location. It was now well past 9 p.m. and I was getting very tired. The landscape was becoming extremely rural and I was beginning to think I'd made a huge mistake booking this facility. Here I was in the city that's supposed to define what a city is, and I was out in the middle of nowhere. After a further twenty-minute drive, we climbed up a short hill to a cement structure with a large iron gate. The gate was locked and the place looked desolate. The cabbie rang a bell and an old woman, whom I never saw again after that night, came out to greet us. She unlocked the gate, showed me into a tiny air-conditioned room located just off the courtyard behind the front gate, and handed me the key. I'd made it to Hong Kong, but what was I going to do now?

The next morning, my predicament got a bit worse. My face had been a bit itchy during the night, but I was so tired that I hadn't thought too much about it. I woke up and felt a huge lump on my cheek. I checked it in the mirror in the shower and was surprised to find that half my face was red and inflamed. Of course, I'd been bitten by spiders before but when I'm in a foreign country I always get a bit paranoid about my health. From experience, I knew that usually these things fade away after a few hours, so I decided to take the wait-and-see approach.

The bathroom was accessible and I thoroughly enjoyed a hot shower, now that I was back in a humid climate. The hostel was huge and resembled a military fortress. There were no other guests around, but there was a refreshment machine and a kitchen. Finally, a thin man named Willie, came from outside, unlocked the gate and spread it open. It turned out that the previous day had been his day off and he'd spent it with a friend in town. He actually lived in an upstairs room of the hostel, as did his father. Over the course of the next few days, we became very good friends, but now, I wanted to get out and survey my new surroundings.

Tai Mei Tuk is a resort area for people who live in Hong Kong. It's located along the Plover Reservoir near the old border with Mainland China. Actually, it fit into my travel lifestyle quite well, since I like to stay in laid back, restful parts of the world. What threw me for a loop was that I wasn't expecting it on this stop and I wondered how I was going to get into the city to take a tour around Victoria Harbour.

Willie had a lot of time on his hands, since the hostel was under booked during the off-season, especially mid-week. This worked to my benefit, as he offered to help me onto a bus to go into the city of Tai Po to do some grocery shopping and sightseeing. The local busses were a lot smaller than the larger one that had initially brought me from the airport. Willie and I waited as two busses with narrow doors passed, before one that was acceptable arrived. I had to board via the back of the bus, as Willie pulled my blue chair up three small steps, but otherwise, there was enough room that I could sit comfortably while hanging onto a rail to steady myself as the vehicle negotiated the roads twists and turns.

Tai Po is the largest city in the vicinity of the hostel and Willie told me that this was where he spent time every day, shopping or hanging out with friends during the afternoon hours when the hostel was closed. We went to the grocery store where I purchased food to keep in the kitchen and beer to drink during the hot evenings. We then headed to an Internet café so I could tell anyone who cared that I'd arrived safely. To finish off, we shared a pot of oolong tea and got to know each other a bit better. It was soon time to head back, as Willie had to clean up the hostel and prepare for a group of women who were expected on the weekend. I used the afternoon to sit by the water and watch as the locals began arriving for a weekend of rest and relaxation. The water in the bay outside the reservoir, seemed quite polluted, but it didn't deter anyone from coming out to enjoy that Friday. There were cement barbeque pits and families could gather to cook their food in the open air. Nearby, there was a pond stocked with fish where you paid a fee for each one you caught. It was popular with the kids. There were ice cream shops and boats for hire. Above the hostel, atop the dam marking the beginning of the reservoir, a group of children arrived with hundreds of kites. There wasn't much wind that day, but it didn't stop them from trying.

On the weekend, the hostel came to life, as did the entire area. The women arrived and the kitchen was taken over with the wonderful smells of Chinese cooking. It probably tasted much better than the toasted cheese sandwiches that were a staple of my diet.

Outside the gates, there was a marathon race in process and tired runners swept past, up the hill and beyond the reservoir above. Parking was at a premium by the afternoon and families found many ways to amuse themselves. To me, it felt like a long weekend in the summer. Chinese people are a hard working lot and I could tell that when they had a day off, they wanted to take full advantage of it. I sat, enjoying a can of beer and taking it all in.

By Monday, the throngs had left and gone back to work. The garbage and mess left behind was incredible. As the early hours passed, a small army of women from the Public Sanitation Department arrived with small, homemade brooms and began the cleanup. By 11 a.m. everything was spotless and the slow pace of rural life had returned.

I'd mentioned to Willie that I wanted to go into the business section of Hong Kong and he offered to take me into Tai Po again, in order to catch one of the modern busses going to Victoria Harbour. I took him up on his offer and soon I was on the road again, this time to explore the CBD. As we drove along the highway to the edge of Kowloon, I was impressed by the number of people living together in such a restricted space yet able to make a comfortable life for themselves and their families. The years since the end of British rule had been very uncertain and traumatic, but the citizens seemed to take the changes in stride and were once again preoccupied with making money.

As I arrived downtown, the hustle of commerce filled the streets. I wheeled up the footpath beside the ferry terminal and was in awe of all the shopping that was available. American fast-food chains were everywhere and if it wasn't for the faces in the crowd, you would've sworn you were in New York City. I finally wheeled down to the ferries and bought a ticket across the harbour to the island of Hong Kong. As we pulled away from the Pier, the magnitude of the skyline became evident. The skyscrapers were huge and construction cranes were everywhere. I looked out at Victoria peak, which had a cable car so tourists could enjoy the view of the city. Chinese junks were on the water and I wondered if they were simply for the tourists or whether they were still used to move goods commercially. I disembarked from the wharf on the island and observed double-decker busses on the streets. I entered a shopping mall selling Gucci and Prada. I was getting hungry, so I went into a small bakery and purchased some Chinese treats to enjoy as I looked back at the skyline. I'm not a city mouse, but I had to see this for myself. It was unlike any city I'd ever been to before, but I began to believe that things had worked out for the best and it was time to make my way back to the peaceful serenity of Tai Mei Tuk.

On my last day, Willie accompanied me again to Tai Po to see me off, but this time we ate at a restaurant where the locals stop for Yum Cha. As the steaming dumplings arrived and Willie began to quaff a cold beer, I knew that for me, being out in the boonies of Hong Kong, had probably been the best place to be.

MALCOLM AND THE QUOKKAS AT ROTTNEST ISLAND

On a recent visit to Oz, I took the opportunity to travel to the most westerly point on the continent, the state of Western Australia and the beautiful city of Perth. For Aussies, W.A. is akin to the wild west of North America. Separated from the rest of the country by the vast Nullarbor Plain, it's distinct, owing to the prospectors, cattlemen, and adventurers who opened the nation to the western coast.

As I landed at the airport, I was happy to see that it offered the customary minivan service to the city. Often, people running these services are reluctant to help me, for fear of getting a hernia, strained back or a lawsuit, if something goes awry. No such worries this time. The energetic young fellow driving the bus insisted there would be "no worries" and after enlisting another passenger to help me on, we were away to my hostel.

The YHA hostel in Perth is located in the trendy area known as Northbridge, which is frequented by yuppies and the well-heeled, upscale dinner crowd. Of course I fit right in, wheeling around in my socks. Actually, the hostel was a charming old building at the corner of the busiest street in town. There were three levels and an elevator or "lift" that my chair barely fit into, to get me up to my room. The interior, on the other hand, was nothing to write home about, as a filthy, dusty old carpet immediately started my eyes watering from some type of allergy. My room was quite large and I had it all to myself, even though there was an extra bed. The transom over the door, which had been a glass fixture, had been knocked out and the management had imaginatively covered the hole with pages from a magazine. I knew it was going to let in a lot of noise, but I had my trusty backpacking earplugs, which are a necessity, especially for those noisy dormitories in which your intoxicated roomies arrive after closing time. Above, the ceiling seemed to be twenty feet high and opened at the top in a small skylight. The washroom facilities were barely manageable for me. There was a slight step up to get into a wide stall with a bathtub, a plastic chair to transfer into and a hand-held shower fixture for ease of use. The toilets were just wide enough to squeeze into, but the doors opened inward and after transferring onto the seat, I had to push the chair out of the stall, just leaving the foot pedal within my reach, before closing the door.

Perth is a wonderful city to get around in. There's a slight drop near the waterfront along the Swan River, but beyond that, it's relatively flat. The city offers two "Cat" services, free low-rise busses to allow tourist and locals move around the CBD. For me, this offered a way up the steep bit near the shore and also let me move easily to points of interest. Kings Park was a large beautiful green space in the heart of the bustle, with magnificent views of the Swan River. I spent a very pleasant afternoon there.

The train station was just moments away from my hostel, so I used the rails to explore the local environs. Fremantle, where the America's Cup was held some years ago, is a former military installation and has an excellent natural harbour. The quaint town that's grown up around it and the spectacular homes rising up from the shores of the Indian Ocean, indicate that this has become a bedroom community for the rich and famous. But beyond that, the shops, markets (with a wide choice of fresh seafood) and dining, make it a must on your itinerary. It's a great place to get those sunset photos that are always in demand too. Fremantle is the jumping-off point for the ferry trip to Rottnest Island, a few kilometers away, home of one of the smallest marsupials, the quokka.

I'd booked a two-day stay at the YHA on Rottnest Island, from my hostel in Perth. Rottnest Island was so named by Dutch settlers, who, upon seeing the quokkas for the first time, thought they were "rotts" or rats. The ferry ride was less than an hour and in some seasons, you may be lucky enough to view whales during the voyage. Upon disembarking, I was met by a free wheelchair friendly bus that regularly runs throughout the island. My hostel was known as the Kingston Barracks, a former army accommodation and offices at the far end of the island. I was unable to get into the office due to the steps, but the dormitories, which consisted of three sets of bunk beds, had ramps. The dining area also contained washroom facilities that looked like they'd meet my needs.

As I wheeled around the site, exploring and investigating the vicinity, I got my first glimpse of a quokka. Actually, the place was overrun with quokkas and with them came all the little quokka poops that I spent the next few days trying to avoid. The little animals were brown, didn't look like rats, had cute eyes, and were about half the size of an average cat. By evening, the animals were out in force and family units of up to eight or nine would slowly hop around in search of food. The ones nearest the barracks seemed comfortable with people and looked for easy handouts, even posing with kiddies for photographs. Further away, they became more wary.

Rottnest has developed a small village near the wharf, complete with a fast-food outlet, ATM, restaurants and a theatre. One of my favourite activities was to hop on the bus in the morning and head to a sheltered cove, since the west side of the island is sheltered from the winds of the Indian Ocean, especially the late afternoon wind (known as "the Doctor" in Perth). I liked to sit under a shady tree and watch families as they snorkelled, swam or played along the beach. Many families rent small cottages for a few weeks during school holidays. For those looking for a more rustic experience, you can also tent at campsites. No cars are allowed on the island and most people bike or walk along the roads. Each day, around 2 p.m., a stingray would glide along the turquoise shore looking for food. What intrigued me was that as the children came toward it, the graceful, gliding swimmer would stop and let the kids touch it. After one youngster came up the hill past me, I asked how it felt. "Like rubber", she happily squeaked. My visit to Rottnest was a great respite.

One famous aspect of Western Australia is the white sand beach. I left the city to venture north to Scarborough beach for a taste of sun and surf. As I waited at the railway station for my bus connection to the coast, I had a religious experience. A man with a limp tried to convert me into a Born Again Christian and a fellow from the Christian Scientists tried to find the "real me". I think he finally got bored with the real me and I was abandoned to await my bus.

I finally arrived at Scarborough beach and was a bit disappointed because a great sand dune between the boardwalk and the beach obstructed my view. The town council is purposely trying to support the natural existence of these formations and I'm always on the side of planet earth, but I was disappointed just the same. The beach was excellent and I enjoyed the view from the change room roof.

The hostel back in Perth had finally caught up with my health and all those dust mites got the better of me. I felt terrible. My eyes were sore and now my throat was aching and I'm sure my tonsils were swollen to the size of golf balls. I wheeled the blue chair north of Northbridge to the Vietnamese part of town. I settled on a small, bright restaurant and ordered a spicy beef soup. It was delicious and made my nose run for the duration of the meal. It did the trick. The next day my throat felt one hundred percent improved and I was ready to roll.

On my return from Fremantle aboard the train earlier in my trip, a late middle-aged man in a motorized scooter struck up a conversation with me. His name was Malcolm and he was a British ex-pat who had once lived in British Columbia, but had settled in Australia in his younger days. I was glad he'd started the conversation; I'm generally not too talkative with strangers. Oh, you can't shut me up once I get going, but initiating things isn't my style. Malcolm worked for the Taxation department, across the street from my hostel and we hit it off right away. After sharing a few cappuccinos over the week, he'd mentioned that his partner was going away for Easter with her family to the Margaret River and that he was free on Easter Sunday. He'd be happy to drive me around Perth on a bit of a tour. It was an offer I couldn't pass up!

On Easter Sunday, Malcolm arrived to pick me up, but the problem was going to be getting into his high van. I'd already concocted a plan. As he arrived, I was lucky that a big, burly backpacker was just exiting the hostel. I hijacked him and asked if he'd mind lifting me into Malcolm's van and throwing my chair into the back. With a European accent, he said it would be his pleasure and soon we were ready to go.

Malcolm drove an old Vauxhall van, but he had some use of his legs, so didn't need hand controls like I use and, with some difficultly, could get around on canes. We toured the Burswood Casino area and then Peppermint Grove, where many of the well-off citizens of Perth reside, near the waterfront. We drove out of the city to John Forest Park, a beautiful drive through ancient western forests, which seemed almost desolate and dry.

One of the most interesting sites on the trip was a view of the water reservoir, known as "the Weir", where one of the more prominent citizens of W.A. tried to build a great pipe to pump water to the interior town of Kalgoorlie. There's an urban myth in Australia that when Kalgoorlie turned the pipes on and no water came out, the engineer took his own life in despair. I was assured that it was a good story, but totally untrue. I've kept in touch with Malcolm and he's in the process of taking his Vauxhall van to the UK and spending the northern summer touring the British Isles. He's quite a guy.

The Perth Food and Wine Festival was on during my stay. It wasn't too far of a wheel from my hostel and there was a huge turnout. Western Australia has some of the finest wine growing regions on the continent and the festival is an opportunity for the small, boutique wineries to show off their excellent wares. Along with great food and entertainment, you can purchase a book of tickets to buy wine samples. Well, the wheelchair seems to bring out the extra large sized sample servings and coupled with the sun, entertainers, music and food it was a great way to top off my trip to Perth.

I must confess, I don't remember much of the rest of that afternoon, but I'll always have great memories of my trip to Western Australia.

THE BUTCHER, THE BAKER AND THE CHEESEMAKER

When I first decided to backpack through Europe by purchasing a rail pass, I remember the thoughts and emotions that ran through my head as my brother, John, and our friend, Phil, picked me up from my tiny apartment to take me to the airport.

"Is that all the stuff you have?" my brother asked incredulously, staring at my small backpack and blue gym bag.

I was scared stiff and in panic mode. "Do you think I'm doing the right thing?" I asked him.

"You'll be fine. If you get stuck, just give us a call on the phone", he reassured, waving me into the departure lounge.

I'd never ridden the rails, never travelled in non-English speaking countries, and never worried so much about the things that could go wrong. I had planned a one-month excursion via Eurail that would take me to ten countries, from France in the west to Hungary in the east. All of a sudden, my confidence abandoned me. One of the reasons I'd chosen to land in Holland, was I felt that in Amsterdam at least, I'd be able to make use of my English and get a bit of Europe under my belt, while getting acclimatized to the new continent and its ways of doing things. The other reason was that I was flying on KLM.

In the days before the invention of the Internet, it was difficult to arrange hostel accommodation, and I'd spent the week leading up to my departure exchanging faxes with various establishments, all informing me that their buildings would be unsuitable for me and my blue chair. That was another reason for panic. As I finally boarded the plane, KLM upgraded my economy ticket to first class and placed me in the nose section of the huge, wide-body aircraft, with a number of elderly people. I never found out if that's the policy of KLM to make it more comfortable for disadvantaged travellers, or if they simply had the extra space (they put me back in economy on the way home a month later), but I appreciated it and my worries melted away with the hors d'ourvres and champagne.

Arriving at the Schiphol Airport on a bright and clear Dutch morning, it was exhilarating to finally be in Europe after all the worry. I cleared customs, exchanged some traveller's cheques and needed to find my way into Amsterdam. At the info desk, I found out that trains pull into the airport and one of the first stops is "Centraal Station", in the city centre, just eighteen kilometers away. The elevator on the concourse took me down one flight to the train tracks, and after asking which train would take me where I wanted to go, I hopped on. It couldn't be any easier. These Dutch seemed to have it all figured out. The conductor looked at my Eurail pass and stamped it with the date. I could now travel almost all over Europe for the next thirty days.

In the central station of Amsterdam, there was a traveller's information desk to help book accommodation for the evening. I told the good-looking young woman my problem and she spent the next fifteen minutes phoning around town for me. After a short while, she smiled from the phone and gave me the thumbs-up. I had a place to stay. She gave me a map of the city, pointing out where I was and where the hostel was. It didn't seem too far away, so I set off to find it, even though it was still morning and I knew it was too early to check in.

Amsterdam is a very flat city and Holland is a very flat country. I guess that's to be expected when most of your nation is below sea level. There were cars everywhere, but they were very small and relatively quiet. What struck me were all the bicycles. Amsterdam had an extensive network of bike paths and citizens are very environmentally conscious, in addition to being very fit. I decided to use the paths for my own benefit. Hey, a wheelchair is sort of like a bicycle—just a few extra wheels more or less. What also caught my eye was the type of bicycles being used. The bikes weren't ten-speed or modern ones. Instead, they looked old and worn out and they all had little bells on them, the type schoolgirls used back in Canada. During my time there, I learned that the Dutch take bike riding very seriously and will use those noisy little bells often, whether you're in a blue chair or not.

As I wheeled toward my hostel, I passed small, well-kept shops adorned with flowers. The Dutch love flowers and use them to brighten their days and the city. I travelled over the small, lilting bridges, which rose over the canals and have become city landmarks. Beside the canals, benches allowed passersby to stop and take a break or watch tour boats and local canal traffic. I finally found the street that my hostel was on, just off the main "Kerk Straat" or Church Street. It was a simple, white building and there were the usual collection of backpackers outside having a smoke after breakfast. There were a few small steps up to the entrance, but they'd also fashioned a ramp, so I was all set.

I informed the staff that I'd be checking in later on, but surprisingly, they had a bed ready that I could check into right away. It was a great relief to leave my shoes and gym bag behind and know where I'd be flopping. They also told me that breakfast was included and gave me a meal ticket for the cafeteria. I dropped my stuff off on my mattress in the four-bed dorm and headed to the dining room. It was huge and had a lot of tables, but only a few eaters were left. I handed my ticket to a man who looked like he was Arabic or Middle-Eastern and he told me to find a table and he'd bring me my breakfast. I don't know whether it was the chair, my haggard look after the long plane ride or the Canadian flag on the pack hanging from the back of my chair (many Dutch and Belgians are fond of Canadians, since our soldiers liberated them in the Second World War), but the man came back with food piled six inches high on the plate. There were at least eight slices of bread, sliced meat, cheese, hot potatoes, stewed vegetables and two hard-boiled eggs. "Make some nice sandwiches and put them in this bag for your lunch", he instructed me sternly. I thanked him, ate as much as I could and ferreted the rest away for later.

After the meal, I felt great. It was time to do some exploring and, full of the confidence that had abandoned me the day before, I exited the hostel. Sadly, I'd forgotten that I had to turn left to use the ramp. I fell head first down the steps, out of my chair and onto the sidewalk, landing on my camcorder. I'd had it on my lap and it received a dent on its audio recorder. Two Japanese chaps who were smoking outside asked me if I was OK, dusted me off and lifted me back in my chair. My dignity was slightly tarnished, but I was none the worse for wear. After checking that I was still in one piece, I headed out. I would like to say that never happened again, but I'd be lying.

The next day, a friend of mine from Canada was also landing in Amsterdam, at the beginning of his tour around Europe by rail. Prior to departing, we'd arranged to meet on the day of his arrival at the Dam Square, in the heart of the city. He said that, like me, after arriving he'd want to look for a place to stay, and that we should meet around 2 p.m. Anyone who knows my friend Lenny, a tall robust blonde fellow with a pleasant personality and a friendly smile, also knows that he's generally less than punctual. So I waited an extra forty minutes and eventually he showed his smiling face. We decided to go for a bit of a walk around town.

Lenny said he'd found a hostel and had already visited the Ann Franke Museum (up a number of stairs, so not on my itinerary). We took the opportunity to renew our acquaintance with a pint of Heineken and a meal at an outdoor café. I convinced my friend that we should take the opportunity to board a tour boat traversing the canals, since I was in dire need of assistance to get onto the boat. He agreed and we made our way down to the launch, but he struggled to lift me onto the craft. The trip was about an hour and we travelled through the heart of the city, past flower markets, trendy shops and streets of small multi-level row houses. Each home had a long protrusion, just below the apex of the roof. The tour guide indicated that they were furniture hooks. The interiors were so cramped, due to lack of space in the small country, that when someone moved in or out, there was no room on the stairs to move furniture. So, when moving, you attached your furniture to a block and tackle on the furniture hook and moved it in and out through the windows!

By now, the jet lag was catching up to Lenny and he was falling asleep. I have some great video of him smiling and trying to stay awake, but he was fighting a losing battle. At the conclusion of the tour, it was all I could do to keep him awake long enough to get myself back on land and into my chair. We decided he needed to sleep, but he insisted that after a few hours, he'd meet me and we would head out and spend the evening in Amsterdam's red light district.

Lenny arrived at my hostel around 7:30 p.m. and we decided to eat dinner in the cafeteria. After a steaming bowl of pasta, it was time for a night on the town. This time, I remembered to turn left down the ramp exiting the hostel. As night fell on Holland, the city seemed to come alive. The two of us strolled through the streets as trams rolled along and bicycles rang their incessant bells. Couples walked arm in arm, window-shopping or just looking out over the canals. We decided to stop into the Marijuana and Hemp museum, which, for six guilders, turned out to be a bit of a rip-off, but at least we could say we'd been there.

Ultimately, we made it to the red light district. It was very clean and not at all what I expected of the area. Sex shows were plentiful and the touts were outside, imploring visitors to come in. As for the prostitutes, they were inside windows and if you were in the market for companionship, you could look them over and decide which one appealed to your tastes. Interestingly, not many were Dutch. They seemed to be Indonesian or from other former Dutch colonies. One of them pointed at me specifically and made a lewd gesture of what she'd do if I would become a client. I was quite sheepish, but Lenny got a huge chuckle out of it.

We capped off our time together at an outdoor pub, hanging around the bar with our pints and taking it all in. That night, I had to kick a fellow out of my bed when I got home. I think he'd sneaked in with one of my roommates to save the fee and he ended up sleeping on the floor. The next day, Lenny was off for the rest of his adventure and I was going to the countryside.

I didn't want to spend all my time in cities, so when the morning came, I boarded a train to visit Alkmaar, a country village known for its cheese making. I also hoped to see some of Holland's famous windmills. Getting to most places in the Netherlands isn't a long trip, so a short while later, I'd arrived. It was quaint, neat and small, but unfortunately, there was no cheese! I learned an important point about being a tourist: READ THE INFORMATION BOOKLETS. It turned out that the cheese market only occurred on Saturdays and this wasn't that day. I was disappointed, but undaunted. I'd make the best of it. I started to look around for a windmill. There was one, but it wasn't spinning. It swayed a bit with the breeze, but turn? It did not. I'm not sure why. It may have been broken or simply obsolete. I wasn't having a good day and it was about to get worse.

I decided to try and find some lunch, but as I crossed the street—THUD!! Once again I'd found a way to fall out of my chair. Looking up at the sky, lying on my back in the middle of the road, I hoped no one would run me over. But what I was really wondering was what had happened? I was in the street already, so there was no curb, no potholes. What was it? As I slowly sat up, I looked at my chair, noticing that one of the two bolts keeping the left front wheel bolted to the frame had been lost. That left the bracket holding the tire to rotate on the frame and turned the device into a three-wheeler. I'd skinned my elbow, but was otherwise unhurt. Just as I'd started wondering how to get out of the road, people started running from shops on both sides of the street to help me. The butcher was there, a fellow from the bakery and some people from a cheese shop. I asked if there was a hardware store nearby, so that I could get a nut and bolt to stabilize the wheel and get myself back on course. They helped me onto a bench and one of the young men rode his bike to fetch the needed parts. I thanked everyone for their help, borrowed a wrench to make the repairs and soon I was on my way.

It had been a bad day, but because of the kindness of strangers, I couldn't say the day was a total loss. It left me with a very warm feeling at the start of my European vacation.

NEW YEAR'S EVE Y2K IN WELLINGTON, N.Z.

Sydney was preparing to host a fabulous party to usher in the new millennium. Actually, I'd been having the debate with my friends back home as to whether it really was a new century or not. My view, supported by many academics, was that new things always start with a "1", so that the year 2000 was actually the end of the century. It didn't really matter who was right, me and the eggheads or everyone else. The main thing was that the year was going to be the first to start with a "2" and that's all that really mattered. Despite the big plans and the fact that I had friends and family in Sydney, I wanted to be in the first time zone to welcome "Y2K", as we programmers and many others called it. I was headed to New Zealand to be one of the first to see if the programming we'd been working on for the last three years would work. Would the lights actually stay on?

Ever since I'd first travelled to the South Pacific, I had thought about coming to this part of the world when the clock ticked past 1999. I even remember as a kid calculating how old I'd be on that date and thinking, "God, I'm going to be thaaat old?" After much internal debate, I finally decided to spend that moment in Wellington, the capital city. Part of my reasoning was that since it was an administrative centre, most government bureaucrats spent lots of money on their own parties, so I was hoping for a lavish affair.

Besides, I'd never been to Wellington and was looking forward to checking out the city and seeing what it had to offer.

When I arrived, it was refreshing to feel how laid back the atmosphere was compared to the craziness in Sydney. I took a short cab ride to the YHA hostel in town and got assigned to a six-bed dorm on the third floor. The hostel was in the middle of town and very convenient for short strolls around the CBD. My only problem with the facility was that they had carpeting in the rooms. I have no idea why anyone running a hostel would want to install a carpet. Don't they realize these kids are drinking and carrying on, not to mention getting sick and that no amount of cleaning is going to be successful? Being in a blue chair, when I wheel along, my hands pick germs from the floor, but since I do the same thing outdoors, I guess I couldn't complain too much. I'm generally pretty good about trying to keep my hands washed, so I'd just have to wash a bit more often.

I spent the afternoon wheeling around town, first picking up a sandwich, some groceries and then sightseeing and deciding what I might do for the next few days. Wellington is located at the bottom of the North Island, in a small bay that affords it a beautiful natural harbour. I loved going down the wharf, wheeling around and quietly listening to seabirds, while watching yachts go out or return. Later that evening, I was enjoying a sunset along the edge of the pier, when I saw something black zipping along in the water. I took very little notice of it, until I overheard a woman talking with her very young daughter, who held a toy fishing rod trying to catch her first "big one". The mother pointed at the sleek, black animal and said, "Watch out for your worm or that baby penguin will get it". Wow! It had never dawned on me that I'd actually see a wild penguin, but there it was. The three of us sat with the sunset while this lonely little penguin splashed about the water looking for its dinner.

For me, it was a very special moment and the child agreed by squealing her delight.

The next day was very sunny and I'd given myself a choice of things to do. I could go to a museum or to a sports event. The decision was a no-brainer. I would wheel to the cricket ground called the Basin Reserve Oval and watch my first ever Test cricket match. I'd followed cricket on TV over my years of travelling to Australia and New Zealand. The sport was probably the precursor to baseball, which is popular in North America. There were two types of matches: the test, which is played over five days that I was going to, or the one-day, which is completed quickly and is more of a traditional sports event.

The wheel to the Oval was very short and I arrived at 9 a.m. I wasn't sure what to expect, but tickets were going for $20, which I thought was a bit expensive. I asked the woman at the ticket booth if they offered a "concession", their term for discount, for the disabled. She gave me a ticket for $10, and that, coupled with the $2 coin that I'd found on the road enroute, meant I had a budget of $12 for beer.

The cricket ground was beautifully green and the stadium was old and historic. I wheeled completely around the field's inside circumference and looked at the pavilion from the furthest point in the outfield. Ticket prices were higher if you wanted to sit in the stands in the shade, but if you were cheap like me, you either stood or spread a blanket on the gentle hills rising from the boundary rope marking the edge of the playing surface. I tried to find a shady place and ended up near the pavilion under a tree. Since the day's play was scheduled to go from 10 a.m. until 6 p.m., with breaks for tea and lunch, staying out of the sun was very important. This was the fourth day of the test and the visiting West Indies team was on the ropes, having failed to score enough runs in their first innings to surpass New Zealand's score, so they had to bat twice in a row.

The New Zealand team was on the field in their traditional black uniforms. Children and fans had great access to team members and came right up to ask them for their autographs. The West Indies great, Brian Lara, was in his batting pads and helmet, ready to head out onto the wicket to try and get his team back into the Test. I've always visited the South Pacific during their summer (my winter), so I end up here in cricket season. I'd rather watch rugby, but it's their winter sport and I'm not going to come during the Canadian summer, which I love.

The game itself was rather boring and the West Indies got bowled out and lost the match, which meant I'd made a good decision, since there'd be no cricket tomorrow. When the players went off for their lunch, children and families were allowed to throw balls and Frisbees around the playing field. You'd never be allowed on a playing field in North America, so that was very refreshing to see. By the end of the day, I wasn't feeling too well from the combination of Tui beer and heat stroke. Oh well, live and learn.

I'd met a few of the hostel's backpackers in the lounge and we were beginning to form a group that would hang out together on New Year's Eve, but now, it was off to the Te Papa National Museum. The Te Papa had recently moved into new facilities near the centre of town and the entrance was quite impressive. You didn't have to pay to enter the museum, but they asked that you provide a donation in the box at the entrance. The largest exhibit on offer displayed the Maori history of settlement in New Zealand and throughout Polynesia. There were large wooden watercraft demonstrating Maori prowess at sailing and navigating from island to island, without the benefit of a compass or any modern techniques. In addition, there were some great exhibits on the geological formation of the country and the impact volcanoes and earthquakes have had on the topography. I took an extremely personal interest in an exhibit on the diversity of the population. One display had pictures of a winery founded by Croatian immigrants. The last name of the family was Babic, my maternal grandmother's maiden name.

The long awaited New Year's Eve had finally arrived. A group of five of us from the hostel had decided to party together and I was happy that, even though I didn't know them too well, we'd be able to share the experience. One fellow was an accountant from Auckland, two other guys were Europeans from Holland and France, respectively. My fourth companion was a young woman dressed in black who was quite fond of spiders was from, of all places, Switzerland. We arrived at Port Nicholson around 9.30 p.m. and the light from the long summer's day was just starting to fade. As the crowd grew and the entertainment heated up, each of my new friends took turns pushing my chair through the army of legs. A spaceship landed on the water and aliens conveyed their greeting to Planet Earth, while a troupe of entertainers hung from the walls of a building under coloured floodlights. A large TV screen showed pictures from other parts of the country and I felt sorry for the people up in Auckland who were suffering under a torrential downpour. The weather held in Wellington and as the man on stage counted down, "Five, four, three, two, one", we watched the sky for the colourful fireworks that lit up the evening.

As I received a few New Year's kisses, I looked up at the light poles and saw that the electricity had remained on after all. In the end, the tiny country of Kiribati had changed time zones to be half an hour earlier than New Zealand, but it was a new century, full of new possibilities and I really didn't care.

ON THE ROAD WITH THE OTHER COLOURED CHAIRS

One of the reasons I became interested in travel in my formative years, was that I was involved for a long time in competitive (and I use the term loosely) wheelchair sports. I played basketball, rugby, table-tennis and even tried pistol shooting. In my later years, I became one of the slowest defensemen in the history of sledge hockey. All of these sports were a great way to keep fit, meet new friends and most importantly for me, travel.

Our little wheelchair sports organization in the beautiful Niagara Peninsula never amounted to much in the way of championships or memorably high-calibre teams, but the cast of characters and some of the road trips more than made up for all the losses. For years, we ran a bingo in Niagara Falls on Saturday mornings to help fund the purchase of sports chairs for those who couldn't afford them and to help sponsor other non-chair bound disabled athletes from the area to attend Provincial, National or International competitions. The main purpose though, was to support the little clubhouse we rented, maintain our van for pick-up of those who didn't drive cars but still wanted to play sports, and cover the expenses of our travels throughout North America for games and tournaments with other teams in the National Wheelchair Basketball Association.

One of my longtime friends and roommates on road trips was Ed, another quadriplegic athlete who also played basketball against paraplegics. Ed was far better than I at the game, had an awesome hook shot and always amazed everyone when he swished it through for two points. He was also well known for being able to snore the paint off the walls, especially after he'd had a few drinks and a tiring day of sports.

We were on a road trip in Rochester, NY and had made our way there on a Friday for a weekend tournament. Another of the players on the team had recently acquired his driver's license, but was slightly tentative about driving with his hand controls on the two-hour trip across the border. I offered to go with Rick in his car, as long as he promised not to kill me enroute. The drive went fine, except for a short distance on the New York State Thruway that was under construction and had numerous neon orange barrels marking the off-road detour around the worst affected areas. Rick came pretty close to driving into a few of them, but that was the worst of it and we made it to the hotel without further incident.

As usual, we weren't faring too well at the basketball games, although there was an expansion team from Binghamton that was even worse than we were. We beat them and lost to the hosts, so after the first day of competition, we were still even at 1-1 and had a reasonable chance of making the finals on the next day.

It was Saturday night, party time for the lads. As usual, one of the rooms was the focus for socializing and I always did my best to make sure it wasn't mine, so that when the time came, I could head off to sleep. If the carrying on was in your room, you'd be lucky to get to bed by 3 a.m. I was a bit of a boring guy in those days and didn't even drink (I've long since discovered the health benefits of a pint of ale). I think it was because I enjoyed driving so much and was worried that if I ever got caught drinking and driving, it would affect my already exorbitant insurance rates and possibly leave me stuck at home without wheels.

We'd ordered a number of pizzas for the team and I'd spent quite a while in the social room, but finally decided I couldn't breathe for all the smoke and was getting tired. I left to go to my room and found Ed sound asleep, snoring up a storm. In those days, I didn't have earplugs, so I had to crawl into bed, put one of the pillows on top of the ear I wasn't lying on and hold my arm on top of the pillow to try and keep the noise out. It took a while, but I finally dropped off to sleep.

We had an early game the next morning and I was the first to get up and hit the shower. I always like to be the first so I could use dry towels. I hopped into the tub and enjoyed a long, hot shower. As I was crawling out of the tub onto the floor, the last thing to come over the edge of the tub was my right foot. I didn't know that Ed had left a glass on the rail of the tub near the wall and as I hit the floor, my foot caught the glass, knocking it down a split second before my leg followed it.

It seemed like the whole episode happened in slow motion and I can still remember vividly the moment my leg dropped onto the broken glass. For a second, I thought I'd escaped injury, but it didn't take long to realize that my hopes were misguided. The top of my foot near the right side had been cut by the glass thus severing a vein. I was now in panic mode as crimson blood spurted out of the injury. I hollered to Ed, who was now up. He hopped into his chair to see what the commotion was. He came in, saw the mess and asked, "What the hell happened?" I was in a real bind because I was nude, there was blood everywhere, and I was surrounded by broken glass so I couldn't crawl away even if I wanted to. The only thing I could do was put pressure on the wound to try and control the blood flow.

Ed hurried down the hall to get help and it was only a few minutes later that he and Bob, an able-bodied member of the team (who helped do repairs on the chairs and drive our van) came to my aid. Bob got a towel and wrapped it around my foot. Shortly, Pat, a leg amputee on the team, hopped in to offer his two-cents worth. "Walt, what the heck? It looks like a scene from *Psycho* in here!" He laughed, trying to re-assure me that everything would be OK. Bob carefully lifted me out of the bathroom and the blood seemed to abate a bit. I carefully got dressed and Bob took me to the local hospital in the club's van.

I spent an hour at the hospital as the doctor put my foot up on a table and carefully plucked all the glass out, while looking through a huge magnifying glass. He finally disinfected it, then gave me a few stitches and a bandage. When I got back to the hotel, the boys gave me the business about what a klutz I was and a few weeks later I received a bill in the mail for $138 that my provincial health care wouldn't cover for U.S. medical services. It was expensive and painful, but it was another story my teammates remembered in they years ahead, much to my chagrin.

A few years later, during March break, our team of snowbirds made our annual migration to Clearwater Beach to attend an annual basketball tournament held by the Tampa Bay entry in the NWBA. We never seemed to do very well in the competition, but when you spend your life in a blue chair, any excuse to head south away from the snowy weather is a good one. We'd been going down for a few years and were old hands at knowing which places offered the best accommodation and where the best vantage points were for viewing the bathing beauties on the beach.

I can still remember the first time we came down to Florida, which was also my first visit to the state. I stayed out in the sun from ten in the morning until four in the afternoon without sunscreen. I was a rookie and didn't realize the effect the latitude has on the sun's strength. My face was horribly sunburned. It was so painful, that I was forced to sleep on my back for a few days because my cheeks were too sensitive to rub against the pillow.

On this visit, I was much wiser and sat in the shade if I could, applied lots of sunscreen and wore dark sunglasses to cut down the glare (and hide where my eyes were looking). I'd decided to move my vantage point and was travelling alone down the sidewalk near the edge of the beach, when I spotted a young woman in a pink see-through bikini. It was quite a unique view and it had all my attention. Unfortunately, it distracted me from watching where I was going and I missed a small curb that allowed grooming and emergency vehicles to enter the beach. I was transfixed by this woman, when suddenly, my chair dropped out from under me. I think I did a complete 360° in the air, before landing unhurt, staring up at the sky. My chair remained on course and continued to the opposite curb. I was just realizing what had happened, when a young, muscular American guy stared down at me and asked, in a southern drawl, if I was OK. I told him I thought I was and he asked if I needed help getting back into my chair. Before I could answer, he picked me up, walked me across the small service road and plopped me into my waiting chair. I thanked him and tried to regain my dignity as I dusted myself off. I'm still not sure whether the woman in the see-through bikini saw any of it, but I hope not.

By the end of the weeklong tournament, I still had some American dollars burning a hole in my pocket. While I was on the beach, I'd watched parasailing tourists getting a tow from the tour boats. Pat and I decided we wanted to give it a go. Actually, I needed Pat because of my lousy sense of balance. I knew he could hang on to me if worse came to worse.

We went out to the wharf to see about a trip. It was within our budget and we boarded the small boat with a few other tourists. Pat and I were the first to get our turn going up under the chute. Pat, with a worker on the boat, lifted me onto the bench seat and then Pat took his place beside me. We were both fitted with lifejackets. I asked where the seatbelts were and was stunned when the staff told us there weren't any. If anything went wrong or a gust of wind tipped the bench, we'd be much safer falling into the Gulf. Maybe he thought it was better, but I sure didn't! Pat held onto me quite tightly and there was a bar in front of us that I could grasp.

Slowly, the line let out and as we rose higher and higher, the noise from the boat's engine began to fade. We were sailing above the beach and water with the parachute hanging out behind us. We drove up along the coastline and had a bird's eye view of the pedestrians and nautical activity. I looked out to sea to try and spy some dolphins or marlins, but there weren't any. Pat had a great sense of humour and cracked jokes about letting me go to see how useful the lifejacket really was. After turning the boat and sailing back to our original starting point, the line began to reel in and we descended back to the ship. It had been a great afternoon and we'd survived another crazy event on the water in Florida.

I still wonder if they've figured out how to fit those bench seats with airbags.

THE BLUE MOUNTAINS AND THE MEGALONG VALLEY

The first time I visited Australia, I stayed with my good friend, Sue, who'd spent over two decades in Canada before moving back a few years before my visit. Sue lived in a suburb of Sydney called Petersham and shared an old Federation era house with an aroma therapist who had the top floor. Thank goodness Sue had rented the bottom flat, which wasn't too bad to get into, as long as I went around to the backyard to enter. As could be expected from an old home, it had lots of character and the rooms were very large. It was also quite drafty and I could see the impact the "rising damp" or mold, on the walls inside. Spring had just started and it was still rather cool in the mornings. The cold inside the house would chill my bones so much, I'd have to go outside to warm up. This area of Petersham in the mid-'90s wasn't the greatest. Some of the houses weren't well kept and when I was there, across the street, were the torched remains of a burned-out compact car. I was surprised that the authorities hadn't towed it away, as would be done immediately in Canada. I'm sure with the booming property prices in Sydney these days, Petersham probably looks a lot better now.

The weekend was coming and Sue suggested we take a tour of the Blue Mountains, which wasn't too far away and made a nice day drive from the city. I'd read and heard quite a bit about the area and was looking forward to getting out of the house and into the countryside, especially with Sue. I've always liked her funny comments, knowledge of interesting facts and upbeat disposition. I'd missed her since she'd moved away from Canada.

We drove out of town along the Parramatta Road and as we got onto the highway, we could see small fires on the grassy medians separating the two directions of traffic. The winter had been drier than usual and as the days warmed, bushfires were already being reported. That didn't bode well for the summer ahead and after I left the country, they had one of the worst seasons for fires that NSW had endured in a long time. The heat that evaded Sue's house, took its toll on her little car. The radiator began to steam and we were forced to stop by the side of the road. Sue had brought water, but a kind gentleman stopped to see if she needed assistance. I felt quite helpless and it must've looked unusual for the fellow to see a man sitting in passenger seat, while the woman tended to the engine troubles. I told Sue that and she mentioned that the guy had seen my blue chair in the boot of the car, so he understood the situation.

We finally got the car working and stopped at a petrol station to make sure everything was all right. As we proceeded, the vegetation became thicker, but it still wasn't as green as I'd expected, due to the drought. We wove along the highway to the top of a ridge.

Sue decided that the Hydro Majestic Hotel at Medlow Bath would be a great place to visit. The hotel was a magnificent construction from the early 1900s. It was actually designed as a health retreat, or spa, which are immensely popular in Europe. The hotel offered wonderful views of the Blue Mountains, which are exactly as advertised and take on a bluish hue the further into the distance you gaze. After lingering around the back and enjoying the sight, which included amazing gardens and grounds, we entered the hotel's restaurant for a light lunch and dessert. The interior of the Hydro

Majestic was even more impressive than the exterior. High ceilings and wide arched entrances reminded me of a simpler and more elegant time, when craftsmanship meant more than getting the construction done as quickly as possible. On entering the intimate restaurant, I was in awe of the large windows that almost reached the ceiling and offered vistas down the sheer drop, to the Megalong Valley below.

We'd picked up a brochure on accessible accommodation in the area. Over the phone, a small campsite told us that some of their cabins were fitted with ramps and were designed to be wheelchair friendly. We thought we'd have a look.

First, we wanted to see the famous and impressive natural rock formation called "The Three Sisters". We stopped on the highway at a look out point by the side of the road and saw the three rocky pinnacles with a bit of vegetation growing from them. The phenomenon was quite unusual, since they jutted from the side of the valley on a small point. An old Aborigine legend says that the sisters were in love with warriors during a conflict and a witch doctor turned them to stone to keep them out of harm's way, but died before bringing them back to life. Throngs of visitors surrounded us, eagerly taking photographs.

We drove down into the Megalong Valley to view the cabins and they were exactly as described. The campground was quite small and most of the cabins were vacant. Sue and I chose one near the edge of the camp and went up the ramp to look inside. The interior was definitely not as luxurious at the Hydro Majestic, but on our budget, it fit the bill. There were two bedrooms, a small living room with a fireplace and a kitchenette. Outside, we found chopped wood and a picnic table on the porch. We'd brought a hamper of food and so we enjoyed our dinner listening to the cackles of kookaburras and enjoying the surrounding gum trees and Aussie countryside. We weren't that far away from Sydney, only about one hundred and fifty kilometers west, but it made for a great weekend and I think we were both happy to be away from the drafty house, if only for a short time.

Sue worked during the week, but after exploring Sydney on my own, we made one last excursion before I departed. Sue had told me about another natural occurrence, on the South Coast in Kiama, that she wanted me to see before I left. It was called "The Great Blowhole", a rock with a hole in it, that as the water pressure of the surf built up, would spray water out, similar to a geyser.

We drove the highways beyond Sydney without incident. Along the way, Sue took the opportunity to visit her friend Ian, who'd worked at Variety Village with her in Toronto. He was now living and working in Woolongong with his wife and young son. We were welcomed warmly into their home and Sue gawked at the garden and at what they'd done with the house, as all good guests should do. I'd never met them before, but they were very hospitable and invited us to share lunch with them, which we eagerly accepted. Ian's son was born in Canada and was adjusting to Australian life, but apparently he missed his favourite hockey team, the Toronto Maple Leafs. We soon said our goodbyes and continued our travels to the blowhole.

Kiama was another forty-five minutes beyond Woolongong and it was a very nice town, totally geared to tourists. We headed out to the blowhole, but were disappointed that the seas were not heavy enough to create the force necessary to push water up through the cave and out the opening for a spray. I think Sue was far more annoyed than I was. I spent the rest of the visit teasing her about how "great" the "Great Blowhole" was. In Australia, all tourist attractions have names like "Big" or "Great" to encourage tourism. I had a co-worker who came to Australia and spent his whole vacation travelling around seeing the "Big Pineapple" or the "Big Banana" and other such attractions. It wasn't how I would've spent my holiday, but it worked for him.

The little village was very cute and we decided to find a café for dessert and a beer. I decided that Sue needed a drink to compensate for the humiliation due to the definite lack of spray at the blowhole from the calm sea. She lamented that I wouldn't hear the roar of water squeezing out. I took the opportunity to tease her even more.

We capped off my visit to New South Wales at a revolving restaurant that offered an awesome view of the great harbour and city of Sydney. As we talked into the evening about our plans, the restaurant slowly turned back toward the water. The Sydney Harbour Bridge and city lights filled the windows. We toasted our friendship and her new future here in her home country. I knew she'd make it a big success. She always did.

PAYING THE TOLL TO CROSS THE BLUE DANUBE

When I was visiting Munich, I ran into an unusual circumstance, one I hope never to repeat. I was kicked out of my hostel! Actually, it wasn't as bad as it sounds, but it was just as problematic. I was in Bavaria at the end of August during the Feast of the Ascension, a state holiday. As a result, all accommodations in the town were fully booked. I had planned on remaining in southern Germany for three days, but the chair-friendly hostel I'd found could only house me for two days. My best efforts at finding alternative sleeping arrangements had failed. They asked me to vacate and I made way for disabled vacationing Germans.

I went off to the train station. I'd prepared for this type of situation. One of the great things about buying a Eurail pass, is that if you're stuck for accommodation or are low on funds, you can save the cost of a night's stay by taking a night train to another destination. I took a look at the list of outgoing trains and noticed that two were headed east near midnight. The first train was headed to Moscow, a city that certainly held interest for me (I remembered studying its city plan in my high school geography course). I decided it would be a bit too cool for me, as my plan was to stay as far south as possible in Central Europe. The second train was headed almost due east to Istanbul. Wow, that would be a great destination! I'd always dreamed of visiting Turkey and I hope someday I'll get the chance, but it was a long train ride, so I decided to get on, sleep overnight and get off at the first stop in the morning. I enquired where that would be and was told that the 8 a.m. stop was Budapest. That sounded interesting. I spent a few extra dollars for an upgrade to a couchette, so I could stretch out and saw a few logs, instead of sitting up all night in my chair. The staff at the station assisted me on board. The conductor made me comfortable and took my passport, so I wouldn't have to be woken during the border crossing in the early hours of the morning. In the train car, there were four places for travellers to sleep. Each of the two bench seats became beds and above them, two more were pulled out and a small ladder was fixed. The arrangement was much like bunk beds and I shared it with three Japanese. I was all set for a visit to Hungary.

I woke up a bit early, but it wasn't because I was uncomfortable or that the noise of the train bothered me. Quite the opposite. I always sleep well on trains and find the gentle roll of the cars and rattling along the tracks serves to lull me to sleep. I just wanted to peek out the window as the day dawned. The countryside was green and flat and homes along the track were a bit weatherworn and unpainted. As we approached the city, the drab buildings and apartment blocks of the communist era were a stark contrast to the bright, new buildings of the west. The train was slowing and as we moved into the station, it finally came to a rest. We had arrived in Budapest and I was again overcome with worry at the possible lack of disabled convenience and what would become of me. I immediately began to think about taking that night's train back to Bavaria.

As I regained my passport and disembarked, I looked for the same type of tourist information booth that the rest of the continent provided for the convenience of visitors. There was a bank office to exchange money, which I did, obtaining a huge sum of Hungarian forints for my Canadian money. But I was unable to find the help kiosk I was looking for. Suddenly, a young man asked me if I was looking for a place to stay. With no other options available, I said yes and he told me that he represented a university dormitory that was idle for the summer and had loads of space. I pointed to my blue chair and asked if it was going to be easy for me to get in and out. He nodded his head and, in very good English, said that there were six stairs leading to the elevator and that I could have a room with a washroom and shower to myself. He also said that the front desk was staffed twenty-four hours a day, so there'd always be someone on hand to help me up and down the stairs. As we talked, his buddies arrived with their recruits, all of them young backpackers, and the van for shuttling us to the hostel. I decided to give it a go, as he seemed interested in helping me and my knowledge of Hungarian was limited and mostly useless. He introduced himself as Csaba, a Romanian student, who was working in Hungary for the summer, as he could make ten times more in Hungary than he could back home. He helped lift me into the front seat of the old van, put my chair and gym bag in the back (my knapsack with my travel documents and camcorder always stays with me) and we were off to the university.

Budapest is named for the two towns that make it up. Buda, where the university was, is on the west side of the Danube River and is the older of the two. Pest, on the other bank of the river is the centre of commerce and nightlife. The university was a bit of a disappointment from an accommodation aspect. As advertised, there were the stairs Csaba had spoken of and there was help to get up and down to the lift, but when I checked out the room, I was in for a shock. It was a draughty old building and the room I was assigned to on the third floor had no light bulbs in it! There were three sets of bunk beds and the washroom facility was up a step and too narrow for my chair to get through. I was in for some problems. On the plus side, the price was right, at about $7 a night. There was a cafeteria with homemade food and a wonderful, hot meat sandwich that seemed to be a staple of the younger crowd and was very good indeed, for the equivalent of about 25 cents. In the evenings, the campus pub was also open and I spent some time down there with Csaba and his friends drinking and listening to Hungarian folk music.

The next morning I was confronted with one of those situations that really test your enthusiasm for travel in a blue chair. I had to go to the washroom but was unable to make my way into the toilet and had to do some fast thinking. Urinating is never a problem, as I can always go in a bottle or cup and then reach over and dump it in the can, but going number two was going to be a challenge. With the uncontrollable urge forcing me into action, I decided to go into a plastic shopping bag! Hey, many dog owners pick up after their pets with bags and then dispose of it, so why not me? After cleaning up and tying the bag tightly the next problem was what to do with it. I had a smaller knapsack with me and carefully placed the unwanted baggage in it and left to call for help down the stairs while hoping they wouldn't notice a strange smell.

Obviously, I wanted to get rid of the bag as quickly as possible, but as luck would have it, I could not find a single garbage can on the street. I was really starting to stink and I needed to improvise. I never litter but sadly I had to make an exception in this situation. I found a small alley and faked opening my knapsack to look in it for something. I took out my unwanted and ripening bag, placed it on the ground beside me, and then pretended to look for something else in my bag. I finished searching and zipped up the bag in the hopes of pretending to forget the bag and leave it behind me. As I made my hasty escape down the sidewalk it was only a few seconds later that I heard shouting behind me. As luck would have it, an old woman had spotted me and thought I'd forgotten a valuable item from by pack. It was all I could do to keep from laughing as this hapless old lady smiled and ran after me waving my smelly bag in front of her. When she finally caught up to me, I thanked her, accepted my trophy and quickly nipped over to the next street to repeat the whole ugly process. I finally succeeded and still can't figure out why the Hungarians didn't provide any public bins. I wonder how they manage to take care of their dogs?

It was time to explore the town, but unfortunately for me, the Buda side was very hilly. The university dorm was across the road from Gellert Hill, a famous and historical Hungarian site. Before modern civilization, the Magyars (Hungarians) were cornered by Asian tribes trying to conquer Europe, who had made inroads as far as Buda. However, the Magyars held the cave at Gellert Hill and turned the tide of the invasion, setting the stage for the founding of the Hungarian Empire.

I decided to cross the Independence Bridge over the Danube to Pest, which was relatively flat. As I slowly wheeled toward the top of the bridge, I heard loud moaning and screaming. When I got to the top, there was an old woman dressed in black, with a dark kerchief on her head. As pedestrians neared her, the shrieks reached their highest pitch and she was generally rewarded with a few coins. I was no exception. As I was a slow target, I made sure I always had some change left to pay her "toll" every time I crossed the Danube. There was no point crossing on the other side, as another woman held that position. I wondered if they were related.

Pest is a beautiful city, very old indeed. I had quite a bit of trouble navigating street crossings, since they didn't have bevelled curbs. I tried to make use of driveways as much as I could, but they were steep as well. Most of the time, I'd smile at someone, point to the curb and receive help up or down the step. After wheeling around the city for the better part of six hours, looking at wonderful monuments and the exteriors of museums, it was time to eat. I headed back toward the Danube, because I'd seen some nice waterfront cafés along the river. Eastern Europe is cheap by our standards, and even though I usually don't like to sit alone in restaurants, I relaxed the rule this once. I found a restaurant a few doors from the bridge and entered. It seemed desolate and as it was getting toward late afternoon, I wondered if I'd caught them between meals or if it was too early for dinner. Eventually, someone noticed me and I looked at the menu. They had lamb, which is my favourite and I also ordered a beer. The prices were extremely reasonable, but I'd been warned of scams in which tourists were presented with a bill with no relation to the prices on the menu. I watched as ferry boats and river traffic wafted through the ancient city and thought about the centuries of life that had lived here. It was unlike anything in the New World, where I was from. The meal consisted of a huge platter of lamb, grilled vegetables with potatoes, salad and an ice cream for dessert. I enjoyed the view so much that afterwards, I treated myself to an after-dinner beer, followed by a cappuccino. The total cost, with gratuity, was less than $12.

I was feeling quite good by the end of the meal. I headed to the top of the bridge and went back to cap off the night with more beer and singing with Csaba and his co-workers. All the while, I made sure I still had money so that the moaning lady would have something to eat as well.

THE PLASTIC FOOD LOOKED GOOD ENOUGH TO EAT

I looked forward to my initial visit to an Asian country, and Japan was going to be my first. It was also the first time I'd been to a country that spoke a language other than English. Despite the problems I'd had finding my hotel in Tokyo, I actually had a very restful sleep. There was a step up into the washroom, but I was able to negotiate it and I was even getting used to all the TV channels, none of which I could understand.

The morning arrived and I received assistance from the hotel staff down the few stairs to street level. It was a bright and sunny November day, and I welcomed the chance to enjoy the moderate warmth wearing my windbreaker. There was no restaurant in the hotel, so I headed out in search of morning coffee. I didn't have far to go. The Japanese are practical and on every block, there was a sidewalk vending machine. What was unusual was what it contained. In addition to the standard fare of cold pop, juice and green tea, there were also cans with varieties of hot coffee. One can had black coffee, another had sugar, still another had sugar and milk, etc. I thought it was a great idea! Needless to say, I took advantage and dropped in my 110Y for a can of coffee with milk. It was delicious and I accompanied it with a cake purchased at a corner store nearby. They also had cold rice wrapped in seaweed, a popular snack in the country and probably one of the reasons the Japanese are among the longest living people in the world, but I decided to give it a pass.

I returned to the hotel, packed up and asked the staff to call me a cab so I could finally check into my hostel in the Asakusa district. A uniformed cabbie arrived and helped me into my seat. We drove for about fifteen minutes and I was in awe at the size of the buildings and the amount of Japanese signage advertising each business. Before we reached our destination, he pulled off to the left and stopped the cab. He pointed to a small building and repeatedly said, what sounded like, "toretoru". He pointed to an entrance, repeating the word about five times, as I nodded, pretending I knew what he was talking about. He left the taxi for a few minutes then returned from the building, finishing zipping his pants. I finally figured it out. He'd been trying to tell me that he wanted to go to the toilet. I felt like a complete idiot, but it was my first experience with the language barrier.

When we arrived at the hostel, it was exactly as it had looked in the hostel guide. It was a huge skyscraper. Apparently the hostel rented out a few floors of the building and had modified them for accommodation. The taxi driver helped me back into my chair and onto the pavement. I took out some paper money to pay him, but he wouldn't accept it. I had no idea why, since he'd run the meter. I took out a credit card and again he refused. He bowed gracefully, shook my hand and then disappeared into the busy traffic. I still don't know why he didn't want my money, but I guess that the hotel owner had paid to compensate for the stairs I'd had to overcome or that he simply wanted to do a good deed. Whatever the reason, it was very much appreciated.

The building housing the hostel had small shops and dining establishments on the main floor, just behind the lobby. As I made my way to the elevator, I noticed that each restaurant had a front window, displaying plastic replicas of the dishes available. The imitation food was quite realistic and perhaps it was supposed to make passersby hungry or maybe it was just to assist tourists with the language barrier when ordering.

The hostel had a pleasant lobby, a fully equipped kitchen and a large, spacious washroom, much like you'd find in a sports arena, with wide stalls. My attention was drawn to a sign on the wall suggesting, "Do not wash your hair in the toilet". The warning was quite explicit, so I made sure not to stick my head in a toilet while I was there. Japan is a rather conservative society when it comes to sex, so here the males were housed on one floor and women on the other. The kitchen was set up so guests could prepare their own food or you could buy breakfast for 500Y and dinner for 800Y. They didn't offer a catered lunch, since it was mandatory that all backpackers be out of the hostel by the afternoon.

I'd tried to phone Aileen, my friend's friend who had booked the hotel room for me the previous night, but I only received a busy signal. It was too bad, since she had the holiday off and wanted to show me around during the daytime. I finally reached her and we decided to meet that night at the nearest JL subway station, get to know each other and then have dinner later on.

I spent the rest of the day wandering around the Asakusa area. Once I strayed from the busy main streets and delved into the narrower ones, a totally different Tokyo emerged. Land is at a premium, due to the high population. Even in the back streets of such a large, cramped city, each family attempts to make their space more personal. As I wheeled along the alleys, old ladies came out to sweep their part of the footpath and water the numerous potted flowers adorning the entrances to their homes. I was surprised that my presence didn't arouse any stares. Instead, people smiled and then went back to their chores.

As I wheeled along a river, watching traffic along a busy bridge, my attention was drawn to the lower edge of the riverbank where joggers and cyclists exercised. An area park was filled with elderly people conducting their exercises and in their midst, was a small shrine devoted to cats. I know many Japanese are Shinto, but I'm not sure how cats fit into it. As I wheeled by a fruit market, I stopped to look at the produce as I was starting to get hungry. The apples were among the biggest I've ever seen in my life, but the cost was 2000Y, over $20, which was far too pricey for my budget. I did buy a bento lunch, but I ate it for dinner. Bento is very popular and is basically bite-sized tidbits of different foods. The one I purchased was mainly seafood, with generous portions of shrimp, octopus and fish.

It was getting dark and I decided to buy a soft drink, find a spot on the busy street to sit and watch life go by. The Japanese are a fascinating people. They're very polite, despite the vast numbers of them living in such crowded conditions. They don't seem to bend to the stresses that many other city dwellers do. I'd expected the Japanese to look like working clones of each other and to a small extent that was true, especially with everyone using cell phones as if they were glued to their ears. But it seemed that everyone made a definite effort to stand out. Instead of all the locals having dark hair, many of the younger ones used a dizzying variety of dyes to colour their locks and they dressed in the strange way that has always puzzled adults about younger generations. As daylight abated, it was replaced by the colourful artificial variety. The air was beginning to cool and suddenly the wind came up. I was tired from my day of wheeling and decided to start back to my hostel.

When I arrived in the lobby, I spent a brief time looking at the plastic food in the restaurant windows. A middle-aged woman, who introduced herself as Miyako, struck up a conversation with me. She was studying English in the area and was walking through the mall to catch her train home. She mentioned that many Japanese like to stop and talk with native English speakers to try and improve their command of the language. She spoke well and told me of her family and interests. We actually met again for coffee the next day, and when I returned home, she corresponded with me for a number of years. It was very nice to connect with someone after such a short visit.

The bed at the hostel was quite narrow and hard, but I was relieved that it wasn't on the floor, as is traditional. I would've had no problem getting down to the floor, but getting back into my chair would've been quite a bother. The next morning, I decided to buy breakfast at the hostel. I was given Miso soup, a large bowl of rice, an egg and a small package, the contents of which were lumpy and the colour of Dijon mustard. It wasn't bacon and eggs, but I was here to enjoy a new lifestyle. I quickly slurped up the tasty soup and then pulled the rice toward me. I looked around to see how other people were eating their meals. The Japanese were cracking the egg, which was raw, and mixing it into the steaming rice. They then opened the package and poured its contents into the bowl also. The entire concoction was stirred thoroughly before eating. I'd never had a raw egg before, but I thought the steam might cook it a bit. The package emitted a weird odour when I opened it and when I put it in my mouth, the flavour was hot and spicy. It was definitely not what I expected from a breakfast, but it certainly was an eye opener so early in the morning.

As I wheeled out of the hostel into the morning, it was interesting to see that each large business employed someone whose job it was to salute each worker at the driveway as they came in to start the day. Since most workers used transit, I speculated that those driving were probably the highest-ranking company officials. I spent the day wheeling about the area again, but in a different direction. I ended up in a large park that I was later told had something to do with the royal family, but I never found out what. The grounds were huge and I was attracted by its wide green lawns, lovely flowerbeds, big shady trees and general peace and quiet. The pond beside me had a number of ducks and geese, accompanied by the appropriate poop on the ground. The silence was broken by a group of cute pre-schoolers all holding hands and following their teacher onto the grounds. The girls all had bright yellow bows in their hair and each one of them carried a blue knapsack. Behind the children, a few grandmothers helped the teacher keep them moving in the right direction. They were quite well behaved, as is typical, and their playful squeals of delight faded as they moved out of range.

I'd planned to meet Aileen after her day's work and so around 7p.m. I waited near the train station. The working day is long in Japan and as I waited for her arrival, I was amused by two co-workers parting company for the night. I think they might have been drinking, but what was funny was that the lower ranking man was bowing so deeply to the senior fellow. They must have spent five minutes talking and bowing before one of them finally went down the stairs to the subway.

Aileen finally appeared, recognizing my description of my hat and the blue chair. She was a funny, smart girl of Japanese descent, who was working as a computer geek on a contract. It was nice to make a new friend and hear a Canadian accent again. She was very enthusiastic about pushing me along the sidewalk and due to her stature we made a perfect match. She didn't have to stoop to reach the handles of my chair and managed the hills with ease. Aileen took me through the nearby areas and we got a great look at the local nightlife. It was another windy November evening and although it was getting cooler, neither one of us seemed to mind. Our conversation was fluid and she was very similar to our mutual friend Rita, who'd put us in touch with each other via e-mail. Even in the late hours, it seemed that the Japanese in Tokyo moved at a breakneck pace. People didn't stroll, instead they walked with purpose under the multitude of neon advertising. Aileen showed me a pachinko parlour, a type of legalized gambling, but it looked more like a noisy pinball arcade. Patrons sat like zombies at the machines, feeding them coins and listening to a strange cacophony of artificial sounds designed to enthuse you to play again.

We were getting tired and settled on a small restaurant where we could enjoy a beer. We both chose a tempura dish, a lightly battered shrimp or other fish. The conversation was great and the company was too. When the food finally came, it looked a lot tastier than the plastic replica we'd picked out at the entrance.

SURVIVING THE CAMPING AND COTTAGE ADVENTURES

In the summertime, from May to October, I'd say there's no place in the world I'd prefer to be than Ontario. In May, the fruit trees blossom in Niagara as the spring rains begin to dry out and vicious late afternoon thunderstorms well up from the unstable atmosphere, as the Caribbean air warms and humidity is suddenly released. The only drawback to the weather these days is the terrible amount of air pollutants that irritate your eyes and lungs, due to our mismanagement of fossil fuels and love of things electric. I'm sad to admit that I'm one of the contributors with my car, as I love to drive through the countryside.

I was first introduced to camping by my company softball team. Each affiliate at the pharmaceutical company I worked for would field a team and every summer we'd play a tournament for provincial bragging rights. Many of the tournaments were held in Guelph, west of Toronto. The players on our team were mostly single and we were all in our mid-twenties or early thirties. We'd rent a group campsite at Elora Gorge Provincial Park and put up the tents. This was our weekend accommodation and camping allowed us to quickly get to know new players on the team and relive old stories, while enjoying music around the campfire in the late evening.

The first year I attended this event, I had no camping gear whatsoever and was told by the team manager, Lenny, that there was enough room for me in the large tent that he was going to stay in. The owner of the tent, Luis, was a part-time scout leader with his church group and had a huge old canvas tent that was quickly dubbed "the Condo" by players on the team. It took quite a while to put the darn thing up, but in time, Luis was able to place all the poles in proper position to finally move our gear in. A fourth person, a summer student employee named Jan, was in the same boat I was, and would also be spending the weekend in the Condo.

After the games that Saturday, we returned to Elora Gorge, anxious to drown our losing sorrows in vast quantities of beer and hungry for a home-cooked meal. In those days at the group site, we'd divide into groups of about four and each was responsible for preparing one of the meals and washing up afterwards. That way everyone contributed, but no one spent all weekend doing domestic chores. After helping create a most memorable barbeque spaghetti dinner with a few of the women on the team, it was time to relax, relive the horrible errors we'd made on the field and enjoy the benefits that camping with good friends under the stars has to offer.

After a few hours, many bottles of beer and numerous songs sung out of key, the stars began to disappear and raindrops began to fall. We finally decided to call it a night and began to disperse to our tents. The only gear I had was an old cloth sleeping bag, which is still in the trunk of my car today. Lenny had said I could crash with him and share his air mattress. Len's a big guy and I hoped there'd be room enough for me, but I wasn't going to pass up the chance to avoid sleeping on the cold ground, especially if it was raining. At 1 a.m., we were all awakened by an amazingly loud crack of thunder.

Not far behind that, was the beginning of a torrential downpour that lasted most of the night.

We found out very quickly that Luis' old tent wasn't very waterproof. In fact, it leaked at almost every tent pole as well as numerous places in the roof. Luis had been sleeping on the ground on a small mat and some bubble wrap. After scurrying around in the tent trying to keep out the water, he finally gave up and we made room for him on our mattress so he could get out of the thin pool of water that was now forming. We sat and listened to the thunder for over forty-five minutes. We'd placed the tent at the edge of a stand of trees and halfway through the storm, Jan piped up and said, "I wonder what would happen if lightning hit a tree and it fell on us?" None of us had thought of that and we fretted until the storm finally rolled away. It was quite wet when we woke up the next morning and none of us had gotten much rest. I'd like to say that's why we didn't do very well in the tournament that year, but I'm not sure it would be the truth.

After a few years of camping during the tournaments, some people on the team, who had access to cottages, began inviting the team up for a weekend during the summer. Again it was Lenny, our manager and second baseman, who started the trend. Leonard's cottage is on Silver Lake, north of Kingston and he shared ownership with his many siblings. The cottage was open to family members during long weekends, but otherwise, they divided the summer up between them, based on holidays or availability.

After a number of years, "Lennypalooza" as it was known, became an event to look forward to. I always took the Friday of the weekend off and headed up to spend a quiet day with Lenny and anyone else who could come up early. One of my favourite activities was to go canoeing with another teammate, Al, and his three boys. Al was quite the outdoorsman and would bring all sorts of gear. I was just being introduced to the joys of the canoe and was very reluctant to head out on the water in such a skinny, tippy craft. I was always encouraged by the group to try new things. Al assured me that we'd stay near the shore and not move out into open water, where the waves sparked up by motorboats could unsettle the canoe. I sat on a soft lifejacket to protect my derriere and wore another. Al was an excellent canoeist and though he was a joker most of the time, he took water safety very seriously. I have problems balancing and held tightly onto the side of the canoe.

We slowly floated past other cottages and then around the nearby Provincial Park. At the far end of the lake, was an entrance to a small swampy reservoir. Al thought it would be a great place to go, since there'd be no waves. We floated past dead logs and water lilies in full bloom. Dead tree trunks had fallen into the water and become hosts for turtles and other amphibians to sun themselves on. As we glided through the scenic swamp, I looked over the edge of the canoe to see small schools of young fish. They spend the summer in the safer shallow water, rather than taking their chances with larger predatory species in the open lake. The only sounds I could hear were the buzzing of a cicada and Al's paddle as it broke the surface. Colourful dragonflies rested on the gunwale of the canoe or on my hand. It was quite a nice voyage.

As we headed home, Al sensed that I'd gained a bit of confidence in his abilities and in my own. He asked if it was OK to venture out into deeper water and I gave him the go ahead. We remained in relatively close proximity to shore and I knew my lifejacket would protect me. I just wanted to avoid getting wet. As we paddled further out into the lake, a fish suddenly jumped to the left. I heard it more than I saw, but I did catch the end of the jump as it re-entered the water. Not long after that, we floated past a dead pike that'd been sliced by the propeller of an outboard. Al thought it would be a great idea to retrieve it and bring it back to the cottage. The only way was to use the two paddles as chopsticks, in an attempt to pick the fish up and throw it onboard in one motion. I almost got my chance to test the buoyancy of the lifejacket, when he nearly tipped the canoe trying to catch the dead fish. After about ten minutes, he succeeded and we drifted back triumphantly to our fellow cottagers on shore.

Dwayne, one of the guys on the team, had decided not to come for the weekend festivities. We got silly that evening over a few beers and placed the unfortunate dead fish in various poses and took snapshots of the pike knee boarding, the pike barbequing, the pike playing ping pong, etc. It was quite hilarious and when we saw Dwayne that week at baseball, we kept calling him "Pike". He had no idea what we were talking about. We finally let him in on the joke when we arrived at the pub afterwards and showed him the photos.

The next year, at the same cottage, I participated in a water volleyball game from an inflated dingy. My friends enjoyed spiking the ball at me, trying to splash me, in a game dubbed "Spike the Crip". After I was lifted back into my chair to dry off and enjoy a beer, the gang continued to play volleyball near the shore or drink on the raft Lenny's family had constructed. I could see a storm brewing over the lake and knew it was headed our way. I was concerned that the swimmers might be caught by lightning and could be electrocuted if it hit the water. Soon I began to bark out warnings, advising them of my weather prognostications. "Fifteen minutes to the storm … Ten minutes to the storm …" and continued the countdown. They had great fun mocking me in my attempt to save them from impending peril, but when the time came and the rain finally hit, they all scurried back to the cottage. As payback for the annoying reminders, they all ran right past, leaving me in the rain for five minutes before finally showing a bit of sympathy. Even then, it was only a few of the women who ventured out to drag my blue chair up the stairs into the cottage. And to think I call them all friends? Is that gratitude or what?

I stayed with the same pharmaceutical company, but began to work with a different affiliate on the other side of town, nearer where I lived. That firm also had a softball team and many of the players were people from the I.T. department in which I worked. Each long summer weekend, the same group of three families, plus or minus other family members or friends, chose a park to camp at and spent the weekend together. By now, many had gotten married and the number of children was growing exponentially.

One park where I've always had dreadful luck was Rondeau Provincial Park in southwestern Ontario, near Chatham. For several years, we'd scheduled Rondeau for the hottest part of summer in early August, when the humidity is stickiest and the weather is stormiest. Three years earlier, in late July, a terrible thunderstorm rolled through the area and knocked down many of the park's trees. For two weeks prior to our scheduled visit, the park was closed to accommodate a cleanup of broken trees and limbs. When the authorities finally reopened the park, we were forced to hide in our tents and trailers for an hour at dusk each day, because of hordes of mosquitoes that hadn't had a meal in over two weeks.

The following year, we returned to the same park, wondering what was in store. Driving to the park, I got lost briefly and had to stop at a roadside vegetable stand to ask for directions. I was guided to a country road that would take me to the highway I needed to be on. I was going a bit too fast on the unpaved road when it suddenly curved to the left. Small nuggets of gravel made the surface very slippery and I came hellishly close to rolling the car into the ditch. I'd been stupid to drive over the speed limit and wasn't paying as much attention as I should have.

I now had my own tent. It was large enough for my blue chair to fit into and my buddy Brad, who'd helped me purchase it, also put it up for me. When I go camping with these friends, I'm adopted on a rotating basis and get to eat with that family and help to either cook or clean up afterwards. It's a great way for me to camp on my own, but still hang out with the group, since cooking for myself is a bother and wouldn't make much sense. After a day of roughing it at the beach on a reclining lounge chair that Brad's wife, Lorrie, had brought for me, we tramped back to camp to relax for a while before making dinner. Brad's daughter, Miranda, rode on my lap on the way back. I was happy to oblige, as long as her swimsuit had dried sufficiently.

We were just thinking about getting out the camp stoves, when the sky began to darken. I don't think I've ever seen clouds come up so fast and as they thickened, they turned a weird shade of green. I was sitting under the awning of my tent, preparing to go inside to wait out the storm, when the wind started to kick up. Brad sensed something big was going to happen and yelled at me to get into my car immediately. The vehicle was parked beside the tent and I opened the door and struggled to get in without benefit of my shoes and leg braces that normally ease the transfer. As I pulled my chair into the back seat, I happened to glance into the rear view mirror, just in time to see my tent flying away above the trees and over some evergreens onto a campsite on the opposite side. The wind had so much force that it had split the seams near the bottom and left the tent pegs holding the floor to the ground. If I'd been in the tent, who knows whether I would've survived? I most certainly would have been badly injured. As the storm continued, a bough from a tree snapped and dropped through the windshield of a new car nearby.

After twenty minutes, the storm blew over. I stayed in the car and asked Brad to survey the damage to see if the tent was salvageable. They went over to retrieve the pieces they could find and just laughed. Brad said there was no way to fix it. After two brushes with death in less than a day, someone was trying to tell me something. I asked them to throw my remaining gear and clothes in the trunk and decided to drive home. They say things happen in threes and I didn't want to remain to find out if it was true.

Recently, at Dwayne and Tina's cottage with Brian and Nancy, I hooked a massive Muskie, using a rod and worm. Dwayne and Brian are still in denial that I caught it, and we always laugh at the story of the big fish that got away!

I don't see as much of those guys as I'd like to anymore, since our lives have gone in different directions. They all helped me enjoy the great outdoors and they never worried about the things I couldn't do while camping or at the cottage. I think that's what good friends always do.

THE SOUTH AND THE NORTH OF IT

Australia, like Canada, is a huge country and it's very difficult to cover all points of interest in one trip. I'd always wanted to see South Australia and the Northern Territories, but had never put them on the list, as other events or friends took up my limited time. This trip finally included the top and bottom of the continent and I was looking forward to it.

Adelaide is the state capital of South Australia and I had a devil of a time finding friendly accommodation there. I rang a number of places from Sydney using my phone card, but most of them warned me away. Reading the guide, I discovered a backpacker's hostel very near the beach, my favourite location. The owner advised me that there were a few stairs to the washroom, but that the accommodation itself should be OK. He had a room on the main floor and told me to call him again when I got to the airport so he could send a vehicle to pick me up.

I arrived at the terminal and was met by two fellows in a van that had definitely seen better days. We drove along the city's outskirts and the first thing I noticed was the extreme heat. It was only 10 a.m., but the temperature was already over 28°C. The forecast was for temperatures to reach the upper 30s by late afternoon. I was also struck by the lack of humidity. Even though it was very warm, it was also quite comfortable.

We arrived at Albert's Hall, the hostel I'd booked, and the location was excellent. The building was right on the beach and behind it there was only a lawn, a pedestrian walkway and a low fence to keep people from toppling into the soft sand below. It was perfect. The problem was the accommodation itself as the wheelchair entrance was through the car park, and upon entering, I found myself in the kitchen which led down a hallway that opened into a living area with sofas, chairs and a large, but old, TV. Continuing, I finally made it to the six-bed dorm. The hostel staff had placed a homemade wooden ramp over the few stairs leading down to the landing. The ramp was quite steep and I knew I wouldn't be able to use it on my own going either way. The room was spacious and I'd been reserved a lower bunk. There was no air conditioning, but there were large fans and since it was on the lower floor, shaded from direct sunlight, I couldn't see the heat being too much of a problem. I did, however, have a big problem with the toilet facilities—they were totally unusable. The washrooms were quite impressive since they were made of marble, but they had a huge step up into them and they were very narrow. I was in panic mode. If I didn't have access to the washroom, I was going to be in big trouble. I decided to stay there for one night to see what happened. In case things get bad, I carry a container in my backpack in which I can discreetly go to the washroom—as long as I can find a private place to do so.

Going outside to admire the view, I noticed that this was an excellent hostel for the able-bodied. The second-floor rooms had wonderful balconies overlooking the beach and would definitely be a great place to party. I wandered along the footpath beside the beach and paused for a long while under a shady tree. I needed my sunglasses because the light reflecting off the sparkling, white sand would've blinded me otherwise. The beach and hostel were in the town of Glenelg, a southern suburb of Adelaide. I was surprised at how few people were on the beach. I guess that when you're lucky enough to live in such a nice part of the world, you take the beach for granted. Of course it was a weekday and I'm sure that had something to with it. There was a long pier to wheel out on as I neared the touristy centre of the beach. I love piers because they let me get out over the water and I enjoy watching fishermen trying their hand. In addition, this is a great place to people watch because I can hover above the bikinis at the waterline.

Numerous bars and patio cafés were clustered in the vicinity of the pier. There was also a small amusement park to one side. The best discovery for me, however, was a McDonald's restaurant with a huge disabled washroom. During my time in Glenelg, this washroom substituted for the lack of accessible facilities in the hostel. In the morning, I'd go there to relieve myself, and then wash my face and torso with a facecloth. I'd then enjoy a copy of *The Australian* newspaper with a cup of cappuccino. It seems that McDonalds is far more upscale in Australia, or perhaps their coffee is more refined. At the end of the day, I'd again visit the toilet to clear my bladder before bedtime. The only disadvantage was that I like to have a beer in the evening near bedtime, but during my stay there I had to put that bad habit on hold, in case I needed to get up that ramp to get outside when no one was around in the middle of the night to assist me.

One afternoon, I met a woman on a park bench with a southern U.S. accent. She introduced herself as Rosalee and mentioned that she and her husband were from Georgia, but had lived in Adelaide for a year or so while he worked as a university professor. I saw her almost every day and I enjoyed talking to her about food. She'd spend much of the afternoon buried in a cookbook on Australian cooking. Some of the pictures and her descriptions of the taste made my mouth water. We spent many late afternoons in a café enjoying coffee or tea and a dessert, exchanging travel stories.

The temperatures reached into the 40s during my visit and it became an evening ritual to wheel down to a small take-away shack on the beach where I could refresh myself with a tasty and cool Magnum ice cream. That's the treat I covet most when I'm in Australia. After enjoying my cool dessert on a stick and watching the sunset, my blue chair and I decided to go for a wheel around the residential neighbourhood to see the homes in the area. Most were modest, but I'm sure that in the hot real estate market along the water, they were worth a fair bit. As dinner was my next priority, I decided to stop at the local pub for a famous Aussie meat pie. I was looking for a real thing, not the ones sold at convenience stores.

I'd watched a TV program about Aussie meat pies and apparently some that are mass-produced have very scary ingredients, but if you find the homemade ones, they're very tasty. The pub was crowded and my only alternative was to sit at the end of a table that was already occupied. I introduced myself and quickly the two sisters sitting at the table with their husbands made me feel at home, as if I'd known them for a long time. The food came and was delicious while pints of beer freely flowed. I left the pub in a few hours, smelling like a cigarette and having violated my "no beer in the evening" rule, but I'd had a good time and would have to deal with that potential problem if the time came.

Soon it was time to leave the sunny south and head to tropical Darwin in the vast Northern Territory. I'd wanted to visit the area since hearing stories from my friends George and Laurie, who'd backpacked in Australia for six months while travelling the world for a year before they were married. They'd told me about Kakadu National Park. On arrival, the plane door opened and the heat and humidity covered me like a sheet. I remembered that I was quite a bit nearer the equator than I had been in S.A.

The YHA in Darwin is more like a resort than a backpacker's hostel. There's a huge pool in the centre of the courtyard, which was the focus of social activity during my stay. Although there are some beaches in Darwin with shark nets, most people don't swim along the coast unless they have a death wish. Many people have tried over the years and many are successful, but there are also numerous reports of people being killed or eaten by crocodiles, notorious for prowling the waters in this part of the country. The four-bed dorm was clean and modern, but throughout the visit, I was forced to sleep in my hooded sweatshirt because the air conditioning was so cold. Unfortunately, the control was out of my reach and my roommates were all Japanese, so asking them to help was difficult. They were very polite. It wasn't unusual for them to come in late at night, but they wouldn't turn on the overhead light. Instead, they had small lights fixed to their caps and would use them like miners.

Darwin is a small town of about 50,000 people, but it's an important administrative centre. Many of the town's historic buildings are painted colonial white and have been kept as reminders of the past. This part of Australia was one of the last to be settled by the Europeans and even now, life is hard. Cyclones have hit with great regularity and in World War II, even more destruction occurred when town was bombed by the Japanese. These former enemies are welcomed today, as indicated by the number of Asian restaurants. I especially enjoyed sitting near the city centre and watching life go by. Local Aborigines would gather at the hottest time of day. Sadly, many of them were not in their native surroundings and seemed displaced. It wasn't uncommon to witness domestic disputes and see the police arrive to sort things out.

I wanted to visit Kakadu as my friends had done years before, but unfortunately all the tours were via bus and I was unable to secure a company that would help me on and off. I was (and still am) terribly disappointed, but it's one of those things that can happen when you're travelling by yourself. In time, I got over it and now I'm philosophical about it. It leaves something on the agenda for me to do and see at some point in the future. I've been to Australia many times and I hope to go there again.

I consoled myself at the pub next door to the hostel. It was close by and it seemed to be a popular place. As I ordered my beer, I noticed an unusual, but familiar looking, trophy behind the bar. I asked about it and was surprised to learn that it was the Melbourne Cup, the famous prize from the country's most important annual horse race. Apparently the owner of the bar had an interest in the horse that had won the last race and so was displaying it.

I didn't stay in Darwin long, but other than not getting on the tour I'd wanted, I was quite impressed with the people and their lifestyle. Hopefully next time I'll get into Kakadu, although I'll probably have to drive my own car. The local kangaroos better look out!

RELAXING IN MOMBASA DESPITE THE MALARIA AND YELLOW FEVER

It was 5:30 a.m. when the buzzer went off in our hotel in Nairobi. It was the day we were to go on our five hundred kilometer trek through the magnificent Athi Basin and over the mountains to the Indian Ocean, ending at the port city of Mombasa, Kenya. Wayne had taken time off work and this was his vacation. We were booked into a resort and I was looking forward to getting some mileage out of all the anti-malarials I'd been taking for the last month. The other worry was yellow fever, also rampant on the coast. The clouds were varying shades of salmon pink as we moved east into an African sunrise along the A1 highway. Oncoming cars flashed their lights at us, warning that we still had our lights on, even though it was barely dawn.

As we moved beyond the plain and into scrubland, beginning our climb into the mountains, the pink clouds darkened and a light rain began to fall. Wayne deftly wove around huge water-filled potholes on the narrow road, while trying to stay out of the way of oncoming lorries. The terrible condition of the roads exacted a toll on the vehicles using it and we passed many drivers standing helplessly beside their motionless machines. Sadly, we were unable to see the famous Mt. Kilamanjaro in Tanzania, as fog had set in, so had to be content to amuse ourselves with corny jokes on the long trip ahead of us.

After six hours of bumpy African roads we approached Mombassa and finally emerged from the rain and darkness into a semi-arid land and the cool, refreshing mountain air was replaced by heat and humidity. We were both amused by a short stretch of road in the middle of nowhere, featuring streetlights on both sides. The road hadn't improved with the weather, but we were within fifty kilometers of our destination and were determined to reach our hotel before the heat of the day set in. As we ended our journey, a sign greeted us with a warning that we were "entering a high risk malaria zone". That didn't inspire much confidence, but since we were now driving past coconut trees and other lush tropical vegetation, we tried to forget about it.

The lobby of the Hotel Intercontinental was a pale yellow colour. We checked into our fourth-floor hotel room overlooking the Indian Ocean, with its waves breaking onto the coral reef clinging to the shore. Shallow pools in the reef held water of varying shades of blue and green, while a breeze wafted over our balcony. The courtyard contained a huge swimming pool and a chess set with three-foot high pieces. A large garden of native flowers and a patio with reclining deck chairs, stood at the edge of the sand between the hotel and the water.

After over six hours of driving, Wayne had earned a rest, so we put on our shorts and made our way to the patio to relax. Wayne fell asleep quickly and I could feel some of his tension from the last few months drift away. It couldn't have been an easy decision to take a job posting so far away, but I had to give Wayne and his wife, Brenda, credit for living here for almost two years. Their two young daughters had attended school with Kenyan children, rather than an all-white facility, and it was in Kenya that his youngest had learned to ride a bicycle in the backyard at Nakuru. Both girls had taken up horse riding and for Brenda, running the household in such an alien environment seemed to have been accomplished with little adjustment or complaint. The whole family had looked on the experience as a positive one.

It was only recently, as the national elections drew near, that Wayne had begun to worry about the political uncertainty and reluctantly decided to send them home for their own safety. Wayne confided to me, after my visit, that my arrival had been a welcome distraction from his thoughts of loneliness for his family and planning to pack up the house for the move back to North America. While Wayne slept under his hat, I looked out at the reef at a dhow floating noisily offshore with its load of tourists. Music blared and the owner of the craft did a crazy dance. I took a long drink from my huge bottle of Tusker and dropped off for an hour or so myself.

In the evening, after Wayne had squashed me at numerous games of chess beside the pool, we decided to enjoy an outdoor dinner with the other guests. The National Dance Company of Tanzania provided live entertainment and the tables around the stage were packed. We had to go to the back with my blue chair in order to avoid all the stairs down to the entertainment area. Drums beat rapidly as three men dressed in warrior garb, with spears and shields, moved along the front of the stage, followed by women singing in Swahili, while later a solo number was performed by an elderly member of the ensemble. He played an instrument resembling a rudimentary guitar or banjo, but he used a bow to tickle the strings and produce music. Strapped to his right leg were small bells to keep the beat. Four women danced in a circle and sang a cappella, making an up and down motion if front of their legs. It was called the "washer woman's song" and I'm sure it told a lament of the hardships of doing the chores around the house while the men were out having a good time. It seems that marriage generally works out much the same on any continent.

The next day, Wayne and I hopped in the car to check out Mombasa. The main street is wide, with a small boulevard separating the opposite flow of traffic. The city is half Christian and half Moslem, with the town of Lamu, to the north, being the centre of Islamic Kenya. When I was there, there were a lot of problems up north in Somalia with Moslem extremists and UN ships could be seen from the shore. As we drove under the famous Mombasa tusks, I foolishly asked if they were real. "Of course", my sarcastic, bearded companion answered in a mocking tone. I fell silent for a while. The residential housing estates, like the citizens, are of course separated by economic class, with most of the wealth still in the hands of white business owners. We drove through their suburbs of oversized homes and high gates for keeping out local thieves and kidnappers. It was a sad comment on the relationship between wealthy and poor in Kenya.

Wayne wanted to take me to the local crocodile park and show me the great beasts. There were no tourist shows, simply crocs lazing around in the sun and partially submerged in the water. There was even a White Nile crocodile. I was struck by the lack of movement in the pen, given the great number of animals enclosed. The fact that it was over 34°C probably had something to do with it. Wayne pointed out that the only thing you could see moving on the reptiles was their tongue moving in and out of their jaw helping to dissipate the heat.

Adjacent to the crocodile village, was a small aquarium with local fish and urchins. I was particularly impressed by the lion-fish, as well as the sea snake, reputed to have the most toxic venom in the world. There were also some wonderful orchids and as I've always been fond of them, I lingered in the garden for a long while enjoying their unusual beauty.

We spent one last afternoon lounging about the patio with our books and beer. It was sad to see the locals walking on the coral and harvesting it to sell to tourists. They would also fish for anything trapped in the small pools by the outgoing tide. Sometimes this would only be small fish and urchins, but often, small octopi could be found as well.

Soon we were back on the road for the long drive to Nakuru. We had planned to stop in Nairobi again, as we were trying to avoid driving at night, but we made such good time on the way back, we decided to chance an hour of night driving so Wayne could sleep in his own bed before returning to work the next day. We passed the towns of Voi and Mtito Andei in the Tsavo region, where a few weeks earlier, a train had crashed into the river after a bridge had washed out, killing numerous travellers in the process. Acacia and baobab trees lined our path home and we were even treated to sights of giraffes and zebras in the fields. We passed the wretched part of the road again and both laughed at the abuse the four-wheel drive vehicle was able to take.

As we drove into the African sunset along the Great Rift Valley, Wayne's long stint in Kenya was drawing to a close. We both silently wondered if we would ever again see or experience the strange pleasures this continent offered. If we never returned, at least we had shared these moments and our friendship was all the better for it.

THE PIZZA, THE MARKET AND THE MOON RAINBOW IN KOROTOGO

I was nearing the end of another of my many trips to the South Pacific. This had been my longest yet, three months, and as usual I was in need of an exotic, yet relaxing destination to conclude my trip. My friend, Bill, whom I had gone to the Yukon and Alaska with many years previously, had returned from his own trip Downunder and had made a stop over in Fiji. He and his wife, Ginny, had quite enjoyed it. I checked its location on the map and decided that it looked like a nice place for some rest and relaxation. It was tropical, not too far from Australia and they spoke English. Though I didn't plan on staying at a resort as Bill and Ginny had, I was hopeful that I would find affordable accommodation somewhere on the island.

The Fiji Islands are located northeast of Australia, almost due north of New Zealand, on the equator. I'd been unable to locate any hostels that were disabled friendly on the Internet or in guide books. They primarily touted cheap beach huts on the little islands dotting the waters not far off the western city of Nadi, where I was arriving. I was going to have to risk it and see if I could find something on arrival. I was fearful of failure and remember e-mailing a friend that I'd sleep under a coconut tree if there were no other options.

The flight arrived in Nadi at about 4 a.m. I was tired when I got off the plane in the dark and entered the low-tech airport. The atmosphere was unbearable. It felt like 110% humidity, which is to be expected this close to the equator, but I was shocked at how hot it was at such an early hour. The customs guard, who was drastically overweight, sweated profusely as he stamped my passport and waved me into the country. I asked someone from the airline if there was a tourist kiosk in the airport and she mentioned there was a travel agency, but that it didn't open until 8 a.m. I'd have to wait. I hit the washroom, which happily had a wide stall, and then looked out the window as dawn began to rise over this new country. After alternately sleeping and being awakened by people concerned about whether I was OK, I finally moved near the entrance of the travel agency to wait for it to open.

When a woman finally arrived to unlock the door, I explained my circumstance and that I wasn't interested in taking a small boat to one of the outlying islands. I preferred to stay on the Coral Coast of Viti Levu, the main island of Fiji I'd landed on. She quickly thought of a place and gave the owner a phone call. I looked at the brochures and it seemed quite acceptable from the picture, but was it? The hotel was two hours away by taxi and it was only going to cost me $F40 per night. There was a hill behind it that led up to the top floor and since there were only six rooms in the hotel, I would be doted on. I asked the travel agent to tell the owner that I would book my entire stay there, sight unseen, if he would agree to pay for the taxi. It was a bit of a gamble. He went for it and I paid the agent my room fees. The owner would send a taxi from his end, as it would be cheaper for him, and I'd have to sit and wait until the middle of the afternoon.

The taxi finally arrived, but it had no identifying marking. I assumed it was a friend of the owner and frankly, I couldn't care less, as long as he got me there safely. We started out to the southwest, around the southern coast of the island to the town of Korotogo on the Coral Coast of Fiji. The green hills and small towns of the island reminded me of other exotic destinations that I'd been to. My driver was Indian. There had been recent problems in Fiji between the native Fijians and the Indians, who were originally brought over by the British to work the farms. The Indian population is now almost equal to that of the Fijians and they are the richer, middle class. Although Fijians own most of the land, there is quite a bit of friction. I read about it in the papers while I was there. Shortly after I left, there was a coup by a Fijian from Australia to remove the Indian Prime Minister.

We travelled along the rough two-lane road, while on the shoulders, Fijians walked to their destinations. As the road veered back toward the coast and away from the hilly interior, I had my first look at the Coral Coast. The water was quite calm and a beautiful shade of blue.

We finally arrived at the white villa called the "Hotel Casablanca". As it was now getting dark, I wondered who'd still be around to greet me. I didn't need to worry. When we stopped on the gravel driveway, four hotel employees came to help me get into my blue chair and take my bags. I was dropped off in the open-air restaurant, the centre of evening activity. The owner was a thin, mustached Egyptian, by the name of Mostafa, and he happily offered me a beer and a menu. I told him that was a great idea and proceeded to order a curry. I was the only person in the restaurant and later found out that they would have closed early due to lack of business, but they wanted to make sure I had a meal before I went to bed. There was a cook named Sunny, a waitress called Jennifer, a fellow who cleaned the rooms and acted as a part-time waiter named

Mansour and a night guard, Ali. They all welcomed me warmly, wanted to hear about my trip and seemed incredulous that I had made the trip from Canada on my own.

I enjoyed the meal and beer and then asked to see my room. I was still a bit worried about whether it would meet my needs. As I had been told prior to my arrival, the second floor was approachable by a steep, paved path that curled around the back. I entered the narrow hall and was led to a one-bedroom suite with a washroom and a very nice balcony overlooking the pool and the sea. I was quite impressed and felt I'd made a good decision. Tired from the day's travels and the early morning arrival, I went to bed.

The next morning, after a very restful sleep, I slid open the balcony door to get my first look at paradise in daylight. The pool was kidney shaped and the surrounding patio was quite wide. To the left was an open space with flowers and palm trees, while to the right, were the restaurant and the office. I could see the narrow dead-end road that led to a new hotel under construction and Fijians were walking toward it on their way to work. Across the road were shallow coral pools and in the distance the open sea. I love listening to the surf crash against the shore. Unfortunately, because of all the coral near the coast, the waves broke onto the reef and the sound was muffled. I lingered on the balcony before dressing, enjoying the cool morning breeze off the water, while a small flock of green and yellow parrots flew noisily from one tree to another.

It took a while to attract the attention of one of the employees to assist me down the steep path back to the restaurant for breakfast. I enjoyed a thick, black cup of coffee with eggs and toast. The staff asked me how I had slept and then Mostafa came to join me, barking the day's orders to the staff. Soon he was admonishing me for paying for the entire stay back at the airport. He told me I should've paid for only a few days and then extended my visit. He would've made more money and I would've received a lower rate. I nodded benignly, but how the heck was I to know this from Nadi? Other than that brief rant, he was a friendly, outgoing guy and I liked him immediately.

The breakfast and conversation were good, but I decided to head out to check the vicinity. To the left, down the road, was a crossroads with a souvenir shop selling items made by local craftsmen from wood and shells. There was a small plaza with a grocery store, a curry house and a public telephone. Except for the construction site, that was about it. As I wheeled back past the hotel, going the other way down the street into Korotogo Town, there was a Kiwi run backpackers' hostel, some very nice homes and a teahouse. I made it to the first roundabout, but there wasn't much beyond that. I was really out in the boonies, but that was what I wanted.

I lingered around the pool reading a book and then crossed the road to look out at the coral during the afternoon. At dinner, I tried one of their chicken pizzas. The restaurant was very good and while I was there I regained the weight I'd lost on the trip, alternating evening meals between a hot curry and a pizza. Mostafa had a special homemade hot sauce that he served on the side as a pizza topping. It was thick, red and oily. It was awesome and I told him he could make lots of money bottling it. He gave me a bottle to take home.

We were soon joined by Mostafa's friend Basil, an older fellow who had recently hurt his leg in a traffic accident. Basil was moving slowly with a cane, but had lots of funny stories to tell. I ended up seeing him almost every night. As we talked into the darkness, bats from the mountains behind the villa appeared, darting about searching for insects. A brief shower came and, just as quickly, passed over and out to sea. Behind the mountains a full moon rose and out over the water, we all saw a strange natural phenomenon that none of us had ever heard of before—a moon rainbow! The bright, evening light from the full moon illuminated and refracted through the droplets of the shower as it slowly moved away. It was an amazing sight in an amazing destination and not one I'll ever forget. I tried to record it on my camcorder, but with the faint light, it didn't record too well. I did, however, capture the sense of awe and excitement we shared.

Mostafa was heading into Singatoka the next day to run some errands and shop at the market. He invited me to come with him to see the town and get away from the hotel for a few hours. I took him up on it and we left by cab. The buildings were unexpectedly ornate for a small town and we passed the mosque that Mostafa worshipped in, as well as numerous Fijian Indian Hindu temples. The town had rough, dirty edge to it. We went for lunch at a cafeteria-style establishment and he ordered french fries, while I had tea. We trooped down the road to his doctor's office to renew his certification that he was healthy enough to run a hotel open to tourists.

We ended up at the market. It was quite laid back, not what I was expecting. That's the way life moves in Fiji; things seem to happen at a slower pace. Live animals, vegetables, taro roots and kava were in abundance. Kava is a mildly narcotic root that is mixed with water to make a drink used in Fijian ceremonies and given to welcome tourists. Mostafa held up a string of crabs and smiled at me. The crabs were holding each other's claws and were dripping wet. He didn't buy them, but it made a good picture. An Indian merchant gave a bunch of bananas to Mostafa to give to me. I offered to pay, but the man wouldn't hear of it and I thanked him. The bananas were only as long as your index finger, but they tasted quite sweet. With the groceries done, we headed back to Korotogo.

A few days later, I was invited by Jennifer, the waitress at the restaurant to participate in the Kava ceremony at her house. Two others accompanied me from the hotel and we strolled into town to visit her on her day off. By inviting some of the guests into their homes, many Fijians are able to generate a bit of extra money, as it's customary to leave a small token in return for lunch and the kava. The home was small and well kept, but a bit under-furnished by western standards. Everyone sat on the floor, except for me of course, and Jennifer's uncle acted as the master of ceremonies. He placed water in a bowl and then added kava in a small burlap bag. He swooshed the bag around in the water and periodically squeezed it, releasing kava infused water into the bowl. The resulting mixture was very murky and I wasn't too enthusiastic about trying it, but I didn't want to be an obnoxious guest, so I accepted a small bowl of the liquid (which he referred to as "low tide") and drank it. In Fiji, kava is in demand and has become quite expensive for the average Fijian. My companions accepted a larger amount ("high tide") and seemed to quite enjoy it. In fact, they had seconds and seemed to get a buzz from it. Even the amount I drank had me worried about getting the runs or hepatitis, since I hadn't seen whether the water was from a bottle or not. As it turned out I was OK. We were also treated to a boiled chicken lunch. It was quite an interesting experience.

In the short time I was at the Hotel Casablanca, Mostafa and I developed quite a close friendship. I'd spend the mornings in his room down the hall from mine, sitting on the balcony reading the papers with him and discussing politics, while eating breakfast and some of the wonderful local fresh fruit. The staff had mocked me for only eating pizza and curry, so I finally relented and asked for a meal of a local fish. Sunny went out onto the coral and bought a Kawa Kawa fish directly from a fisherman. Grilling it to perfection, he served it with the traditional taro root, a starchy replacement for potato in the Fijian diet. It was a delicious last meal for me in Fiji.

The hospitality had been great. Every time I wheeled around the road by myself, Fijians would approach me and ask if I needed a push. They were extremely gentle and kind. Actually, I commented about this in a letter to the local paper that Mostafa faxed to them. It was published in the paper the next day.

At sunset on the final night of my visit, Basil came one last time to say goodbye. We all sat across the street on the green grass looking out over the Coral Coast. Bats flew over us and the conversation ran well into the night along with my beer. The next day, Mostafa, the Egyptian whose family was back in Australia, personally took me to the airport.

I had a great time in Fiji and it was all due to the wonderful people I'd met. That, to me, is one of the best things about travel and one of the most lasting.

BORDERING ON AN ILLEGAL ALIEN

I have always prided myself on my knowledge of the world and of geography in particular. I think my interests in both are my main reasons for wanting to travel. I must confess that prior to doing research on possible destinations for travel in South America I had never even heard of Iguazu Falls along the border between Argentina and Brazil. It was only after a friend of mine, who has an Argentinean boss, asked him to point out possible places to visit, that I learned of Iguazu's existence and immediately made plans to visit.

After Buenos Aires, the long bus trip to the south of Chile and the adventure in Ushuaia, the trip to the tropics was to begin my last leg of my trip to the continent. I had been having many problems with the national airline of Argentina, but the flight up to the border between Brazil and Argentina, where Iguazu Falls is located was to be a pleasure. For the first time on the trip, I had been upgraded to business class on the small airplane and was served food on china plate while relaxing in an oversized and comfy seat. As we made our descent toward the Falls, the pilot swooped down to allow the passengers on the left of the plane a chance to view the cataracts and then he banked and turned the jet around so that those of us on the right side were able to enjoy the sight of the Falls from a distance. Although the natural landmark was not really very close up, the sight of it really gave me a feeling for how large of a tourist attraction it was. The cataracts extended up and down a long length of the escarpment at the confluence of the Iguazu and Parana rivers and there were 285 waterfalls in total. Against the dark green tropical jungle backdrop, it was really impressive to see. I had no idea at this point whether or not the Falls would be accessible for a blue chair, so I was really happy and excited that I had been able to get at least one sight of Iguazu even before I had landed!

After a long taxi ride into town from the remote airport, it was once again time to do some quick thinking when the hostel that I had booked over the internet, which had indicated they were chair friendly, ended up having the dormitories located down in the basement. It was really too bad as the hostel was more like a resort and had a huge pool and club bar. I asked the lady at the reception desk to contact the local YHA hostel to see if they had any availability. The YHA indicated that they could accommodate me and so it was back into the cab for another ride, this one closer to the center of town. The hostel was actually quite flat except for the fact that down the main hallway toward the dorms was a small flight of three steps. I knew this wouldn't be much of a problem but for the fact that the person working when I arrived was a lady and it seemed that I was the only person staying at the place. Not to worry, in a few minutes out popped an older Englishman who had been around back sunbathing in the 32C heat. Don was a retired schoolteacher who had spent over 40 hours on a bus from remote Brazil and was now taking it easy prior to his return to that country.

I received some assistance from Don in getting down the step to see the dorm rooms. It was an extra two pesos a night to get a room with air conditioning and so I decided to splurge. As I would find out later, it became very annoying because when ever I was out of the room the staff would try to save electricity by turning off the air conditioner! It definitely defeated the purpose of trying to stay cool. Don made me a cup of tea and we got to chatting by the side of the small pool which was off to the side of the main building, while we watched some lovely French backpackers enjoying its use. I mentioned that I was hoping to see Iguazu Falls and was unsure of my ability to do so. Don suggested that he push me into town so that I could contact some of the tourist operators to see if they could help. Don had said that he had some shopping to do anyway and that pushing me would be a good bit of exercise for him. So, in the late afternoon, when the tropical sun is at the hottest, we began our trek along the red streets of Iguazu, Argentina. The soil in the area is very iron rich, and so the roads are made out of iron bricks. But I must confess that for some reason the brick are not smooth, but rather very pointy and seem to be laid irregularly so that traffic basically has to slow down to a crawl in order to safely cross. It was definitely not good for both car and wheelchair tires alike. Luckily the sidewalks were in considerably better shape and though they were broken in certain spots they were generally in a very good state and Don had no trouble navigating. After a short time in an internet café while enjoying a cup of coffee that was included in the price, we located the tourist office which in turn pointed us in the direction of one of the main guide operators in town.

On arrival I explained to the woman at the desk that I was interested in a tour of the National Park and that I was unsure as to whether it was possible to do while in a chair. She waved her hand an said that it would be no problem as most of the upper track of walkways on the Argentinean side of Iguazu were built with the disabled in mind. Furthermore, she said that on the Brazilian side there were elevators that lifted you to the same height as of the top of the Falls so that you could see all the wonder close up. Wow, was I ever excited and relieved! I was going to get to see Iguazu Falls after all. She explained that in order to fly in a helicopter it was necessary to go to Brazil as in Argentina helicopters were banned in the National Park so as not to disturb the wildlife. I gave her my credit card and booked a full day tour for the next day, the morning in Argentina and the afternoon in Brazil. After ringing up the sale and handing me my receipt, the lady asked to see my passport. She noticed that I didn't have a visa to go to Brazil which Canadian travelers need. I told her that in the guidebook that I was using, it said that travelers without visas could still travel over the border for a day, just to see the Falls as long as they were returning afterwards. She shook her head and said that it wasn't true at all. I was hugely disappointed and asked her to add a credit to my card for the afternoon trip to Brazil that I wasn't going to be able to use. The woman headed into the back room with my card, but returned in a short time and said that if I wanted to go to Brazil they would get me across the border. She said that the guide went over the border every day and knew all the guards and that they should have no problem getting me there at least for a few hours. I was quite happy to hear that and it goes to show that in any country, once a good saleswoman has your money, they are always reluctant to give it back. After all, a happy customer is the best customer.

The next day I woke early and even though the hostel breakfast was not supposed to be served until eight in the morning, the fellow in charge loaded me up on strong coffee and toast an hour earlier as he prepared the meal for the rest of the sleeping backpackers. The temperature was forecast to rise to about 42C and although there were a few clouds about, I was sure that they would burn off. Right on schedule my tour guide, Emilio and driver Jose (their names have been changed since they smuggled me across the border) arrived in a large van that was too high for me to get in and out of easily. When I explained that a simple car with a large trunk would suffice, Jose radioed the problem to headquarters and they quickly told him to head back and pick up a car. It gave me a chance to get to know Emilio, and I liked him right off the bat. Emilio had a big smile and seemed to be very friendly, in addition he was a big guy and since he was going to be pushing me around for the entire day in the oppressive heat, I was glad that he was young and fit. After only a short wait, Jose returned and the three of us headed towards the National Park to get our first look at Iguazu Falls.

The park was only a short drive from the town and I was quite impressed with how modern the facilities were. The entrance welcomed you with a large map of the Park and there was a restaurant, gift shop and washrooms. As we walked through to hop on a toy train that would take us up to the walkways that lead to the Falls, local indigenous vendors lined the way spreading out their wares on the sidewalk for the tourists to see. The toy train was completely accessible and I thought that this was a very neat way of moving the visitors from the outskirts of the park to the interior in the heat of the day. Of course, along the way, one of the stops was at another restaurant and souvenir booth, where guests were encouraged to disembark and have a look around or enjoy a drink or light snack. Emilio and I stayed on the train as it ran along the river through the lush jungle vegetation, to the edge of the falls.

Emilio and I finally got off at the end of the line and you could immediately hear the sound of water nearby. There were a huge number of different tracks that tourists could follow, but generally the system was divided into two, the upper track and the lower track that went down a long series of step to ground level and was where you could head to spend the day on the beach, take a jet boat trip to the base of the main Falls or even rent a canoe and go paddling over the tropical river. I would have to stay on the upper track, but that didn't bother me in the least. One of my main views on travel is not to worry about what I can't do or see, but dwell on what is available to experience.

Emilio started pushing me along the steel grated paths, and my chair made a funny sound as it rolled along. Huge rapids leading up to the Falls were the first thing I saw and I stopped to take some pictures and video and then just paused to enjoy it for myself. There is a calming effect of running water that cannot really be explained. Maybe that is why so many people have fountains in their backyards these days. As I listened to the roar of the water and looked upstream at some of the boats in the water below, colourful butterflies flitted by in the now late morning air and one landed on the rail just beside me, possibly to enjoy the magnificent view too! When we finally moved on toward the Falls, it wasn't long until we arrived at the highest and grandest of all the Falls in the entire series of cataracts—The Devil's Throat! I was actually a bit disappointed that this was the first waterfall that I saw but on the other hand, many of the other visitors that day were quite elderly and since the Devil's Throat is the big draw, I guess that it's important to make the feature attraction as accessible to them as possible. The Devils Throat was a towering monster and there was a huge volume of water going over the edge. The really neat thing to me was how close we were to it from the walkway and we were getting soaked from the spray. My hometown of Welland, is less than a half hour's drive from Niagara Falls and I must say that sitting there looking at the Devil's Throat and then gazing past it at all the other waterfalls that ran up and down the confluence of the two rivers in that tropical setting made me wonder what all the fuss is about in North America. Niagara Falls is a wonder, but Iguazu Falls, which many people in the northern hemisphere have never heard of, was truly awesome.

I ended up spending about half an hour there watching the Devil's Throat, enjoying the sights, and Emilio always was great urging me to take my time and enjoy the view as much and as long as I wanted since we were going to be around for the entire day. We finally moved on and along the narrow walkways, many of which had small rest stops with park benches so that older visitors could pause and take a break from the heat and humidity. The Argentinean side offered a side view of the gorge below and from our perch we could see many other people on the lower track or those who had made it all the way to ground level itself. There they could hike on walking paths or enjoy a dip in the water that was protected from alligators by a net. Jet boats zipped along and did their best to thrill the younger crowd, as they made quick and sharp turns near the base of many of the Falls. After a few hours of marveling at the wide variety of foliage, birds, and many of the 285 waterfalls we decided it was time to begin our trip to Brazil. Emilio pushed me down a long path inland, toward the Sheraton Hotel, which offered its guest a distant view of the Devil's Throat, though from what I could see of it from the coffee lounge, the most one could really see was the water spray rising up. Jose had arrived with the car and I think both of us were happy to relax in the air-conditioned comfort, at least for a brief time.

It was only a short drive out of the park, onto the highway and over to the bridge that marked the border between Argentina and Brazil. I was still quite worried about getting over the border without the proper Brazilian visa that a Canadian requires. Emilio smiled and seemed totally unconcerned, probably because he knew the border guards quite well and dealt with them six days a week for many years, and his affable personality helped quite a bit. He asked me for my passport and he went into the border hut without me. It only took about five minutes and he returned with a huge smile on his face saying there would be no problem. I flipped through my passport and found no stamp in it, and being the worrywart that I am, I now began to fret about getting back into Argentina. We crossed over the Parana River into Brazil. What was cute was the fact that the bridge was painted in white and baby blue stripes on the Argentine side and then yellow and green stripes on the other half. I had made it into Brazil after all. Emilio then informed me that we were running a slight risk because if I got caught without a visa, the fine would be $1500 US. Oh well, I guess that is the price you have to pay, when you are an illegal alien!

It did not take long for us to arrive at the entrance to Iquazu National Park of Brazil and after paying the entrance fee we left the car to enter a large pavilion to await our completely wheelchair accessible bus. I took the opportunity to treat my two companions to a coffee and some lunch. After waiting a short time for some other tourists to show up, we boarded the bus and began to slowly make our way along the tropical road toward the many waterfalls. What was interesting was the fact that the bus was not a direct trip, rather, the Brazilians had set up a series of interesting stops that you could hop on or off and enjoy a hike along marked routes or disembark at a beautiful hotel perhaps for lunch or a capuccino. We left the bus at another pavilion alongside the waterfalls and Emilio directed me to an elevator that lifted us to the highest level. It was completely remarkable because as soon as the door opened you were situated beside a roaring waterfall and getting completely soaked by its cool spray and mist. There were a series of suspended walkways that meandered around the face of three of the falls and into a certain area where you seemed to be equidistant from the front of all of them. It was absolutely thrilling. The roar of the cataracts, the proximity to them, the spray on your brow, the warmth of the southern sun on your face, and the beauty of the lush tropical scenery was unlike anything I could ever have expected. In addition to all this was the fact that the walkways ended with a magnificent panoramic view of all the waterfalls including the Devil's Throat. I spent quite a long time enjoying the experience and trying to photograph as much as I could without ruining my equipment due to the watery mist. Afterwards, I took advantage of my brief visit to write some postcards to some friends back home. By now it was getting late in the afternoon and regretfully it was time to leave Iquazu Falls so that we could take the helicopter ride above it.

The helicopter field was nearby and Emilio again left without me to enquire as to whether the trip was suitable for a disabled tourist. His big smile as he walked back to the car spoke volumes and the two of them assisted me into my blue chair and into the reception area. There were two trips on offer the cheapest was a fifteen minute ride and the expensive option was for an hour, but would include a trip over the hydro dam. I opted for the cheapie ride and then took my place in the queue with the others. I waited for a half hour and then it was my turn. There were three others on my trip, one sat in the front left of the helicopter and the two others sat in the back with me at the left side. Emilio and one of the trip employees grabbed me and gently placed me into the seat. I had barely got settled in, put my safety belt on and was reaching for my knapsack with my camcorder when the vehicle began a sudden ascent into the sky.

It was my first time in a helicopter and the feeling of "g-forces" against my body was something I had never felt before as I am used to the long takeoff that is usual in plane rides. We were suddenly rising at an alarming rate and as I was getting used to that, the vehicle suddenly turned on a dime and swung around to the right, leaving me squished into the door owing to my poor balance. But after regaining my composure and looking out of the window, I must say that the view was breathtaking especially as we flew over the canopy of the southern fringe of the Amazonian rainforest. The dark green of the foliage against the blue of the sky with a few clouds scattered in made for quite a scene. The helicopter sped its way over the canopy of the rainforest toward the confluence of the two rivers and the awaiting waterfalls. As we approached, the falls were on the side opposite to me and I strained my neck to catch a glimpse of the natural wonder through the arms of my companions who were busy snapping photographs and exclaiming Germanic phrases of amazement. It only took a short time before the pilot looped the craft around in a semi-circle and I finally got to view the Devil's Throat on my side of the helicopter. The white power of the natural forces were quite astonishing from this unique vantage point, and I tried to capture some of it with both my camera and camcorder, while also making sure to view some of it without the benefit of a viewfinder. It was well worth the trip across the border. Sadly a fifteen minute flight is only a brief treat and in short order we were headed back toward our landing pad. As I looked out though the window I smiled, knowing that I had accomplished all my goals at Iquazu Falls.

The landing was as swift as the takeoff and Emilio, with his ever present smile, welcomed me by helping me into my blue chair. He knew by my smile that I had had a great time. In fact, due to his help I had a great day and the trip across the border back to Argentina and the hostel was a great time to relax and unwind prior to some wonderful dinner with three Swedish backpackers, followed by another with two French backpackers and a pair of German students.

Who could have asked for a better day? It was definitely time for a beer and I was buying.

KURANDA, THE ATHERTON TABLELANDS AND THE CROCS

The far north of Queensland is a magnet for young backpackers due to its proximity to the Great Barrier Reef, but one of its other attractions is the tropical rainforest nearby. For those of us from the frozen north, it's a sight that has to be experienced.

One of the best ways to travel to the rainforest from the coast is to take the historic, scenic train from Cairns to Kuranda. I investigated whether the train car would be accessible for a blue chair, as many older trains are inaccessible to the disabled. The person behind the wicket at the train station informed me that the last car would meet my needs and that many older tourists liked to use its wider spaces. I booked a ticket for the morning's trip and was all set. I even had enough time to stop by the café for a flat white coffee and a muffin.

My train car had an authentic, vintage wooden interior. There was just enough room for my chair to squeeze between the parallel bench seats and as I faced the back of the car, I was able to look out the windows on either side. There was a speaker system mounted on the ceiling of the car and during the ninety-minute trip, Queensland Rail's taped tour guide let us know what we were looking at as we viewed the vistas. The train climbed over 300 meters up to Kuranda, past the communities of Freshwater, Stoney Creek and Barron Falls.

As we moved along the tracks, the city faded from sight and was replaced by the thick, leafy vegetation commonly found in areas that receive huge amounts of rain, as the Cape York Peninsula does in the rainy season. The car rattled along, climbing to Stoney Creek over a large bridge. As we passed the waterfalls at Barron Gorge, we were treated to magnificent tropical panoramas. The trip's soundtrack noted the lives that had been lost in the manual construction of the fifteen tunnels we were passing through on our way to Kuranda. I could only imagine the hardships those workers had faced in the days before modern medicine and sanitary facilities. Bugs and disease must've taken a toll, in addition to accidental deaths. The railway was finally completed in 1891 and at the time, was considered a marvel of modern engineering. As I looked down from the train into the vast gorge below, I felt respect for the people who'd had the nerve to work at such heights without the benefit of safety equipment.

After travelling over thirty kilometers up the side of the mountain, we arrived at the little town of Kuranda in the middle of the rainforest. The station itself was quite beautiful, displaying flowers and plant specimens native to the area. It was a short wheel along a slightly rough road into town and I felt I was a world away. The tranquility and sounds of birds in the trees made my travel stress fade away. It was a pretty town and it was supposed to be. The train and the cable car I was going to leave on, were specifically designed to bring tourists here each day. That was the real reason the town existed. The fine restaurants and cafés, tourist activities, Koala park, bird aviary, Aboriginal Dance Centre, Noctarium (which I thought was an innovative word) and obligatory Butterfly Sanctuary, all ensured that your visit to Kuranda would be an active one that would lighten your wallet. Some of these attractions were included in the tour ticket price, but not mine, so I contented myself with window-shopping the craft stores, although I did treat myself to a tea and scone on an outdoor deck overlooking a tropical paddock. The rest of the afternoon was spent rolling around or watching the sedate life go by. It was a nice place to visit and I suspected it was an even better place to work.

When the afternoon was nearing its end, I arranged to head back to Cairns via the recently constructed cable car. I'd wanted to make sure I was on the cable car during its descent, since that's generally the best way to view the scenery—on the way down. When I wheeled over to the station, the attendant asked me if I minded sharing a car. I accompanied a couple from Calgary and we got along quite well. Some of the views from the hanging cars were even better than those on the train. There were several stops with walking paths so passengers could learn more about the flora and fauna at different altitudes. We took advantage of this feature and my new friends didn't seem to mind pushing me around along the rough paths. As we neared the final stop, the striking blue colour of the Coral Sea stood out against the coastline. At the foot of the landing, the Aboriginal Centre housed exhibits and had demonstrations of crafts and techniques used by local Aborigines. Outside the Centre, I stopped to watch an older gentleman instruct students on the finer points of throwing a boomerang. It was the first time I'd seen one actually return to the hands of the person throwing it! It was getting late and I had to grab a taxi back to the hostel to cook my supper.

A few days later, after spending some time around town and on the wonderful wharf that Cairns rebuilt following a recent cyclone, I found a coach company with a young, fit driver who was happy to lift me onto the front seat of the bus. I was quite pleased, because most drivers are understandably reluctant to do strenuous lifting in case they're injured and end up missing work. The driver, named

Rick was a friendly Aussie in the traditional summer working garb of the country: a pair of shorts. There were two air-conditioned buses travelling in tandem on the trip through the Atherton Tablelands that loomed over the coral coast. With two coaches and two drivers, it meant that if my driver began to feel the strain from lifting me onto the bus, there would at least be another person along to assist.

We moved out of the city and drove east up the slopes that had previously lifted me to Kuranda. Upon reaching the top of the hills, we were greeted by wide-open spaces and fertile lands that reminded me a bit of Ontario in the late summer. As we moved toward one of the main points on our tour, we stopped at some large mounds that huge colonies of termites had created. I remained on the bus, but listened to the information regarding the termites and noticed that the mounds were taller than most of the men in the group. The eerie scene reminded me of artists' renditions of the Martian landscape I'd seen in fantasy books as a boy. The main stop on the morning trip was at the famous Curtain Fig tree. It was a rough trip down a long path, so again I stayed on the bus, but I gave my camcorder to Rick and asked him to document the site. The fig sends down roots as it grows up along the trunk of a host tree. This host had fallen over under the weight of the fig or died an early death. As a result, the Curtain Fig sent its shoots down perpendicular to the host tree. When I returned home and looked at the footage, I finally saw how interesting it was.

We had lunch at the wharf beside the shore of Lake Barrine, a water-filled volcanic depression. We boarded the boat for a one-hour tour around its circumference. Animals and birds seemed to appear on cue. I'm still not sure whether they were wild or tame, but one of the birds flew about the deck and waited for the crew to throw food into the air. I enjoyed the appearance of crocodiles near the shore on the far side of the lake. The staff didn't feed them, but they were awesome to look at. I've enjoyed watching these prehistoric creatures ever since first seeing them in Africa. The tour was quite relaxing and the deck of the boat was nice and flat. It was good to spend some time back in my chair and out of the bus seat. After a day's drive through the Tablelands, we had a lovely green drive back down the mountain roads. In the distance, we could see shimmering waters as the late day sun hit the waves of the Sea toward Cairns.

I was so impressed with the crocs that I decided to book a tour the next day of a crocodile farm. The visit was on a small ferry, sailing inland from the city of Cairns. At least I wouldn't have to spend any more time on the bus. The tour took us past an Australian Navy installation and some little towns. The further inland we went, the more prominent the mountains in the distance became. When we arrived at the crocodile farm, I was surprised at the number of crocs in pens, behind high fences. We were reminded on the tour that this was a working, for-profit farm and not a wildlife park. I was hoisted out of my chair and onto a narrow bench on the back of the pickup truck that would take us through the farm. I was amazed as the keeper called out some of the males and threw them dead, whole chickens, complete with feathers. These were the breeding males, usually kept separate from other crocodiles because of their size and territorial nature. In other pens, females who'd laid eggs were guarding their nests from predators such as birds or small marsupials.

We saw how the farm worked and that most of the animals were used to generate income. The leather from their hide was highly sought after by high-end shoe and purse manufacturers in Japan and Europe. The meat was popular with Asian consumers and a growing number of tourists to Australia who could find it on offer in some local restaurants. Other parts of the animal, such as teeth, were made into trinkets, such as key chains. At the end of the tour, I was handed a live, baby crocodile to pose with for my camera. I gave the poor animal back to the keeper, just as it relieved itself all over me.

On the way back to Cairns, we were offered coffee or tea and samples of crocodile meat. I selected a crocodile sausage that tasted a bit spicy, but otherwise had no distinctive flavour.

In the end, I guess the croc tasted better to me than I would have to him. He would have broken a few teeth on my chair.

SLALOMING MY WAY UP THE CHAMPS-ÉLYSÉES

Paris is a beautiful city, but if you're travelling the world in a blue chair, it's a very big city. I arrived at the "Gare du Nord" train station at 8 a.m. as the overnight sleeper pulled in from Amsterdam. Usually, backpackers are met by numerous touts employed by hostels, each waving brochures while enticing you to follow to their accommodation. This was no exception, but I ignored their advances and dutifully found my way to the Travel Bureau, which most towns offer to assist weary travellers looking for places to sleep. Unfortunately, the door to the office was up six stairs and there was a queue of about twenty-five others waiting for service. After waving my hands about for over a quarter of an hour in a vain attempt to attract the attention of attendants behind the desk, I struck upon the idea of asking for help from backpackers who were coming out with their sleeping arrangements already fulfilled. I asked two lovely, young Norwegian women to go back up the stairs and mention to the attendants that I was outside looking for help. I thought that if they at least knew I existed, I was halfway home. Finally, the French woman in the office waved at me and then made me wait another fifteen minutes before emerging to meet me.

She was a pleasant woman in her forties and came armed with all sorts of information and a map of greater Paris. She said she had booked me into a hostel that was on one level and that I would "love it". I asked where it was and if it was far. "Oh no!" she exclaimed with her heavy French accent. So I set off happily, another worry gone from my mind.

Since it was "close", I decided to head east along the sidewalk to the hostel. I generally don't like to take cabs because I travel on a tight budget and for me part of the excitement of travelling is viewing life and scenery along the way. In addition, I feel that by wheeling along, I'm able to burn enough calories that I can enjoy all available local food and drink.

I slowly moved through the streets of Paris with my backpack hanging from the back of my chair and my blue gym bag on my lap. The old streets were straight and busy. Morning commuters rushed down into Metro stations and broom-handling African immigrants from French-speaking former colonies swept the streets of the evening's mess. Some of the bevelled curbs at intersection corners were too steep for me to negotiate on my own, so with my dreadful high school French, I asked these fellows if they could "assiste moi?" up them. With smiles on their faces, they happily obliged. I passed the Bastille where, in 1789, mobs of angry people stormed the prison, starting the French Revolution.

After wheeling for over an hour at a constant pace, I was also becoming rather hungry. I wondered what this crazy woman at the Tourist Info kiosk was talking about when she stated that the hostel was close. The ancient city seemed to have weathered the years and wars well. The facades on the buildings were layered with small, ornate sculptures and entrances were adorned with summer flowers. Finally, I found the hostel and entered a courtyard surrounded by doorways leading into the dormitories. My dorm consisted of two sets of bunk beds and an ensuite washroom with a stair trying to impede me. It didn't work. I couldn't close the door, but I didn't care. I could still get the job done.

My roommates were two Italians and a South Korean. As breakfast was included, I was lucky to get fed. Normally when checking in you receive the next day's meal and check-in time is usually after lunch. Many of the hostellers were milling around speaking their languages and some were seated at tables eating their meal. It wasn't much to write home about; a coffee, a stale, rock-hard roll and some marmalade. I was starved and made the best of it.

As the hostel was closed from 11 a.m. until 3 p.m. for cleaning, I decided to head out to see some of the city's sights. Of course, Paris has many attractions. The main ones have to be the River Seine, Notre Dame, the Champs-Élysées, the Arc de Triomphe, the L'Ouvre and of course, the landmark Eiffel Tower. I was determined to see them all.

Armed with my map, I headed west toward the centre of the city. Happily for me, Paris is a relatively flat place and the wheeling was very good. Honking horns, an auditory mainstay in any metropolis, were loudest when lights changed red. I became more adept at getting up curbs onto the sidewalks. The people seemed friendly and helpful, which contradicted the traditional notion of Parisians as cold and aloof. I peered into the storefronts of famous "patisseries" or bakeries that seem to abound in great numbers. As it was nearing lunch, I entered one and asked the woman to make me a baked roll with meat and cheese filling. I also purchased a fruit juice. Before the introduction of the Euro, the franc was, for me, a puzzling currency. I was used to dollars and the franc seemed almost worthless, as its denomination was so low. What really annoyed me was the large value notes, the higher the value the bigger the note. The largest one I had, worth about $100, had to be folded four times just to fit into my wallet. I got my sandwich and was all set to begin to look for a place to eat my lunch.

One of the most wonderful things about Paris is the small, but plentiful, public "jardins" or gardens seemingly on every block.

They're a welcome refuge from the noise and bustle of the city. I found one, wheeled through rows of brightly coloured flowers with bees buzzing around and sat under a shady tree to enjoy my lunch and take it all in. It was a scene from a movie, as young lovers strolled through the garden arm in arm. Elderly women with canes struggled to walk, but took the time and made the effort to bend down and enjoy the brief fragrances the flowers offered. I savoured my lunch.

You cannot visit Paris without attending one or more of the fabulous museums in the city and the greatest of them all is the L'Ouvre. I was quite excited to be visiting this wonderful landmark but was astonished to see some modern glass pyramids in the front courtyard designed to advertise the Egyptian exhibit. I entered, paid the admission and set out to explore. Many of the paintings were spectacular, although I cannot pretend to be an art fanatic. I did find myself in the company of a number of long dead nobility and I decided that many Egyptians have travelled more in death than they ever did in life and that deceased royalty must be one of the country's greatest exports. After a number of hours of gawking at all manner of art and artifacts, it was time to see the Mona Lisa. I contacted one of the ladies employed by the museum to help guide me to the famed smile. It took about twenty minutes of navigating up half a floor on an elevator, walking down a narrow aisle and then finding another elevator to take us up or down another half floor. This process was repeated at least three times until we finally arrived and Leonardo da Vinci's work presented itself to me. It was a great way to end my trip to the L'Ouvre and although the protective glass in front of the painting slightly distorted the art due to the reflection of light off it, and we were kept at a distance behind a rope, I could finally say that I gave Mona a smile too.

Finally, it was time to make my final assault on the Champs-Élysées. I was now wheeling uphill and that was not good. It was late afternoon and I was tiring fast. There were no lack of offers from passersby wanting to give me a push up the street to my destination. Normally, I would graciously accept, but for some reason, I'm still not sure why, I wanted to make it there on my own. By now I had another problem. Parisians are also well known for their affinity for small dogs and poodles. The sidewalks were booby trapped with dog poop left by the pampered pooches. Culturally, it seemed Parisians feel no obligation to clean up after their pets and I was left to slalom my way up to my final destination. My journey was made even harder by inattentive pedestrians who had failed to miss one of the little bombs and had smeared it across the pavement. One mistake and I would have it all on my hands!

Strangely, the sidewalk garbage bins had their openings welded shut, forcing people to put their trash on top and thereby littering the street. It made for an unsightly mess and I wondered if it was due to worries about Algerian terrorists, who were in the news at the time, possibly placing bombs in them. As I neared the Arc de Triomphe, I decided to do something stupid. I tried to cross the street into the famous median to snap a centered photograph of the historic landmark. There must've been five lanes of traffic going one-way and I got past four of them when the light changed. A sympathetic motorist graciously waited as I finished my hectic crossing and I framed the picture I wanted. It was only a short trip across the Seine to the Eiffel Tower to complete the day's exciting, but tiring, sightseeing.

I was so happy that I'd avoided the dog droppings that I decided to break one of my rules. A few hours later, well into the evening, with my hands and arms filthy black from the city streets, I broke down and took a cab home.

AOTEAROA, THE MAINLAND AND THE ISLAND

The first time I ever went on a long trip overseas back in the mid-1990s, I chose to make New Zealand my initial stop. I didn't know a soul there, but everything I'd ever seen or read on the country, made me feel it was a pretty mirror image of Canada, where I'm from.

After a long flight from Los Angeles, the plane circled the airport, swinging around to align itself with the runway and I saw my first glimpse of this beautiful country. In those early morning hours, it seemed an oasis in an endless shimmering ocean. I was quite tired, but also very excited. I'd booked into a hostel via fax. The hostel, according to the map I had, was close to the harbourfront and each fax I'd received from the young woman who worked there came with the friendly salutation "Kia Ora". The hostel was not chair friendly, but the lass assured me that staff were always on hand and that usually there were young backpackers around smoking or waiting at the bus stop, just outside the door. That suited me fine. As I arrived in my taxi, the Maori driver unfolded my chair and helped me into it. As the promised throng outside didn't seem to be evident, I asked him if he would mind rolling me up the steps backwards. He was happy to do it and I was set to check into my room. As it happened, the woman who'd been sending me faxes over the previous few weeks was the one to check me in and she showed me up the lift to the third floor of the building and my four-bed dormitory. I was all ready for my first solo adventure abroad, but I was a bit too tired to continue. I took a nap.

Aotearoa means "land of the long, white cloud" and is the Pacific Islander's name for the country. I found out over the next few days that if you're looking for clouds, New Zealand is the place to be. I was prepared though. I'd read in all the tourist information about the maritime climate. It wasn't unfamiliar to me from visits to the east coast of Canada, which is very similar. I was decked out in a weatherproof spring jacket with a waterproof hood. Actually it wasn't as bad as all that. Most of the time, the wind blew the clouds and the light rain in, and then in fifteen minutes the wind would blow it all away and the sun would come out to dry things again. I immediately made a beeline to the water to explore the area around the harbour. The centerpiece of the waterfront is Queen Elizabeth Square. It's only a short wheel down to the harbour, most recently famous for hosting two America's Cup competitions. It's sad that New Zealand eventually lost the Cup and I wonder what the impact on the local economy will be.

I decided to take a boat tour of Auckland Harbour. Although the wind and showers played havoc with my attempts to balance my chair on the deck, it was an impressive tour and the views of the "City of Sails" with the green volcanic hills all around were quite startling. We headed to the west for a short voyage onto the Hauraki Gulf, a brief stop at Rangitoto Island, a popular spot for families and picnicking. Heading back towards town, I disembarked on the other side of the water in Devonport, an upscale bedroom community with a lovely promenade and excellent cafés. It was a bit too hilly for me to explore fully, but I did wander away from the pier and into some neighbourhoods. The homes were small, more like cottages, but they were well kept and I got the feeling that this would be a great place to live. I boarded the boat again and we headed under the bridge to Waitemata Harbour for some magnificent views of the city and the Sky Tower, which dominates the city's skyline. For the low fare, which included a free hot coffee, it'd been a great first day.

The next morning, I ate breakfast in the hostel restaurant. The décor was interesting, as there was a vertical beam from the ceiling down to the floor. Someone had painted the beam brown and where it met the ceiling, green and bushy to represent the crown of a tree. It was all very artistic. I had breakfast with a young woman from Vancouver who was travelling alone. She was quite fit, a runner and mountain biker. I mentioned that all the hills surrounding the city made it difficult for me to try to explore. She kindly offered to spend the day with me and push me around. Of course when a lovely, young woman makes you an offer like that, you have to take advantage. I told her that we'd have to make a deal and that lunch would be on me. We moved to higher ground and explored "The Domain", which I believe is the largest park in Auckland. After lunch, we headed up to the museum, which boasted a terrific exhibit of Maori and Pacific native canoes or "waka", from which the aboriginal inhabitants came to Aotearoa from other Polynesian islands. The Maori, who were ultimately conquered by the British, form a large proportion of the population and the two cultures have merged into the most harmonious and inclusive society I've ever seen. In addition to these Native artifacts, there was also a very good exhibit of Egyptian relics, including a mummy. I bet that Pharaoh was the furthest travelled of his lot.

In the evening, I met a couple from the UK. Dan was a Kiwi and Fiona was a Canadian. They were back visiting his family and touring around the country for a few weeks. We decided to see what the nightlife was like. The hostel was located on the fringe of the red-light district, but it was the tamest one I'd ever seen. I saw a few

Asian massage parlours and that was about it. We ended up in a Maori bar and were the only "Pakeha" (those of European descent) in it. That seemed to make us the object of attention and we had a great time. The Maori patrons all offered to help get my blue chair down the stairs on the way out.

The following day, I was off to the South Island (known to the locals as "the mainland") and Christchurch on the east coast, which is the largest city in Canterbury. I was originally attracted to the area because I'd read that it was the flattest part of New Zealand. At the airport, I was met by a cabbie named Rex (read more about him in other chapters). We'd met via computer correspondence and I'd mentioned that I was unable to find acceptable accommodation. He graciously took it upon himself to tour around town looking for somewhere that would be accessible. He found that the YMCA would fit the bill and so when I got to town, he was waiting with a sign with my name on it. That had never happened to me before. I was a bit nervous about meeting someone over the computer, but as time (indeed years) went by, we've become very good friends.

The "Y" was quite good, except for a having a bit of a messy washroom. It was right on the edge of Hagley Park, the centre of recreational activities in the city. Within its grounds there's a magnificent Botanical Gardens and the historic Christ's College. Wheeling away from the park, I crossed Montreal Street, which made me think of home. Crossing the Avon River, the atmosphere reminded me of old England. On the water, a popular tourist activity is "punting on the Avon". Punting has nothing to do with football, but is the activity the proprietor of the boat uses to propel the craft along the river with a long pole, similar to the way they do it in Venice. I moved along to Cathedral Square where a choir was conducting a free concert to the appreciation of passersby. I decided to do some "pinting" and entered the old Victoria Hotel, which became my haunt while I was in town. They offered horse race betting and a delicious meat pie. I quickly fell into a crowd of gamblers, one of whom was an older guy with the greatest job in the world: he was a salesman for women's lingerie. Excellent.

Rex met up with me at the pub the next day and we made plans for an excursion in his Peugeot. The weather down on the South Island, or the "mainland" as the locals refer to it, was much drier than in Auckland and apparently the driest in the country. Rex and I drove down to Lyttleton Harbour, not far from Christchurch, then we continued south to an even prettier harbour, known as Akaroa. Rex told me that this was originally a French settlement that was ultimately taken over by British forces. This interested me because of the historic relationship between the British and the French that helped to form, and still influences, Canada. As we got out and I wheeled around, I noticed many of the streets had French names. We drove to the top of the hills around Akaroa. I remember it as being one of the most pleasant views I'd ever seen.

The countryside became quite scrubby as Rex and I drove out to the boonies to visit a friend of his and his dog Babe, a white English Bull Terrier. The fellow was renting a farm and trying to make a go of it, but didn't seem to be doing too well from what I could see. Still, he was friendly and offered us a beer. He and Rex spent some time catching up, while I played with the dog. It was time to head back to Christchurch.

New Zealand had been a wonderful experience for me. The country was green and beautiful and the people I'd met were even better.

GRASS SKIRTS IN THE PARADISE OF THE PACIFIC

I'd never dreamed about visiting Hawaii, but I'd heard so many good things about the islands from friends and family who'd either gone there on honeymoon or vacation, that it sounded like a good place for a stopover on my way home from my first visit to the South Pacific.

I was definitely not a seasoned traveller in the mid-1990s, so I wasn't sure, as I planned my trip, what to expect from the hostels that would make up most of my accommodation. I decided to take the last week as a real holiday and that when I got to Waikiki, I'd stay in a proper hotel and not do much other than enjoy myself in the sun. There was a hostel in Honolulu, but that was a tad distant from the beach, where I like to spend most of my time. I settled on an Outrigger Hotel and when I arrived, the taxi dropped me off and I was surprised at how many Outriggers there were, at least back then, in such a small area. It seemed that almost every block contained a hotel from the same chain and that they had cornered the market in the affordable price range. It didn't matter to me, as long as my room was OK for my chair, which it was. The view wasn't great, since I was a block away from Kalakaua Avenue. The main things for me were that I could get into the bathtub easily and it was only a short trip down to the water. Everything was going to be perfect.

I rode down to the beach in my blue chair and checked out the main strip along the waterfront. There were several posh hotels on the other side of the street. What I liked was that there were not too many hotels adjacent to the sand. The development of the beach was geared to tourists and the public beaches were probably the most centrally located. I've been to some resorts where the public access to shore is far away from the amenities and most of the hotels own the best beaches. That's the way it was for Kuhio Beach. On the other hand, Waikiki Beach was hidden to some extent behind buildings, but it was public as well. I wheeled the length of the strip and was amazed at how nice the weather was. It was late November and the temperature was in the low 80s. The sky was blue, although punctuated by a few puffy white clouds, while the humidity was very comfortable. The Hyatt Hotel was the centerpiece of the strip and inside was an upscale shopping mall where I gawked at the expensive baubles on offer. Toward the south, I could see Diamond Head, the famous extinct volcanic that always seemed to be the focus of the old TV show *Hawaii 5-0*. To the northern end of the beach was the Ala Wai Harbor and Yacht Club, the jumping-off point for tours around the western end of the island of Oahu.

I decided to spend the rest of the afternoon at the beach looking at the lovely ladies or, when I needed a change of pace, turning around and facing the street to see what amazing cars and people were showing off on the main street. As I was sitting there, an older gentleman struck up a conversation and asked if I was enjoying Waikiki. I mentioned that I'd just arrived, but that so far, it was as advertised. He turned out to be a Canadian from Vancouver and told me that he tried to visit Hawaii almost every year to escape the rainy season in British Columbia. His name was George and he said he'd been a merchant seaman in the South Pacific in his youth. It was nice to meet someone from home and hear a familiar accent.

As the afternoon was getting quite hot and I'd been sitting in the sun for a while, I decided to head along the pavement for a wheel to get some exercise and a new point of view on the beach. I directed my travels back toward Diamond Head and left the strip behind as I passed the grounds of the zoo on the left, with the beach on my right. I wheeled up a slight grade for about fifteen minutes before deciding to take a break and look out over the sand onto the water and take a short rest. It was then that I noticed something peculiar, at least to me. I scanned the beach and noticed that there were a lot of people in thongs, but none of them were women. I'd stumbled onto the gay beach. I was a bit surprised, because I hadn't wheeled far and back in Canada most gay beaches are usually further away from the main ones, either for privacy or to avoid the heterosexual crowd. Anyway, there was nothing here I was interested in looking at, so I made a hasty retreat back across the street to a location where women in bikinis were plentiful.

The next day I met George again at the beach and we decided to go into the Hyatt for a coffee. He was an older guy, but he was a talker and very outgoing. I enjoyed his outlook on life and that he was still quite a lady's man. It gave me a bit of hope, as I've always been pretty inept when it comes to women. I enjoyed his stories and he suggested that we get together one evening during the weekend, when local entrepreneurs run an outdoor market with food stalls. For now, I was off to a boat tour of Pearl Harbor.

The harbour at Waikiki is quite large and, as you can imagine, some of the luxury yachts moored there are quite pricey and impressive. I boarded a tour boat headed to Pearl Harbor to see the port and war memorial to the 1941 attack that marked the U.S. entry into the Second World War. The boat wasn't very large and I like to sit on deck when I'm at sea. I found an area wide enough to position my chair sideways between the cabin and the rail, so I could smell the sea air, listen to the birds and watch the scenery on the land as we floated by.

Visiting Pearl Harbor was a somber experience for many of the tourists on the boat. For many of the Americans, it turned out to be quite emotional. The U.S.S. Arizona was bombed, along with much of the port, and almost 2,400 people were killed. The battleship is still underwater and tiny droplets of oil still float up to the surface from the wreck on the sea floor. Above it is a unique white memorial, rectangular with a curved roof, narrower at the centre and higher at the ends, with a solitary U.S. flag in the middle. The memorial stands as a silent reminder of the terrible destruction and waste, both in human and economic terms, of war.

On the Saturday evening, George and I got together for dinner and browsed the International Market Square in the middle of the tourist track on Waikiki. Many of the foods were authentically Hawaiian and I did get some macadamia nuts, even though I knew from my earlier visit to Australia that they were native to that continent, not Hawaii. We both chose a stall selling Japanese sushi, which I bought, while George ended up with Chinese food they were also selling. We had another great conversation and then as daylight began to fade, we eased back across the street to the beach to sit and wait for one of the amazing sunsets that this island is renowned for. It seemed everyone there had a camera or camcorder and I didn't want to disappoint my friends back home by not coming back with a Waikiki sunset photograph.

With the state of Hawaii six hours earlier than the Eastern Time zone, it was very strange getting up at 7 a.m. to watch a morning of NFL football. On the other hand, it was finished by noon and I could go out and enjoy the day without spending it all inside. I had another day of roughing it on the beach with all the lovelies, but I had planned in the afternoon to attend a luau. The arrangements for the luau had been quite hasty, as I'd been debating whether to go to one or not, but George had finally convinced me. It was a bus tour and they had agreed to assist me on and off the bus. Since it was on and off only once, I didn't think it would be too bad. The dinner was to the north and we drove through the countryside gawking at the beauty of the island and its tropical plants. We arrived at the coastal resort where the dinner and entertainment were to occur, but unfortunately for me the area was mostly sand, except for the dining area, which had a floor. I asked some of the other guests to give me a push through the sand to the area near the sea, so I could enjoy the show while listening to the waves. Somewhere along the way, I must've been driven over a sharp seashell or a bit of broken glass, because my left tire started to lose air. Great. Not what I needed!

The entertainment was amazing. The dancing was spectacular, much of it involving lit torches being juggled. In addition, ancient stories were told of the King of the Hawaiian Islands and how he dealt with the first sailors and missionaries visiting the islands. I was a bit disappointed in the food. A luau is a meal of pig, roasted by hot stones buried underground with the animal for most of the day. It was quite tasty and they made quite a fuss about getting it out of the ground, but when it finally ended up on my plate, the portions were pretty skimpy. I would have to content myself with the free drink that came with the luau. I drowned my sorrows about my skimpy meal and flat tire with a beer.

The next day, I tried to find a place to obtain a new tube for my chair. I asked everywhere, but there were no medical supply or bicycle repair shops in the vicinity. I still had two days left and I didn't want to spend it limping around. In the end, I did just that. Honolulu has a wheelchair accessible bus service. The buses are normal sized, but they are low-rise and a chair can easily get on. The problem is that if they pick up a patron in a chair, the bus driver has to get off his bum to help you in. Many of the drivers drove right past me when they saw I was waiting. That really left a bad taste in my mouth, and coupled with the fact that the wheelchair friendly busses only came around every fourth or fifth bus, I finally gave up trying to find a place to fix my tire.

I contented myself with limping down to the beach, sipping on cool drinks, watching the waves, working on my tan and watching beautiful models in skimpy bathing suits. I decided I'd worry about my tube when I got home and was a little less busy.

THE GIRLS, THE KNIGHT AND THE HOT CARS

I've been a big fan of Formula 1 racing for years. I never used to be interested, but a good friend of mine, Cyril, got me into it. Now it's become common for me to wake at 8 a.m. on Sunday mornings back in Ontario to watch all the action. The fact that a Canadian, Jacques Villeneuve, won the championship a number of years ago also helped to pique my interest. When I last went to Australia, I specifically made sure I was in Melbourne in March, so I could attend the annual race that kicks off the international open-wheel racing season.

Melbourne has a wonderfully accessible mass transit system, except for the trams that run along rails down all the main streets of the city. Not that I am unfamiliar with them, they have exactly the same type of trams in Toronto, although back home you're allowed to drive on the tracks in front of the railcars. In Melbourne you must stay off them and trams have the right of way at all times.

I wanted to get out to St. Kilda, a suburb famous for its trendy restaurants, shopping and great beach as well. The Melbourne Transit System, or MET, didn't have a rail line that went directly there, so they set up a method whereby a patron in a chair had to phone an 800 number and book a trip to St. Kilda and back on a small wheelchair friendly bus. I did that and talked to George, a pleasant and helpful man of Greek descent, who asked me to meet him at a pickup point beside Flinders Station, the historic centerpiece of the entire transit system. I met him there and as we drove by Albert Park, where the F1 race is held, I mentioned that I was planning on attending the race. He seemed happy that I was a fan and asked me if I wanted to take a spin around the track. Of course I did. We proceeded along the race route, as construction crews erected the stands and pedestrian barriers for the race. It was very cool.

George instructed me on what to do race day. I was to head down to the Spencer St. Station and the MET would be running a series of accessible vans to help shuttle wheelies effortlessly between the subway and the track. I thought that was quite a simple and smart system. As he dropped me off, I told him that I'd see him again on race day.

I slowly pushed back up Elizabeth St. to my hostel behind the Victoria Market. It was a slow push up hill, but after half an hour, I was back in North Melbourne at the YHA hostel. The next morning, I was enjoying my traditional breakfast of tea and a toasted cheese sandwich, when a young woman sat down opposite me all decked out in F1 gear. Using my vast abilities at deductive reasoning, I guessed that she was going to the F1 race on the weekend. She introduced herself as Belinda and mentioned that she was from New South Wales and came to Victoria every March for the race. She was very knowledgeable and knew a lot more about all the intricacies of racing than I did. She asked me if I was headed down to the mock pit stops and car shows that were being held in front of the Town Hall later in the morning. I said that I hadn't even been aware of them, but that I was interested. We decided to head there together. Since she was relatively short in stature, it worked out quite well; smaller people are the best at pushing wheelchairs because their backs don't get sore from stooping down to reach the handles. We finished breakie and made our way to Swanston St. to see what was going on. The pedestrian traffic had increased enormously and we tried to maneuver to the front of the line to watch some of the Minardis run mock pit stops. The cars were quite amazing and to be that close to them was great. After watching for a while, we made our way to a coffee house for a cuppa and noticed that something was going on across the street. We finished up and decided to check it out.

It turned out that Australia Post was using the event to launch a new series of stamps honouring Australian motor racing greats. Some very interesting historical racecars were on exhibit and I was struck by how small many of the early models were. Sir Jack Brabham, the Australian former world champion, was in attendance as he was going to be honoured. Belinda was quite excited and got his autograph. A woman spotted me looking at the cars and handed me an envelope with the first-day run of stamps on it. I was shocked at the gesture and thanked her. I then decided that since I had this envelope with the stamp on it, I should try to get Sir Jack's autograph on it too. I waited in line a while and then talked to him briefly while he signed my paper envelope. I ended up giving it to my buddy Cyril when I got home, as he was the fellow who got me involved with this sport in the first place. Both Belinda and I had quite a good day and it was all because she'd sat with me for breakfast. I didn't see her much after because she was going down to Albert Park for all three days of practice and racing, whereas I only had a ticket for the race on Sunday.

It was two days before the race and I had another problem. The hostel I was staying in was booked solid for the Grand Prix race long before I made my booking, so I had to move out for two days before returning after all the race fans had exited town. Luckily, I'd found a place that was about halfway closer to downtown than where I was now. The International Backpackers was brand new, or at least the interior was new. I'd been lucky to find it, especially since it was chair friendly. The ambience left a bit to be desired, but the rooms were larger than where I was and the window opened onto a noisy courtyard where all the smokers hung out. I had my earplugs so it was no big deal. The washrooms were huge and perfect for the disabled, but if you wanted to prepare your own meals it was necessary to leave a deposit for a set of plates and cutlery. I decided not to bother for the two nights I was going to be there.

When you buy a disabled ticket to the F1 race in Melbourne, they give you an extra ticket so you can bring a "helper". It was a nice gesture, but for me I hadn't met anyone other than Belinda who was interested in going with me. I was at an Internet café bragging via e-mail to Luke from England, whom I'd met in Phuket, that I was going to the race and that I had this extra ticket for him if he could fly down to use it. He called me a derogatory so and so in reply, but also mentioned that a woman he'd gone diving with in the Whitsundays was in town and might like to use the ticket. I told him to give her my e-mail so we could hook up for the race.

The next day, I received a message from Luke's "tall, blonde Dutch friend" as she described herself in the e-mail. It was a blatant attempt to influence me into giving her the ticket and it worked perfectly, of course. I wanted to arrange a beer before race day, but she was staying with friends out of town, so it was impossible to hook up in advance. I told her that I was leaving the hostel for Spencer St. station at 8 a.m. as I wanted to arrive early to find out where to pick up my ticket, get settled and then watch the warm-up laps in the late morning.

I waited for her, but she'd slept in, so I started out right at 8 a.m. I'd paid for the ticket, so I wasn't waiting around for someone I'd never met. I headed down the street to the subway to get to Spencer St. I thought I might pass her on the street, but I didn't. When I arrived at the station, I found the busses, but not my driver friend,

George. I asked them to drop me off where I could pick up my ticket and they obliged by dropping me off near the gate. I picked up the two tickets, entered and was shown the way to turn 3, where the disabled wooden stand was. I'd never attended a race before, but we were right at trackside behind a high fence that had been doubled in size since a tire flew over and killed a race worker the previous year. It was slightly rainy and there were dark clouds passing rapidly. I'd always watched the race on TV and envied the sunshine from my couch in Canada. It figured that the weather would be crappy when I was in attendance.

I was watching some of the other types of car races they hold before the warm up laps, when Esther, the Dutch girl, tapped my shoulder! She'd made it after all. It turned out that she had partied with her friends the night before, slept in, gone to my hostel up a parallel road, then gone to Spencer St. station and asked the drivers if anyone had taken a guy in a blue chair with a Canadian flag on his backpack to the track and if so, where had they dropped him off. They communicated via the radio and she was told where I'd been left and they let her on to give her a lift to the same place. When she got to the track, she told the gate keeper the whole sad story and asked if she would accompany her inside to see if I was there. I was and I gave the official Esther's ticket. Talk about not taking "No" for an answer. It showed how easygoing Aussies are. That would never have happened anywhere else. Of course, the fact that she was as beautiful as she described herself didn't hurt either.

We watched some of the preliminary races and got to know each other. We had quite a bit in common since she was a Project Leader in IT, as am I, and of course we talked about Luke quite a bit. In fact I got the impression that she was quite hung up on him, which was bad for me, but I e-mailed him the news when I got back to an Internet café and they became an item when she finally got back to Europe a month later. Esther suggested that we wheel around the track, as she needed to pick up some film anyway. We made it down about five turns, but the mud began to be a bit thick. Actually, it was good that she did make it because she was a nice girl and I enjoyed talking to her.

The race commenced, the sky cleared somewhat and the track dried out. It didn't help driver Ralf Schumacher as he caused a huge smash at turn 1 and they had to rerun the start with the cars that survived. Sadly, there was no TV screen where we were, so we couldn't see what had happened until we got home. When the race finally started again, the Ferrari driver, Michael Schumacher, won as usual and the Aussie driver was fifth, which was celebrated wildly by the local fans.

Esther and I decided to join all the motor-head fans on the track for the party afterwards and we both got some great pictures of it. It'd been a great day and we made our way back to meet the buses and return to Spencer St. station. One of the other guys in a chair was a fellow named Ray, who used to be an Aussie champion motorcycle racer and competed on the European pro tour until he crashed and broke his back. It turned out that he owned a motorcycle shop near my current hostel and he mentioned to us that his favourite team was playing Australian Rules football in Colonial Stadium, just opposite the train station we were pulling into.

I asked Esther if she was up for it and she was. It was only suppertime so we bought our pre-season tickets and went in to hit the food stalls. The stadium is huge and the oval that they play "footie" and cricket on is a monster pasture. Each team has eighteen players on the field, but when you're watching the game, it doesn't look like there are thirty-six men out there with all the green pasture you see. When they're playing at one end of the field, the water boys are out on the field at the other end rehydrating the rest of the players. The Kangaroos squashed the Magpies by about 120-60, but it was only an early training game. The only people taking it seriously were the fans from either team that we saw fighting with each other outside the stadium on the way home. The game itself was created in Victoria to be an off-season workout for cricket players and is most popular here in the Melbourne area. In the end, I followed the season to its conclusion from my home and the Magpies made it to the "Grand Final", but lost the big game.

Esther and I had a great time and before she said goodbye, I received a kiss. In the end, I felt it was a fair trade for the ticket. We'd called Luke on her mobile phone during the race. That left him eating his heart out.

THE RELATIVES AND ROASTED LAMB OF GORSKI KOTAR

Croatia is an excellent destination for tourists. I'm biased of course, because my family's from that part of the world. Since the war for independence was concluded in 1991, more and more tourists are discovering the Adriatic coast known as the Croatian Riviera, as well as the rest of the country. By comparable European standards, Croatia is still quite affordable, without conceding any of the usual amenities that experienced travellers expect.

My arrival at my mother's village was indeed a bit harrowing, but once I settled into it, there was a great deal to enjoy. Located in the little suburb of Dolenci, my mother and her sister, Aunt Darinka, co-owned the house that they grew up in and where we stayed. I arrived by car from my Uncle Josip's place nearby, but not an easy wheel along the unpaved back roads of rural Eastern Europe. I can still remember my first look at the house from the inside. Basically there were only two rooms, a combination kitchen and eating room as well as another large one used as a bedroom. That was about it. There was a small patio around the side of the house, but the grounds were not navigable in my chair, since the backyard fell away steeply from the side of the road. There really wasn't much of a view either. Sitting outside the front door, we stared across the narrow dirt road at the grassy side of a hill. Up the hill to the left, was the family barn.

The first night in that little house was a happy one for me. I'd heard all the stories of my mother and her family growing up here and I was beginning to meet some of the relatives I'd heard so much about over the years. We enjoyed some strong, thick Turkish coffee and cakes my aunt had made. I was told that the kitchen is where the family would sleep during long winter nights. The stove looked like it should be gas fired, but they were feeding it small pieces of wood to support the fire near the bottom of the cooker. There was no television, but the blare of the radio in Croatian made me feel like I was in the house I'd grown up in back in Canada. The one major problem was the number of flies or "muhas" buzzing around. They drove me nuts. The front door was left partially open most of the time and flies had free reign of the premises. There was a no-pest strip hanging down from the ceiling with a few trapped insects on it, but it wasn't making much of an impact. My mom and I crashed in the bedroom while my aunt slept in the kitchen by the stove, just as she would in the wintertime.

I spent the next few days exploring the little town and the friendly relatives and family friends in it. Just down the road, was my other uncle, Zvonko, a thin, tanned man with a rough edge to him. When I first saw him, he was wearing a French beret and carrying a pack of pesticide on his back, with which he'd spent the morning spraying fruit trees in his orchard. He only had about an acre of land and his red brick home was unfinished, with many of the openings still windowless. I had only a passable grasp of Croatian and relied on my mom for most of the translation, but I told him that I thought his plot of land was very beautiful. The orchard ran downhill away from the back of the house and I could see most of the property from where we sat. The fruit trees were full of ripening peaches and plums and my uncle wandered off to retrieve some of the bounty. I made a pig of myself while I was there and probably ate too much of the fruit for one day, but it was so fresh, sweet and tasty that none of us could resist. He and his sister talked for a long while and my mom had brought him some clothes from Canada. He drew long puffs from his cigarette and he reminded me a little of my dad back home, because of the way he gestured when he spoke.

Further down the road, but not within walking distance, was my mom's first cousin Branko, his wife Nevenka and their son Bozidar, who was slightly younger than I. They came to my aunt's house to pick us up for an evening at their home. Bozidar drove a small compact and it was all we could do to fit in and find enough room in the trunk for the blue chair. We finally had to leave the lid open during the short drive. We had a great night of conversation, most of which I could understand a bit of and what I couldn't figure out, I got translated. Nevenka brought out a plate of "shunka", cured ham, a very popular salty treat for special occasions. I remember when I was a kid, my mom tried to smuggle one through the airport on her return to Canada, but the customs agent found and impounded it. Importing meat that hasn't been inspected could bring serious animal infections into the country. She was quite upset and complained that they would be eating very well that night. Anyway, it wasn't long before we heard a knock on the door and some other friends also stopped by to pay their respects to my mom. I made the mistake of passing the plate with the cheese and shunka over to them to be polite. When I got home, I was severely admonished because apparently the host is to be the person to pass the plate of food to the other guests. I had my first lesson in Croatian etiquette. At first it didn't make sense to me, but it puts the hospitality that they showed us into perspective.

That night, we watched the little TV in the kitchen. The show *M*A*S*H* was on, in English with Croatian subtitles. I thought programs would be dubbed verbally, but they weren't.

A few days later, my Uncle Josip, Bozidar, my mother and I, headed to the restaurant that Josip's son's partner Snezana worked in. Actually Snezana and my other cousin, Josip's daughter Djurdja, both worked at the same restaurant, but they worked a whole day on and a whole day off. They were scheduled for opposite days so they never actually worked together while I was visiting. Before going to the restaurant, we drove around the district, which is called Gorski Kotar. The largest town in the area is Karlovac. On a sad note, we passed a hospital that had been bombed in the war in 1991 and had been left demolished, as a memorial to the suffering during the war. The town was quite nice and what I liked about the whole country was the relatively laid back lifestyle, even though most of the population were quite poor and had to work hard just to feed themselves. The hills and narrow winding roads overlooked picturesque little villages of white houses topped with red clay tiled roofs. The tallest structure in each village was invariably the church steeple and each night at 6 p.m. the church bells rang throughout the country and people crossed themselves and said a prayer for those who had passed away.

We arrived at the restaurant on the side of the highway and were greeted by an automated rotating barbeque with pigs and lambs on the spits. I don't know how any driver could resist these places. I've never driven a car in Croatia, but if I did, I don't think I'd ever get anywhere because I'd be stopping all the time to eat these wonderful roasting delicacies. We decided to sit outside on a covered patio attached to the front of the building. I'd developed quite a fondness for a pint of Karlovacko beer, while my uncle preferred a drink of half wine and half ginger ale. Snezana served us and in a short while our meal arrived. The four of us shared one kilogram each of pork and lamb and made sure we had enough to take home to my aunt. As side dishes, bread, tomatoes and onions made the perfect accompaniment to the salty meat and I had to order a second beer to wash it all down. In Croatia, each slice of bread eaten is charged on the bill, unlike most western countries that offer it free of charge. Also, when paying a bill, it's considered rude to pass money from hand to hand. You learn to lay the bills and coins on the counter and then let the employee pick them up.

Most of the time I was in the country visiting my family, I went with the flow and did whatever my mom wanted to do. One thing I had on my agenda was to visit the local Catholic church for Sunday service. Across the road from our house, was a lady named Zjelka, who was a good friend of my mother. They had been schoolgirls together and Zjelka had spent quite a long time in France, working during the years prior to the war. Of course she spoke excellent French and I was able to exercise my schoolboy command of the language to communicate with her independently. She owned a small, pale yellow Zhastava compact car, a model that was only manufactured in the former Yugoslavia. Zjelka agreed to give me a lift in her car to the church in town and on the way she escorted me on a short tour of the local area. We stopped at a lookout that loomed over some of the other villages and she reminisced about playing in those same fields when she was younger.

The church was quite small and I was the youngest person in attendance. All the worshippers were rather elderly, but the women's choir singing the liturgy was very memorable. In small towns like this, the Priest is one of the most respected figures and wields a lot of power over the congregation. At the end of the mass, I was introduced to him and we had our picture taken together. I'm not the most devout person around, but that service took me back to my roots and I think I started to understand a little more about where I came from on that day.

The time had gone by all too quickly and in a short while it was time to think about heading back to Zagreb to catch the return train to Western Europe. On my last morning in Dolenci, Branko stopped by on his tractor in his white undershirt to say goodbye. As we toasted my trip, Branko had tears in his eyes. He is an old gentleman and my mother told me it was because he said he liked my sense of humour and didn't know if we would ever meet again. That was a very sad time. I also said goodbye to my Aunt Darinka, with whom I'd been staying and then my cousin Zjelko came to pick us up in his small car. Finally, we stopped by Uncle Josip's to bid another teary farewell.

Zjelko took us along the same rural highways that I took by bus on arrival from Zagreb, but he was unsure of the route to the train station. I remembered the way and pointed out all the turns until we got there. He was quite impressed at my ability to remember and commented that I knew Zagreb better than he did.

We were still planning on staying here one more night, but I needed to purchase a ticket back to the Austrian border. We enjoyed lunch at the café attached to the station and then parted ways with the last of the relatives on my mom's side. We had booked ourselves into a Zagreb youth hostel, which was not far away from the centre of town and the famous Ban Jelacic Square. As we arrived at the Square, with all its shops and restaurants, we paused to sit and watch life go by. A tall man dressed in the costume of the province of Lika, wore a traditional pillbox hat and my mother waved to him as he walked past. It was noteworthy because my dad was from Lika and had great pride in his native district. We decided that it was such a nice day that we couldn't let it go by without having a coffee and cake in one of the cafés on the Square. I couldn't believe that after all these years hearing about Croatia, I was sharing a Turkish coffee with my Mother in this, the most famous landmark in the nation.

We found our hostel and although room was small, it was bright, clean and airy. There were two single beds, a desk and a washroom with towels. For the small amount of money it cost, it was great value. My mother got on the payphone downstairs to see if my dad's cousins, who lived in the city, were available to come and meet me. We couldn't visit their house because it's up a huge flight of stairs that would be impossible for me. It turned out that they were home and we arranged to meet outside the hostel around dinnertime.

Soon, Ivan, his wife Jelka and their daughter Ana, came to meet us and we found another outdoor restaurant in which to dine. My mother had brought some pictures of my dad and Ivan shocked me when he started kissing the pictures. It turned out that when Ivan was very young, his father had died suddenly. They had a flock of sheep, but no one to watch them since he was too small. My dad took his family's sheep out with his flock each day and watched them until Ivan was old enough to do the job on his own. It had meant a great deal to him and it was obvious that to his family my dad was highly thought of. I'd never heard the story before and it was very touching. I learned something new about my father's character in the tough economic times they'd grown up in.

Ana was a lawyer in Zagreb and had just returned from a holiday in Europe. She was fluent in both English and Italian. I was asked about my work in the IT industry and they shook their heads in amazement. In the old country, most disabled people don't work for a living. Instead, they stay at home and are taken care of by the family.

After the meal and a few drinks, it was time to say goodbye, but I was quite happy that I'd had the opportunity to meet some of my relatives from the other side of the family. My mom and I found our way back to the hostel. The next day, I'd head off to Switzerland via Austria and would be back in Canada long before she'd arrive home. We talked about all the week's activities and the relatives and people I'd met.

All my mother's siblings have passed away now and I'm very grateful to have had the opportunity to meet them at least once in my life.

I never felt as close to my mom as I did that week in Croatia so long ago.

CHINESE NEW YEAR'S EVE AT WAT CHALONG

After a few days in Bangkok, I'd had my fill of the noise and pollution and was looking forward to my excursion into the Andaman Sea on the island of Phuket. I'm not a city person, even though I've lived most of my life in them, but when on vacation, they're even less desirable. It was only a one-hour afternoon flight to the south of the country and as the plane approached the lush jewel of green in the tranquil blue sea, I knew that whatever awaited me would be something I'd enjoy.

I'd arranged to stay at the local youth hostel, which I was told wasn't perfectly designed for wheelchairs, but would be OK for most of my needs. I'm always a little skeptical when I hear things like that, but the Bangkok YHA was totally inaccessible, so this hostel's willingness to host me was at least a good sign. I knew that if the building was unacceptable, I'd easily be able to find somewhere to stay near the beach, though at a much higher price.

I'd arranged to be picked up at the airport by transport from the hostel, but when I came out of the terminal, I was surprised to see a full-sized van waiting for me. I'm not too adept at getting in and out of vans, but I locked my leg braces, tried to stand up as best I could and asked the driver to grab my legs and give me a boost up to the seat. We made it into the van and after stowing my chair in the back we were off. The trip was forty-five minutes and we travelled along lush roads and into a mountainous area. All along the trip, numerous motorcycles honked and weaved around us. Most of those on bikes were not wearing any headgear and to their credit, the majority of them stayed on the shoulder of the road, probably because their bikes didn't have the power to keep up with the traffic. We drove to the other side of the hills and in the distance the blue waters of the sea came into range. The hostel was on a busy road and it was definitely not close to the beach, which disappointed me. We travelled down a long gravel driveway to a white, two-level villa. The driver went into the office to inform the employees of my arrival and before long, three tiny Thai women came out with a wooden ramp and placed it over the three stairs at the entrance.

It was a hot January afternoon in the middle of the "cool season". I was dripping with sweat and the woman in charge, with the unusual name of Meow, asked me whether I would like a room with a fan or air conditioning. That was a no-brainer. I think that Thais call it the cool season because the humidity is slightly less than 90%. I'd hate to be there after March or in the rainy season. At least my research on when best to visit Asia had paid off. I was led down a long porch outside the building to the last room before a set of small steps into the backyard. The room was large, but not very spacious because there were three beds crammed into it. The most important thing was that I'd be able to go to the washroom with no difficulties. I wouldn't be able to close the door, but since I was going to have the room to myself anyway, that didn't matter. I was told breakfast was included, which was a nice bonus. Meals were served in the small roadside restaurant that I'd passed at the end of the driveway. It was a bit secluded and I couldn't see any other backpackers, but I was out of Bangkok and it was warm and sunny. What more could I ask?

In the evening after a brief rest, I was in the lobby reading tourist brochures, when I finally ran into some other backpackers. First I met a lovely woman, Jorja, from Melbourne and then two blokes, Luke from Bristol, England and Leighton who was another Aussie. It seemed that Jorja and I were the newbies, while the two guys had been there for a while. After talking for a bit, we decided to walk down the highway to Chalong, basically a few buildings down by the roundabout. Walking by the side of the road in Thailand is no easy feat. I convinced Luke, who was by far the tallest of us, to give me a push. We were halfway down the road, walking on the left shoulder, when one of the small motorcycles that like to stick near the shoulder of the road, away from traffic, came a bit too close for comfort. The driver or bike actually brushed the sleeve of my shirt. At the speed they were going, that would've been a recipe for disaster. Luke and I were incredulous at our close call and when we finally got to the German restaurant and the end of the road, we both needed a stiff drink.

I thought of my friend, John, from my university days, who had moved to Thailand later in life and after settling down with a Thai and starting a family, had died in a traffic accident. I think that he was one of the reasons I had come to Thailand and I toasted him before my first sip.

The hostel offered a taxi service and the driver's name was Saharat. This fellow was actually an employee of the hostel, not a licensed vehicle for hire. He simply had a car and would drive guests if they needed a ride. I did. I wanted to hit the beaches, so he dropped me off at the famous Patong Beach and, after arranging a pick up time for the early evening. I was on my own for the day. The beach itself was quite good. Women sat near the promenade with towels and scented oils, offering relaxing Thai massages. For a fee, you could rent a cabana or a lounger and would be waited on if you wanted a drink or an ice cream.

I was saddened by some of the people on the beach. It wasn't unusual to see an older man in his fifties or more, walking hand in hand with a young Thai girl. Many tourists come to Thailand for the sex trade and in fact, though the authorities deny it, it's an important part of tourism and the economy. I was getting thirsty and decided to head over to the local variety store for a juice. I went to the cooler and saw a brownish liquid in a plastic milk container and bought it, thinking it was chocolate or flavoured milk. When I opened it, I noticed that the flavour was a little weird, but I thought nothing of it. After drinking it, I looked at the Thai writing on the container. The expiry date was 04/02/45, which didn't look like any date that would expire soon. Later, when Saharat picked me up, I asked him to translate the label for me. He said that the drink was "sour milk". I guess that explains it. Sour milk never expires!

After spending most of the day at the beach watching life go by, I decided to check out the shopping and restaurants along the main street of Patong. As I wheeled down a narrow pedestrian mall, looking up at the ornamental woodwork, I failed to notice a slight dip in the cement and I fell, arm first, onto the pavement. I checked myself to see if I was OK and some people who were in the shops nearby assisted me back into my chair. I had a cut on my elbow that was bleeding, but I was fine otherwise. I took the first aid kit from my backpack and cleaned and disinfected the abrasion before putting a bandage on it. It was sore, but OK.

The next day, I was in trouble. I must've missed part of the cut when I was cleaning it or maybe something had gotten into the bandage, but part of the cut had become infected. I knew the telltale signs of infection—hot, red and itchy. My elbow had them all. I spent the next two days watching the infection get worse and trying to decide what to do. I had little faith in the Thai medical system and thought seriously about returning to Australia before things deteriorated. As luck would have it, two Swedish women, with their three kids, had checked into the hostel. At dinner, one of them noticed that I kept looking at my elbow and seemed in some discomfort. It turned out that she was a fourth-year medical student. She gave me a clear liquid to place on the infected area to kill the bacteria. In only one day, it made a real impact and soon the heat and redness had abated. My arm was better, I had some new friends and I could stay in Phuket.

One of the Swedish women had a son who wanted to see Thai kickboxing. They asked if I was interested in attending with them, so we all stuffed ourselves in Saharat's car and drove out of town to the boxing arena. It turned out to be a bit more expensive than we were expecting, since Thailand is usually quite affordable, but we paid the admission and entered the packed, brightly lit arena. "Mui Thai" is the country's national sport and they take it seriously. When the boxers enter the stadium, they wear unique headgear and slowly walk around the ring to the rhythmic drumming and chanting of a musical troupe. It seemed more like a Buddhist festival than a sporting event, but eventually the fighting commenced and we got our money's worth. The chanting continued throughout the fight, as the boxers tried to punch and knee each other into submission. Saharat was thoroughly enjoying himself from the floor seats they'd given us. He got in for free since he was with a disabled guy. The bouts lasted for the better part of three hours, but we left early as the younger children were becoming tired. It was a great night of entertainment and had offered insight into the important role religion plays in the lives of the people, even in their sport.

Saharat and I had become good friends during my week in Phuket and he'd begun to drive me around for free, worried that I was spending all my money on him. He graciously took me up to Sunset Point to watch the sun drop wonderfully below the horizon and he also brought me to the long pier that jutted into Chalong Bay. I had also gotten to know his Filipina wife, Christina, who was employed as a singer at a lounge on Kata Beach. He was going to pick her up from work and I asked if I could go with him to listen to her perform. A German fellow, who spent most of his time scuba diving, also accompanied us. Christina was quite good and it allowed me to buy Saharat a few beers to help repay him for all the kindness he'd shown me on my visit.

It was my last night in Phuket and the cast of characters at my hostel had changed again. It was a very young crowd, who all seemed to converge in the lobby at the same time. We found out that it was Chinese New Year's eve and that most of the community would be at the local temple or "Wat" to celebrate. Eight of us decided to go down and see what all the fuss was about. As dusk approached, we walked along the shoulder of the road a short distance to Wat Chalong.

The temple grounds had been decorated and there were food and merchandise stalls everywhere. We wandered around for about two hours, taking it all in, music blaring, the night market, and we decided to try some of the foods offered. One of them was a brown pea-pod fruit that tasted like a cross between a date and a fig and was just as sticky. Some stalls sold dried goods that looked like every fly in town had been on them. Some of my companions purchased bootleg CDs for their Walkmans. Before we headed back to the hostel, I made sure we purchased an ample supply of beer. The beer I drank there was called Singha, but this time I bought the other major brand, Changi. I'd been warned that Changi was the more potent of the two. I bought a large bottle for later.

When we arrived back at the hostel, the others had already returned and were choosing which video to watch in the lounge. Another backpacker, from Singapore, arrived from the festival with a bag of cooked and dried insects. He offered a free bug to anyone who wanted to try one. There were no takers, but we made sure we saw him eat one. He did. We concluded what had been a great last night in Thailand with some dried durian chips. I washed them down with my huge beer and before I knew it, I was totally plastered.

It'd been a university-type atmosphere and typical of those days from my own experience, I wandered to my room to sleep it off.

ACROSS TO THE PACIFIC ALONE IN MY OLD BUICK

Prior to departing for my backpacking adventure of early 2002, I decided that fifteen years in the same apartment was enough and that it was time for a change. It was a hard decision to make, because living in a co-op I knew most of the members, it was only two blocks from Lake Ontario and I enjoyed wheeling along the lake each day for fitness while taking in the natural beauty. I'd made many friends there as well, who provided a great support system. But, they say change is good. As Christmas passed, I threw out or gave away most of my useless belongings and stored what was left in my friend Wayne's basement. When I returned, I'd head out west in my car and move to Vancouver.

When the overseas trip was over, Wayne picked me up at the airport in the middle of the night. I was tired and looking forward to a long sleep on his couch, but he was pepped up and suggested we go to my old apartment and pick up my car from the underground parking. We woke up my buddy Cyril, who lived there, and he opened the garage door. Even though I had no insurance, Wayne coaxed me to drive it to his house, so that the next day I'd be all set to head back to my parent's house. I was to stay there with my mum for a few months, until the weather warmed up and the Prairies thawed out from the long winter.

After a few months back in Welland with my family, having relaxed and fattened up with some home cooking, it was mid-May and I decided to head out west. I planned on spending some time in Omaha, Nebraska visiting relatives on my mother's side and then heading back north to Canada and along the Trans-Canada highway to the west coast. The plan was to make it there by early June and stay at the hostel while trying to find an apartment to start my new life.

I kissed my mom goodbye, my sister Frances saw me off and I headed along Highway 401 to the border with Detroit. My main concern was the ability of my old, white Buick Regal with almost 300,000 kilometers on it, to successfully complete the trip. Before backpacking, I'd had the transmission rebuilt and it seemed to work well, but would it be fit enough? I had my mechanic check it out and give it an oil change, but that was about it. I thought that if it conked out along the way, I'd have it fixed and then carry on.

At the border, the guard asked me where I was headed. "To Omaha" I replied and he waved me past. I was a bit surprised that it was that easy, since it hadn't been long since the tragic September 11th bombing of the World Trade Center. I'd obtained a route map from the CAA and the way was laid out for me in magic marker. I resolved to stop frequently when tired and if I got really bagged, I'd spend the night in a motel wherever I was.

As I left Canada, I pressed the button on the dashboard and the digital speedometer (which I hated when I first bought the car) automatically switched to miles from kilometers per hour. The roads in the depressing ghettos of Detroit were terrible and I wondered why they didn't clean it up since it was an international border. Once I finally found the I75, the road improved and it was clear sailing for the rest of the day. I drove for about an hour and then headed west on the I80, which would take me directly into Omaha. At least I couldn't complain that it was a complicated route. The first day's driving was uneventful, except for hitting Chicago around rush hour. It was terribly slow, crawling along for about thirty-five minutes, but I'd been in worse traffic in Toronto. Once it passed 6 p.m., the traffic abated and I pulled the hand control down toward my lap. I was speeding again, but I wanted to get to Iowa by sunset.

As my car rolled along the roadway through Illinois, it felt like a breath of fresh mid-western air had filled my lungs. The concrete mountains of the east were behind me and as I moved toward the setting sun, the scenery turned green and leafy and the towns were far less populated. Darkness fell and I realized I'd been on the road for about ten hours and was getting tired. Spots of rain began to fall in the darkness and I thought it would be a good time to find a motel and let the gathering storm pass as I slept. One neat thing about driving in the U.S. is that the country is totally geared to the automobile. Roadways are well marked for gas and lodging, but the days of full service gas stations are long gone. Each time I needed gas, I'd have to drive up to the payment shack and ask someone coming out if they could go back in and let the attendant know that a disabled traveller needed gas. They always helped me with a smile, but it was a great pain regardless. Although the motel I found wasn't just off the road, it wasn't far and I kept my eye on the sign from the road, as it must've been thirty feet high and brightly illuminated. They had a room designed for the disabled and even had a roll-in shower. I'd stopped at a fast food place before my arrival, so I was all set. A hamburger, a baseball game on TV and a hot shower—it was Americana at its best. I hadn't quite made the Iowa state line, but I was happy nonetheless.

The next day, I woke up refreshed and eager to get on the road, but first I had the continental breakfast that was included in the price of the room. I had my coffee, orange juice, cereal, toast and even took a bagel and coffee with me for the road. It was only six more hours across Iowa to Omaha and my uncle's smiling face. The sun was back and I was off through the rolling hills to get there before supper. I remembered Iowa from my first drive to visit my relatives, many years ago. I'd always thought it would be as flat as a pancake, but was pleasantly surprised to find that it undulated wonderfully as I passed immaculate farms with open pastures. The car radio blared out country and western music and the farm report. I felt like I was in an episode of *WKRP*. Finally, after driving through lunch, I arrived at the town of Council Bluffs, the last Iowa community, and crossed the Missouri River to the state of Nebraska. I pulled off the highway and into the parking lot of a restaurant to phone my uncle, since I didn't know how to get to his place. I woke him up from his afternoon nap and at first he didn't realize who it was. "Wait there and I'll come out to get you", he suggested. I reclined my seat and had a snooze myself. I'd made it to Omaha and I was one-third of the way to Vancouver.

My Uncle Otto is a big guy, but the years are starting to catch up with him. He's a bionic man. He has a mechanical device in his heart, a metal shoulder, a new knee and a rebuilt hip. I think he may be the only person in the family with more hardware in him than I have. He brought along his little charcoal Shih-tzu dog, Buddy, and escorted me to his home in the suburbs. We arrived at a split-level house with a full basement and there were about four small steps to the door that he was able to roll me up. My Aunt Eleanor was there and some of my cousins' children who came there after school. Before long, I was enjoying a barbeque and getting reacquainted with my family as they dropped by in turn to pick up their children. It seemed an informal schedule was made up to have me over for dinner.

I spent a wonderful five days there and it was super to see all my cousins and their kids. I saw my nephew's baseball game, played in the backyard with the twins, had dinner at my cousin's house, had a pizza feast at another's, and visited Boy's Town where many midwestern orphans grew up. My uncle drove me out to Lincoln to see the stadium and campus of the Nebraska Cornhuskers college football team. My cousin Steve and his wife Val and her family, treated me to a delicious Omaha steak dinner and took me to see a small amateur theatre troupe dubbed the "Borne in a Barn" players, out in a cornfield. I wanted to leave on the Sunday, but they coaxed me into staying over to Monday, so everyone could say goodbye at a family gathering at my cousin Cheryl's new house. As my time there grew short, I began to miss them already and started to become a bit fearful. Up to now, I'd had family to look forward to seeing, but after this, I was on my own. The next morning, I took Otto and Eleanor to breakfast at the Iowa casino across the river, then kissed them goodbye and got a lick from Buddy the dog. I was back on the road again and headed north to Canada.

The open road beckoned and I drove along the highway north through the state of South Dakota. The terrain was slowly losing its vegetation as the last three years of Prairie drought had taken their toll. Grey, shallow hills seemed to stretch out to the horizon and it was all I could do to keep from falling into a trance. It was also starting to become very hot in the car. My Buick has a very small roof and large windows, which are great for visibility, but it also acts like a greenhouse, magnifying the sun's rays to steaming proportions. I stopped for something to drink as much as for gas and had to ask someone from the convenience store attached to the filling station, to come out to pump gas, but also grab me some water on the way back with the change.

I continued north until I got halfway through North Dakota and then I headed west again toward Montana. I was in what is called "The Badlands" or "The Black Hills" and there wasn't much greenery beyond some prairie grass. The landscape was almost featureless, but for these nondescript dark mounds, but somehow it was very beautiful. I placed my camcorder on the dashboard and recorded snippets of the trip for posterity. I was now going eighty-five miles an hour and violating my rule against going over the legal limit. I'd been on the road all day and it was time to find accommodation. I was ten miles shy of Montana, but it was time to pack it in for the night. I needed some rest and my hand was cramped from gripping the hand controls all day.

The next day, I crossed into Montana briefly and resumed my northern migration back to the Canadian border. I stopped at another self-serve gas bar and asked for some assistance. A beautiful, young blonde with long, windswept hair and tight faded jeans, filled up the car and I wondered about the stories you hear of goddesses found in the boonies who end up making it big in Los Angeles. She seemed like the type. I drove until about lunchtime. It was the first time on the trip that I was off the interstate highway system and back on a two-lane road. The speed limit was still sixty-five miles an hour and it seemed strange being approached by oncoming trucks. I got lost briefly in a small town as I neared the port of entry and ended up wandering back into North Dakota. Regaining my bearings, I found the hut that marked the national line and a chubby, old customs agent came out to question me. He asked if I'd repaired my car while in the States and I shook my head. He warned me that the next sixty kilometers were under construction and that I should take it slowly.

I was in Saskatchewan for the first time in my life and I wasn't impressed by the quality of the road. It was terrible. As time went by, the kilometers slipped away and the parched prairie seemed to long for a single tree. The province seemed a poor one, as many of the road signs were faded and poorly maintained. However, I was just passing through, as I had to get to Calgary, where I'd reserved a bed in the local backpacking hostel.

I finally found the Trans-Canada Highway (known as the #1) and made my way around Regina and past Swift Current. By late afternoon, I'd crossed into Alberta and the highway was back down to two lanes again. I was surprised, as I expected the national highway to be four lanes all the way across the country. Some of the names of towns out west are very inventive. Medicine Hat was the first strange one in Alberta and I knew the town from watching their junior hockey team on TV. As I searched for a new channel on the radio, I was warned of an incoming weather front from the mountains. Apparently cold weather was coming and when it combined with the hot air that I was in now, they were expecting very bad winds and SNOW! It was the end of May for God's sake. I hadn't seen snow since Christmas and having been overseas the first four months of the year, I'd successfully avoided it. Snow this time of the year? That was not good news.

As I moved west, out of the flat prairies and into the foothills of the Rocky Mountains, the winds began to buffet my car as predicted. Suddenly, in the distance, I saw a coloured fog through my windshield. Within ten minutes, I was in the middle of a dust storm and the tiny red particles were ticking against the roof of my car. The temperature was dropping as well. I turned on my headlights and hoped I could drive through it before the snow started to fly. I found out later that the winds had reached eighty kilometers an hour and though the dust storm didn't last long, I was happy to finally be within an hour's drive of Calgary.

One great thing about summer in Canada is the long hours of sunlight. It was 8 p.m. and I still had a lot of daytime remaining. I entered the city, which is spread out over a vast distance on either side of the Trans-Canada. It seemed odd that I couldn't see the large peaks of the Rockies, but there were hills. After a half hour of going around in circles on one-way streets, I finally broke down and asked someone for directions. As darkness fell, I parked the car outside the wood panelled Calgary YHA, right downtown, and got out for the first time in sixteen hours. The temperature was now just above freezing, but I was home and I hoped that the predicted snow would pass by.

I woke up the next day to six centimeters of snow and I was getting really depressed. The weather was slated to stay cool over the weekend and I knew I wouldn't be able to wheel around Calgary with this white stuff all over the place. My next stop was to be Lake Louise, but I was leery about heading out on the icy highway into the mountains. When I have a schedule, I like to keep to it, but after trying to head out on the road to Banff, it was just too icy. As far as I could see, there was no sand or salt on the roads to improve traction. Perhaps all the cars had studded tires, which are banned in Ontario, but after crawling along for ten kilometers on roads with no guardrails, I decided to head back to Calgary. Instead of going all the way downtown, I checked into a motel to wait for warmer weather and improved road conditions. I wouldn't be able to stay in Lake Louise, but the next two days were booked for Banff and I hoped I could still make those reservations.

The next morning, I looked out the window to spy the sun. The roads were wet, but fine for driving. I left the foothills behind and headed through the Rockies to the tourist town of Banff. I was less than two hours drive from the city and people entering Banff overnight were required to buy a pass for Banff National Park. I hadn't seen these mountains up close for almost fifteen years and it was my first time driving through them. The gradual incline surprised me. On either side, snow-capped peaks guided me along the valleys and into scenic little town. As I drove into town, elk lined the gullies beside the forests, grazing and resting on the deep green carpet of spring grass. I felt like I was on safari in Africa again.

The hostel in Banff was great value. For $20 a night, I stayed in a mountain lodge with a restaurant inside, not far from the centre of town. In an area that's famous for being overpriced and a bit too trendy, I couldn't go wrong. The town was not large and catered mostly to the tourist trade. Backpackers like to stay here because part-time work is plentiful and the idyllic surroundings are great for the off hours. There's hiking, skiing, white-water rafting and a host of other activities. I parked my car downtown, pulled out the blue chair and decided to wheel around. Cottage-style storefronts on the wide streets sold everything from sushi to maple syrup. Wherever I was, there was a mountain looking over my shoulder. I hopped back into the car and drove around town to see the famous Banff Springs Hotel and the surrounding golf course. It was a very pretty town and a lovely part of the world.

The second day was spent at the hostel, reclining on the deck with a beer. It was a welcome respite from all the driving. The cool mountain air and the abundant bird life made me giddy and I couldn't help feeling a sense of spring fever. In the late afternoon, I drove out to see some of the fabulous homes and condos for the vacation set. I was told that many high fliers from the western U.S. and Canada like to come up on the weekends in the winter to ski. The homes near the riverbank were overrun by elk as the animals grazed in front of doorsteps and took no notice of me as I passed close by. They'd obviously adjusted to urban life, but I wondered how the homeowners coped with the elk poop on the lawn, especially if there were kids around. It was a small price to pay to live in paradise.

I left for Lake Louise and British Columbia the next day. The drive to Lake Louise wasn't a long one. The lake was largely frozen on the day I visited. It was very scenic, nestled amongst the mountains and flanked by the large hotel where many Canadian politicians have made bad decisions over the years, but I was glad that I'd chosen to spend a much longer time at Banff. The parking lot was jammed with busses of Japanese tourists and after staying for a short while I was back on the Trans-Canada, beginning the final leg of the journey.

I never tired of the magnificent scenery as I drove through the Rockies. In fact, it was all I could do to concentrate on the road. I was very careful as my old car climbed the last bit of altitude and I entered Rogers Pass, which marks a dangerous point on the highway. During the winter, this area is often closed due to heavy snowfall and the risk of, or clean up after, avalanches. I had to wait my turn as the road was under reconstruction and down to one lane.

I began my long, slow descent to the Pacific Ocean and had entered my favourite province, British Columbia. The driving was slow as I weaved the car along the western edge of the range and soon the famous BC drizzle covered my windshield. There were numerous tunnels to navigate and when passing through Revelstoke, I decided to stop at a high school car wash to wipe a continent's worth of dirt and bugs off of my car. The boys laughed while the girls scrubbed the grill and headlights to no avail, before taking their turn to help with the wash. I continued on until reaching Kamloops for the evening. I was now in the semi-arid interior of the province, sandwiched between the Coastal Mountains near the sea and the Rockies to the east. This part of Canada is reputed to be among the sunniest in the country. The hotel was located along the highway and I relaxed in preparation for my final assault on the lower mainland.

I'd decided to take the slower, scenic route along the Fraser Valley, as most people who'd made the journey had advised me this was the best way to go. They'd recently built a toll road into the Okanagan Valley, as a quicker short cut for commuters and industrial traffic. The Fraser route was down to two lanes and there was no speeding on pain of death. If the road sign advised sixty kilometers per hour, I'd go slower. I think I developed a bit of vertigo as I started to get fearful that I'd slip over the edge and become food for the salmon. The drive was spectacular and the valley was unimaginably beautiful. Although it was a very long drive and I had to concentrate enormously, I think I made the right decision. By mid-afternoon, I was out of the valley and back to four lanes.

The skyline of Vancouver is one of the prettiest in the world and as I'd been here many times by plane, it seemed to welcome me back. The traffic got worse and I crossed the various bridges into the city. From my car, I looked out at English Bay and Stanley Park. The mountains in the distance seemed to rise out of the Pacific as I left the exit ramp. Of course, I got totally lost, having never driven here before, and ended up in the rundown East End. Before long I located my hostel at the corner of Thurlow and Davie streets and rounded the block five times before finding a place to park the vehicle.

It'd been fifty hours of driving across seven states and four provinces and I was completely spent, but I was the happiest driver on earth and my car and I were still in one piece.

THE BEACHES, FERRIES AND TRAINS AROUND THE HARBOUR

There are a number of great things about visiting Sydney as a backpacker or tourist with a disability. The subway line is almost completely accessible and the ferries are an easy mode of transportation that take you to interesting points all along what has to be one of the most amazing and beautiful harbours in the world. I've been lucky enough to visit Sydney many times over the years and each time I hop on and off the local transit system, it gets better and I discover new and interesting parts of the city and its suburbs.

I've had my share of problems on the rails over the years, especially before the Olympics. My hostel was just across the street from Central Station. One of my favourite things to do was head down to Circular Quay to hang out around the Opera House or wheel to "The Rocks" where a great deal of lively city activity can be found. The problem was that the elevator at Central, which moved you from the higher inter-city trains to the underground city subway, was out of order. As a result, when I wanted to take what would normally be a five minute train ride on the subway, I was forced to get on the inter-city line and go way out to the first station with a stop connecting to the inner city underground. I'd head out to

Strathfield Station, change platforms and generally wait from twenty to thirty minutes until a train heading to the City Circle came by.

Many of the trains have older cars, so an employee would come out with a portable metal ramp to help me on board. I was asked where I was getting off, so they could then radio ahead and arrange to have another ramp waiting for me at my stop. I didn't mind that so much, although it was a bit of a pain after awhile, especially when I was tired after a long, hot Aussie day in the sun, but most of the time the main Station elevator from street level up to the platforms was locked up. The elevator car was inside a vestibule with two huge old wooden doors that had obviously been there since the time the historic station was constructed. If I used the station during regular business hours there was no problem, but for some reason, when the hour got late, the doors were locked and I'd have no way of getting back down to street level. My only alternative was to head out to the escalator and ask someone going in my direction to hang on to the chair while I held on to the handrails and glided to the end. I just had to make sure I timed a wheelie properly as we both reached the bottom, to ensure that my chair didn't get stuck on the metal prongs that disappeared into the other side of the machine.

There are a number of interesting ferry rides available in Sydney. When I go, I purchase a weekly pass, good for all the local methods of transit whether it be rail, water or land. On my first visit, I took the ferry up the Parramatta River to the city of the same name. The mode of transport wasn't one of the older, historic green ferries, to which most Sydneysiders are accustomed. Instead, the newer River Cat is used. The Cat is a wider vessel, designed for calmer, shallower waters. The trip took about twenty minutes and like many of the trips, departed from the wharf near the Opera House and sailed west under the Sydney Harbour Bridge. The bridge is known affectionately by the locals as the "coat hanger" and is the launch site for magnificent fireworks each New Year's Eve. In fact, you can spend $100 and be taken up to the top on a tour called "Bridge Climb". It looks like fun, but a fellow in a blue chair would have to have awesome arms to be able to pull himself up to the top of that structure.

The voyage was quiet and pretty, while the town at the end is quite nice and has numerous relaxing green spaces along the edge of the river in which to enjoy a nice picnic. The trouble was that I had nothing to eat. No worries. I went off to a local eatery to rectify that slight oversight. The small restaurant had a variety of hamburgers on the menu and one of them was the Great Aussie Burger with "the Lot". That's slang for a burger with the works and it sounded like something that would fill me up. Little did I know that a burger with the works in Sydney includes a fried egg on top and a condiment would be a slice of a beet. I couldn't believe the size of the thing by the time she was finished cooking and putting it together. It also came with chips on the side. I wheeled back to the edge of the river and found a shady spot. I shared my chips with some of the seagulls, knowing that there was too much food for me to eat. I did finally get through the hamburger. The egg on top was a bit unusual, but the beets were good and added a nice flavour. The whole thing made quite a mess as the grease and oil from the egg and burger mixed with the red beet juice. Of course, I ended up wearing most of it on my shirt. I must've looked like a pathetic tourist on my way back to ritzy Circular Quay that afternoon.

I had the opportunity to meet a computer pal named Kerry, whom I'd corresponded with via an old Internet service for people interested in the Asia-Pacific area. I'd asked for help with some train timetables and such and trying to find accommodations outside the city centre, nearer the beaches. Kerry was one of the people who'd responded and we made plans to get together when I was going to be in Manly. I phoned the number provided and was surprised to find that Kerry was a woman. I'm not sure why I expected a man's voice on the other end of the line, but it didn't deter her and we made our arrangement to meet. I told her when I'd be getting off the ferry at Manly and told her to watch out for a fellow in a blue chair and a white Tilley hat. We hooked up and she escorted me along the Corso, a great pedestrian mall running between the ferry terminal and Manly beach. I'm ashamed to admit it now, but the first time I ever came to Manly, I mistook the small kiddie beach near the ferry terminal for the famous Manly beach and stayed there all day, without even discovering the mall or the real beach.

Kerry and I got along quite well and she turned out to be quite an interesting individual, having spent a long time backpacking and travelling around the globe with her husband and kids in such places as Eastern Europe during the old communist days and for rather long periods of time as well. We looked out over the large, white sand beach, while at one end some of the sun worshippers played games of volleyball on courts that were set up by the local town council. We had a very nice conversation and shared an ice cream. I suggested that if she had time later in my visit, we could get together with her husband for dinner. She thought it was possible and we could arrange it.

After Kerry left, I stayed and wheeled the length of the promenade along the edge of the ocean. Around the far end, condos looked out over the lovely blue water. As the sand started to disappear and it began to get rocky, the footpath turned uphill. People offered me a push, but I was determined to do it by myself. I did make it, but not without a great deal of effort. The rocks to the left smoothed out and had created shallow salt-water pools that parents could bring their children to. Here they could enjoy the water without worrying about waves or jellyfish. I found a small seaside restaurant which was a tad expensive, but that is to be expected, and sat to enjoy the late afternoon with a beer.

Heading back to Manly, I happened upon a weekend market that the town hosts for locals and tourists. It was all I could do to make sure I didn't run over other shoppers' ankles due to the crush of people. There were quite a few booths where artists were selling their paintings or sculptures. Others were hawking the typical tacky fare that is always found at such events. At the end of the market, I stopped into a fruit and vegetable shop to replenish my supply back at the hostel. Even though I wasn't heading back just yet, I knew I could stuff it in the bag on the back of my chair until it was time to leave.

As the sun began to set and people on the sand gathered their belongings to head home, I decided to stick around and see what the Corso was like at night. After a dull few hours spent in one of the pubs with another pint of local ale and a boring game of cricket on TV, the pedestrian traffic began to pick up. Gone were the bathing suits of the daytime and the kids had put on their finest threads for a night of dancing and revelry. Families, with their children, were walking together eating kebabs or take-away pizza and getting in some window-shopping as well. It was quite a nice evening.

My energy was beginning to fade and I knew that there was a limit to when the last ferry made its final trip back to Sydney. Instead of the older ferry, on which I could sit outside on and smell the salt air, they were using one of the Cats that only had inside seating. It was a nice quiet ride, since the motor seemed to be much more modern than the noisy older one. The lights of the city and the view of Harbour Bridge, along with the illuminated sight of the Opera House, made for a very memorable trip. I'd never been out on the water at night and for me it was one of the best ways to see Sydney.

Sadly, not all of my excursions on the water have been so successful. On one of my first trips to Sydney, I asked one of the women who worked at the ferry terminal where a nice stop would be, as I looked down at the route map. "Oh, Neutral Bay is quite nice", she replied. So, being a trusting tourist, I took her advice. It was nearing dusk and, as we arrived, the wharf seemed to be abandoned and no other passengers were getting off. I disembarked and the ferry departed. When I got off the wharf and turned the corner, the only thing facing me was a steep road up to the top of a hill. With no one around to help, I was out of luck. I've always wondered what's so nice at Neutral Bay, as I've never been back.

I had to wait another hour for the ferry to return and retrieve me, but it was quite entertaining that evening, watching the giant cockroaches scurry across the old wooden wharf while I hoped they wouldn't start crawling all over me and my chair.

QUITE A RHUBARB AT MIDSUMMER IN THE MIDDLE OF SWEDEN

When you are backpacking in Chile with Sara, a Swedish girl, and she invites you to the biggest party in Sweden, you make sure to go if it is possible. I usually stay near Canada in the summertime, but recently I had the opportunity to go to England for a wedding so I took Sara up on her invitation.

    I bought one of the cheapie flights that are all the rage in Europe these days and arrived in Vasteras, Sweden at 9.30 am. I was a bit bleary eyed after being up all night at the airport. I had paid the equivalent of $30 for the flight, but the downside was that takeoff was scheduled for 6.30 am, which made it easier for me to just sleep at the terminal, but the only thing I hadn't reckoned on was the fact that there were only a few rows of chairs to stretch out and sleep on! Vasteras is about one and a half hours west of Stockholm and it was actually closer to Sara's town of Bjursas, so it worked out quite well. There is no train station from the terminal, so I took a cab to the station and then bought a ticket for the two hour ride to Falun, which is the nearest city I could get to by train. I was still struggling to cope with my leg in a cast and had a large belt looped around the back of my chair with two bungee cords holding my bag to the belt. Since I had broken my leg a few months earlier in Zambia, my lap was no longer flat and could not hold the bag steady on its own.

As the train rolled along, the flat farmlands of southern Sweden gradually gave way to lovely, green pine and birch forests and wonderfully rolling hills and blue lakes. On arrival in Falun, I asked the lady at the wicket to call the number that Sara had provided in order to let her know that I was nearby. Sara told her to tell me that she would drive over and pick me up in under a half hour.

In a short while, smiling Sara arrived in a van, which was not the best vehicle for me to try to get into, but she asked a taxi driver to help and he helped pull me in from the inside. We headed back up the highway which was lined with thick forests and reminded me very much of northern Ontario back home. Her house, which she was sharing with her boyfriend, Mikael, was idyllic and situated on a quiet sprawling farm, which actually had no crops or animals, but two dogs, that he was training for hunting purposes.

Sara showed me around and rolled my blue chair up the four steps onto the patio where she made a quick pasta lunch and we got caught up in conversation, each updating the other on what had happened in the time since we had last seen each other the previous winter in South America. After lunch we switched cars, this time into a green station wagon, which should have been easier for me. The problem was that all the driveways in this part of the world were made out of gravel and this is generally not the best surface for me to get traction on with my left foot. I almost slipped, but I did just manage to get my bum onto the seat and Sara laughed, wondering whether I would fall out. This scenario was to repeat many times over the week and twice Sara had to rescue me from falling out onto the road, while another time it was Mikael to my rescue.

I knew from talking to Sara in Chile that she worked at a ski resort, but it turned out that her family actually owned the resort and she was helping to manage it. The resort was usually full in the winter but was not in the summer. My accommodation was a wheelchair friendly ski chalet that was high on a hill overlooking a number of other chalets. Each building had four residences and the one I was in had two bedrooms, one with four bunks and the other with a double lower bunk and a single upper bunk. Additionally, there was a huge balcony, a sitting room with two couches, a large washroom with grab bars and an emergency switch, and of course, a sauna!! I didn't think I would need to use that. Sara had come prepared and loaded the fridge up with bread, cheese, milk, juice and coffee and had brought over an extra toaster. I was all set and was quite impressed with the facilities at the ski resort.

After leaving me so that I could freshen up and enjoy a short nap, Sara returned to take me back to her house. She wanted to prepare a big meal for me. Mikael was spending the week in Stockholm working until Friday, so I was getting the benefit of all the attention. I helped her chop up some ham, but most of the time we just talked while she spent the late afternoon working on a delicious quiche and a rhubarb pie. As she prepared each dish, she would complain that she didn't know how to cook well, but it all came out great. In fact it was the best quiche I ever had. She was worried that her pie was not working out well, due to the fact that some of the sugar had bubbled up as caramel, but it looked OK to me. After dinner, we bundled the dessert into the car and headed out to her parent's summer house on the lake. Immediately, her mother noticed the caramel and told her she had baked it at too high a temperature. Everyone laughed but the pie was quite good under the ice cream and I enjoyed it with her wonderful parents out on the deck in the middle of the Swedish woods. I must say there were quite a few mosquitoes, but they didn't seem to itch as much as their Canadian cousins. It had been a great first day in Bjursas.

I had not intended to stay with Sara for the whole time I was in Sweden, as I had hoped to hook up with a Swedish family that I had met earlier that year in Cape Town, South Africa. Sadly, I was unable to contact them so I stayed at the ski resort the whole time.

Most mornings I was left to my own as Sara worked or did her normal tasks of the day. She worried that it was boring, but I assured her that sitting on a balcony, enjoying a coffee with some cheese and toast, while looking at green mountains, smelling the fresh air and being buzzed by fearless swallows, was the most pleasant way to spend a morning that I could ever have imagined.

Sara had an appointment, so I was off to see more of Falun than the train station. She dropped me off near the town's pedestrian shopping area and I spent the morning in a cafe, drinking a cappuccino and reading a Swedish newspaper that I couldn't understand. It didn't matter. I looked at the pictures, watched the people go by, wandered the streets slowly, bought some strawberries and postcards and generally enjoyed my return to continental Europe. I couldn't believe that it had been ten years since my month of backpacking on the trains. One of my goals in life is to spend a year of my life in Europe somewhere, possibly in Spain or Italy, where the weather is the most suitable for me, but it really doesn't matter where. As long as you are where you want to be in life, happiness will always follow.

After the morning in Falun, we stopped to pick up Sara's parents, Per and Helen and sister Anki, who all work together in a construction business. We drove to a nearby restaurant that Sara used to work at and had a great buffet lunch. That evening, Sara's girlfriends were having a BBQ and so we arrived, though a bit late, and enjoyed some delicious salads and grilled meats, which got washed down with rhubarb juice and finished off with another rhubarb pie. I must say that from my brief time in that country, it appears to me that Swedes are the world leaders in rhubarb consumption!

The couple that was hosting the event, in the nearby little village of Andersbo, had recently returned from a trip to Iceland and brought out their photo album from the trip. The landscape reminded me of the moon, since none of the pictures from the trip seemed to include a tree, but it was ruggedly beautiful anyway, and is another country I will have to try to get to in the future. One of the couples in attendance included Sara's brother, Goran and his wife and two children. The children played happily into the long daylight hours and by 10 pm. there still was no evidence that the sun was inclined to drop below the midsummer horizon. We said our farewells and returned to the ski resort. I was successfully able to get out of the station wagon safely and Sara pushed me up the portable metal ramp that she had placed over the two steps up to the chalet. Sara left, and I stayed out on the balcony for a few hours waiting to see the sun drop down, but a dusky light is all I could see until I finally gave up and hit the sack.

The midsummer weekend was quickly coming up and Sara was getting very excited about it as it was one of her favourite holidays, but she still had a soccer game to play in. After a pleasant afternoon of sitting down by the lake watching the swimmers and enjoying a relaxing coffee break with my hostess, I helped Sara work on an advertisement for an autumn special directed at city dwellers looking for a retreat from the bustle of city life. Following work and a quick supper we headed out to the soccer field which was located by the side of the highway. Sara's team was quite young, and she was the veteran in the match lineup. The visitors arrived in their red outfits and promptly squashed the home team 13-2, but Sara scored a magnificent goal that Ronaldinho himself would have been proud of, looping a long ball from the left wing just under the crossbar on the far side. After the game the home team provides cake and drinks which I enjoyed while Sara changed. In the distance a game of Swedish "bramball" was going on. The game is similar to baseball but definitely not as competitive as everyone participating, young and old, were laughing hysterically during the match.

The following day was Friday, the first day of the "midsommer" weekend but the sky was threatening rain and I hoped that the weather would hold off. Early in the morning Sara brought Mikael over to meet me. Mikael had been working all week in Stockholm with Sara's uncle, who's home we were to visit later in the day for the family's midsummer celebration. Mikael was a shy, quiet guy, and unfortunately for me, he didn't speak English, and so with my horrible command of Swedish, we couldn't communicate too well. They returned at around 1 pm. to bring me over to his farm for lunch, and then we proceeded to her uncle Gosta's residence. From what I could gather about the weekend, the first day is basically dedicated to the family, the Saturday is the community day and when all the younger Swedes really party into the wee hours and then finally, Sunday is the day to recover from all the drinking that went on the previous two days!

After lunch at Sara's it was off to her parent's house for her to change into the traditional costume that many Swedish girls in the countryside wear on Midsommer Day. While she was in the house I had a chance to talk to her father, who showed off his new little two seat convertible sports car. For the rest of my stay, Per would constantly say "We've got to get Walt into my car so that I can get it up to 240 kph.", at which point I would say "You can get me in, but I'll never get out with this cast on my leg!!". Sara returned with her ornate costume on, which her mother had made for her. She told me that when she gets married she wants to wear the costume as a wedding dress, that shows you how much she loves the country life.

We drove up to the mountain where the raising of the midsommer pole would take place and it was already a hub of activity. I was concerned that we would have to park far away, but Sara told the parking guys that I was in a wheelchair so we got a spot right beside the hill leading up to the entrance. It was a really wonderful sight seeing all the ladies and small children walking into the grounds in their costumes. Each different type gave an indication of which village you were from or even what country, as there were some Norwegians in attendance. Sara's sister, Christina, brought her boyfriend, Bjorn, from Falun, and he was in charge of wheeling the blue chair up the dusty incline and to a nice spot near the top of the hill, where the pole would be hoisted. Anyone in costume or in a wheelchair got in free, but I had all this Swedish money left, so I made sure to buy Bjorn's admission. The family gathered in one spot and we took some great pictures of all the ladies of the family and Alma, the two year old, in their costumes.

There was a band playing music and finally the tall pole began to move. Starting from the far end there were four pairs of wooden forks, each spaced about two feet apart and the fellows holding them would then lift and walk toward the grounded end of the midsommer pole. After everyone cheered and chanted for a move, those furthest away, would then move to a place inside of the nearest pair of lifters and the process was slowly repeated about ten times until the pole finally was perpendicular to the ground. The midsommer pole itself was a cross covered with garlands of flowers and on either side of the cross, circles hung down. A big cheer went up from the crowd and the lifting was done by men in the traditional costume, which included a large top hat. I asked why more men didn't wear the costumes on the day, but the general feeling was that they weren't as becoming as the ladies outfits. It was time for the dancing to begin and there were many of them, but the most memorable was the "Frog Dance" which included many gestures, most of which consisted of waving beside your ears, because frogs have no ears and waving behind your bum, because frogs have no tails. It was quite hilarious but everyone was having a great time on top of that mountain and though a huge black raincloud approached us menacingly, it finally detoured away and the revellers were left with sunshine to complete the afternoon.

It was off to Uncle Gosta's house for the meal and family festivities. We were greeted by Sara's little niece who offered us a glass of strawberry wine and then we toured around the property to answer questions on papers that were posted to different barns and buildings. We answered ten questions in all, most of which were about Swedish or Nordic legends and the questions were all in Swedish. My strategy was to mooch answers off the smartest one of all, which I felt was Sara's mother, Helen, but she was guarding her answers very carefully from my eyes. In the end I did quite well by getting seven correct. Not too bad for a Canadian who is completely illiterate in Swedish.

The family began to construct and decorate their own midsommer pole and it was wonderful to see the little girls gathering flowers very carefully and then the mothers instructing them on how to place them. That is how traditions pass from on generation to another and it was great to actually see it happen. When the pole was decorated everyone cheered as it was lifted up. The celebration could now officially begin!

I'm not sure how many people were in attendance there but it was likely close to 30 with all the kids and I felt really honoured to be included. Uncle Gosta was really friendly and trying to get me drunk even before I had eaten anything. The selection of food was astounding and it was a buffet. The salmon mousse pie fell on the ground but tasted great once they got all the grass out of it. There was a large selection of pickled herring and summer potatoes as well as salads and sausages. After eating a piece of sausage, Sara asked me if I liked it. I said I did and then she asked me if I knew what it was that I had eaten. Now, you know you are really in trouble when someone asks you that question. She finally told me that it was horse sausage. Well, it tasted OK at the time, but I generally try to make it a policy not to eat anything that had a name during its life!!

Much more conversation and drinking followed the meal. I wanted to put some Bailey's in my coffee but Uncle Gosta said it was a girl's drink, though he finally relented in the end. I was really starting to get looped but it was time to work off some of the calories with a game of "bramball", which was similar to baseball, but had two sets of bases, inside for the kids and more distant ones for the adults. The batter throws up the ball and hits it with a stick, and the fielders throw the ball back to a person standing in front of the hitter. When he gets the ball, he yells "BRAM!", at which point if you are between bases you return to the previous base. Each base gets the hitting team a point and the fielding team also gets three points for a catch with one hand and also other ways that I can't remember. There didn't seem to be any "outs", rather each team hit for 10 minutes. Per was the umpire and seemed to make up the rules as they went along, but there was lots of laughter and I even got to hit once. The final score was around 64-35 for the guys, but I suggested that the girl's score should be doubled. This won me lots of friends with the girls but Per wasn't listening. After a few more drinks, dessert and coffee, it was time for Sara to drive her grandmother home while I chatted with the remaining guests. When Sara returned to pick me up it was midnight and it was still not dark. It had been quite a pleasant day and a great kickoff to the midsommer festivities.

Sara had to work the next day, Saturday, which was fine with me and allowed for a quiet sleep in and finally a relaxing late morning on the balcony with my coffee and toast with cheese. The swallows were buzzing around my head and a young girl on horseback strode in front of my chalet and passed to the left up the mountain path. The resort has gotten quite busy, which was to be expected over the holiday weekend. Sara was spending a lot of time overseeing the dune buggy track where guests could pay for 10 laps. There were a group of drunk guys in their early twenties, and after Sara banished them from the track, they kindly bought a little kid a spin around the track. You've got to love the Swedes!

After Sara finished work, it was off to Mikael's friends Johan's house for another party prior to heading back up the mountain for the concert. Actually Sara wasn't sure we would go as she thought it would be too rough for the wheelchair with all the crowds, but since this was the first day she was drinking the whole week, she quickly changed her mind and decided we should go. Now that was the Sara I remembered from Chile! We had another questionnaire game, though this one was trying to remember the order of objects hidden under a blanket. Our team lost horribly. Mikael grilled up some pork chops and Sara and I finally jumped into the Gato Negro wine for the first time in over a year. There was an American hippie in attendance, but he wasn't the most talkative, so we decided to join the soccer game, which basically amounted to penalty shots. Sara was in goal and I got to throw one at her since my leg, which was in the cast, probably couldn't kick too far. It was hilarious when Mikael kicked as hard as he could and Sara simply screamed, laughed and jumped out of the way.

Sara's sister, Anki came and picked us up to drive to the mountain and as the day turned into dusk, the concert was getting started. The area was totally crammed with partying young people and although alcohol was not allowed, I had suspiciously brought my knapsack, which hung on the back of my chair and was loaded up with vodka coolers and beer. I really enjoyed the band and Sara was really having a good time and headed down the hill with her younger sister, Christina. I just enjoyed watching all the people have so much fun at the festival. The concert didn't really last long, about an hour, and then we moved over to another part of the mountain where they had a D.J. and a wooden, outdoor dance platform. Sara really loved to dance. I remembered her dancing when were were at another outdoor festival, drinking "chi cha", in Valdivia back in South America. Once again she was the life of the party and all the guys were asking her to dance. She would always apologise for leaving me, but I was just happy she was enjoying herself. Johan and his wife finally showed up and handed me a hot dog, which really hit the spot as it was getting real late. It was about 3:30 am. when we decided to call a cab and head back. I will always remember my weekend on top of that mountain in Bjursas, when the day never got dark. What a party!

I got up quite late the next morning, but thanks to drinking lots of water before bed the night before, my head was in rather good shape. It was mostly a day of recovery. Sara came in the afternoon and we did some shopping and then got some pizzas from the pizzeria to bring over to her brother Goran's house. After dinner, someone suggested that it was time for a ride on the family boat out on the lake. It was quite a drop in elevation on the gravel road but Mikael negotiated the trip with my chair successfully despite all the bugs going into his ears. Goran's wife brought along the two girls, and considering that the youngest was only a toddler, I was impressed that they didn't worry too much about the cool, late evening breeze blowing in off the cold lake waters. We spent quite a long time out on the lake and at times Goran really cranked up the engine. We stopped to chat with some of their friends on the other side of the lake and then returned to the quiet waters at the end of the lake where most of Sara's family lived. We decided not to try to push the blue chair up the steep gravel incline and instead, Goran backed down his sport utility vehicle. Again the rain had barely held off and the midsommer weekend had sadly come to an end.

It was my last full day in Sweden, Sara had the day off and planned an excursion to Rattvik to see some of the sights. Mikael's 10 year old daughter, Hana, came with us and as we drove to the end of the first major highway surrounded by green forests, we came upon the sparkling blue waters of Lake Siljan, Sweden's fourth largest lake. After stopping to take some photos we headed up to Nusnes to watch the artisans make the famous Dala Horses, which are wooden and decorated with the special marking of each town that has its own, representative horse. There were a series of partly finished horses leading up to the finished one and we could ask the craftsmen some questions. Outside we munched on a hotdog and Hana pretended to ride on a large one that was situated in front of the gift store.

We stopped back at Lake Siljan for lunch. Hana romped in the playground while I wheeled near the banks of the lake and admired the view. It was hot and sunny, the best weather I had in Sweden and Sara suggested it was time for an ice cream. After our treat it was back on the road to visit the Dalhalla Amphitheater, which was constructed from the pit left by a quarry and had wonderful acoustics. We were allowed to drive right down to the seating area and a volunteer gave a speech in Swedish about the facility. I didn't get much out of that but she also spoke English to us privately and said that each year more and more events are conducted. At the bottom, under the stage was a pool of deep green water. What a great treasure for the people in the region of Dalarna.

In the late afternoon we returned to Mikael's house and Sara prepared a dinner of lasagna. While Sara was back in the kitchen, a deer emerged from the forest behind the house and Mikael alerted me to it. What a way to finish my visit. For dessert, it was appropriately—RHUBARB!! Actually it was growing like crazy in the front yard so they were doing their best to eat it as fast as it grew. Sara made a rhubarb pudding that looked awful, but really tasted delicious, I had to have a second helping. Who knew I would end up liking rhubarb so much?

The next day Sara picked me up to take me to the train station in Falun, we stopped for lunch and then the train finally arrived. They had a unique way of getting a wheelchair on board as a circular platform rose me up and then rotated me so that I could wheel onto the train car. Sara was chatting away to the conductor when he finally told her she'd better get off, or she would end up in Vasteras. So it was a quick hug and a wave through the window, and then Sara and her ever present smile were gone once again. I was left with my memories of the trip and the magnificent lakes, green forests and pastures on the trip back to the south.

I never thought that I would make it to Sweden and it is funny how things that go around, come around. The last time I saw Sara in Chile, she was waving goodbye through a bus window and now I had done the same on a train. Her family and friends had welcomed the stranger in a blue chair into their lives for a brief time. Often times it is the memories of events and faces of friends that one remembers the most.

For me, that is the way I will always remember Sara, her family and her little town in the middle of Sweden. That reminds me, I'd better go out and get a rhubarb pie!

CAMPING AT THE MASAI MARA ON THE SERENGETI

One of the things that interested me most when I was a disabled kid sitting in front of the TV, was nature programming. I saw many far off places and unusual animals. It was the thrill of a lifetime when in 1993 on a visit to Kenya, my friend Wayne suggested that we fly out to the Masai Mara, Kenya's portion of the Serengeti Plain, for two days of camping. I didn't know if I could do it, but if he was willing to take me, then I was definitely going to give it a try.

We travelled for two hours in the early morning on a trip from Nakuru, where Wayne was working, to the Kenyan capital of Nairobi. Just before lunch, we arrived at a small airstrip to catch our Cessna flight to the Masai Mara, which is located near the western border with Tanzania. Wayne is a notoriously bad flyer and would've been much happier on the flight if he'd been drunk. Of course I took advantage of the opportunity to mock him and hand him my camcorder, enticing him to film some of the landscape.

Small clouds passed as we ascended over the African countryside. Green trees and thick forests gave way to open pastures. I could never have imagined the wondrous beauty of this continent and I looked down, wondering what animals were playing their daily game of life and death. The Africa of open fields and animal migration is slowly fading into history, as fences are erected and forests are brought down to clear land for planting. This is exactly what happened in North America and ultimately led to the end of the buffalo and the First Nation's way of life.

We arrived at the Mara Safari Lodge on the Mara River and found the way to our "tent", which was to be home for the next few days. Inside were two large, single beds, a shower that I could easily get into, a toilet and a marble vanity. It was not exactly roughing it in the wilds of Africa, but Wayne and I decided we could tolerate it. I'd purchased a bottle of Bailey's at a store in Nakuru before we left, paying an outrageous $50 U.S., but Wayne had never tasted the drink before and I knew we'd have to share a special toast when we arrived. He loved it and to this day, when we get together, it's a tradition to share a Bailey's on renewing our friendship.

We headed into the lounge for a beer, following a short afternoon nap and met a fellow wildlife enthusiast from Sri Lanka, named Hamza, who worked for a packaging company and had travelled to Canada numerous times with work. Hamza had a slight speech impediment due to losing part of his lower jaw to cancer, but we could understand him perfectly and he fit right in with the two of us. We enjoyed a Tusker out on the patio overlooking the fast rushing brown Mara River, while a blue kingfisher serenaded us as he scanned the water for a meal.

The three of us congregated outside the Lodge with a British couple and their two young children for our first safari in a Land Rover. As we moved out into the long, brown grass of the savannah, raindrops began to fall. Our Kenyan guide stopped by the side of the road to manually put up the top. We were all set as the rain started to pound down and it wasn't long before we were rewarded.

A pair of young male cheetahs became our first quarry and they looked so cute as they huddled together for a long while in the rain. The guide suggested that they'd just been abandoned by their mother and were setting out for the first time to stake out a territory. We moved on and it wasn't long before we spotted a hyena. They're not large and their back legs seem shorter than the front, but when the animal yawned, we gasped at the sight of its massive teeth. As the terrain moved from grassland to green scrub, we finally saw a herd of gnu, also known as wildebeests. It was exciting to see the topi, zebra and Thompson's gazelles congregate and I wondered what predator's eyes might have been watching from behind a rock or shrub.

The driver obviously knew his game park quite well, as he revved up the engine for a short ride to where he'd spotted a pride of lions the previous day. Sure enough, as we rounded a bend and came to a stand of trees near the edge of a forest, we were treated to the sight of a pride of lions. They were quite comfortable with people watching from the truck as the male, with his magnificent mane, gently licked a cub as he lay on the wet ground, under a tree, out of the rain. I'd never realized how gentle a male could be. I knew that the lionesses were excellent protectors, but this seemed rare to me. The lion was quite cute as he groomed his paw. For the most part, the five or six lionesses stayed off to the side, away from the male, but the cubs romped all over the distance between them. The rain finally abated and some of the mud and water holes that were left became so large, I thought the Land Rover would become submerged, but we made it home. It was time for a Bailey's and dinner in the lounge.

As we ate our chicken and potatoes while sipping on a cold Tusker, some of the local Masai, dressed in their traditional red garb and brandishing spears, entered the lounge and began to chant and sing in their native tongue. Masai warriors always wear red, so if they're injured in battle, their adversary won't know they've been hurt. The Masai are nomadic shepherds and a staple food is a drink made from a combination of milk and blood from the cattle they own. They have perfected a technique to draw blood from the neck of the animal without causing injury or long-term negative effect to the beast. In one of the main movements of the dance, each member in turn would sing and then jump up as high as he could. I think this is probably important because in the rainy season, when the grasses are high, it's important to be able to jump to keep a lookout for predators that may attack and reduce the size of the herd. Even though it was totally staged for the tourists, I must confess that we enjoyed it immensely. We were told that the songs were authentic.

After a great night's sleep, at least for me, we gathered again in the lobby for another day's safari. Wayne pointed out a huge Nile perch that weighed 175 pounds, caught in 1968, mounted on the wall of the lobby. He suggested that the guy who landed the fish was either eaten by it or was a complete maniac. It was just daybreak when we departed and the African landscape was beginning to stir to the sound of excited birds in the cool breeze. We moved easily through more herds of antelope and then glimpsed an array of crowned cranes and secretary birds. Suddenly, a jackal sprang out of the grass, attacking one of the hapless fowl, but was denied its meal, as the alert birds quickly made flight. Rolling along the open spaces of the Mara, we happened upon a herd of ominous looking Cape Buffalo. These animals must be a wonderful meal for lions, cheetahs or leopards, but taking them down is likely risky. The fearsome curved horns, sharp hooves and stocky muscular bodies, made it apparent that any animal trying to make a meal of them would have a heck of a fight on its hands.

The weather was much better than the previous day, but some of the huge water-filled depressions in the road were still present. We approached each of them with dread, but our driver maneuvered the vehicle deftly through the waves without getting stuck in the mud. We watched from the front to see what it looked like as the next truck in the convoy made its way through the huge puddle. As lunch approached, we came upon a flock of huge ostriches loping along the terrain. As the large birds moved by, a herd of zebras barely blinked and continued to graze.

Next on the list of Africa's "Big Five" animals, were two rhinoceroses that were not wild, but part of a captive breeding program to help increase the numbers of this highly poached animal. They're impressive beasts with poor eyesight and nasty tempers, but these specimens were relatively docile and Wayne took the opportunity to get out and pose for a photograph. After two days out of my blue chair and in the front seat of this bumpy ride, my sore bum was starting to get the better of me. We began to make our way back to camp and as we did, another herd of antelope seemed to gather to bid us farewell.

The Mara River, which ran beside our tent, had unusual residents each afternoon. As we returned from the day's excursion, we decided to go to the edge of the safari park and observe a group of hippos wading in the muddy water. These beasts are massive, but they're also quite slow and rather quiet, except for low grunting noises. They're so big and have such small legs, that they require the buoyant force of the water to keep them upright, although in the evenings, they come out on land to eat grass. There were about fourteen of them in this particular pool, but they all seemed to be getting along very well. The only sound was of them expelling their breath in a heavy fashion from their lungs or the occasional splash. The scene was very tranquil and while lazing about, they occasionally opened their mouths to yawn, revealing amazingly large canine teeth.

Our trip to this portion of the Serengeti was coming to an end. As we made our way to the landing strip for takeoff, a group of giraffes watched and short rain showers put in another appearance. We still had a bit of Bailey's left and I gave it to Wayne to finish off. This time I decided to leave him alone and let him sleep on our return flight to Nairobi.

DON'T SHOOT DOWN MY PLANE!

I'd always wanted to try my hand at one of those tourist resorts that have become so popular over the last decade or so. It was during a winter in the mid-'90s and that year I hadn't planned an exotic trip away from the snow and ice. I thought I could make it through, but by the end of February, the weather had finally begun to take its toll. Unfortunately, I was again travelling alone and that meant paying a single supplement, but the week in Cuba was quite affordable. It was all going to be new to me, since my trips are generally on a shoe-string budget and my homemade meals are not too elaborate or tasty.

The three-hour flight landed and we were greeted by a huge painting of the face of Fidel Castro, the leader of the revolution who brought communism to the country decades ago. When we passed through customs, instead of a normal stamp in my passport outlining the arrival date and the allowable length of stay, the customs agent flipped to the back page and stamped a small symbol on it. Nowhere on the symbol was there any writing, much less the name Cuba. I believe this was to make it easier for tourists travelling to other countries, where diplomatic relations with Cuba aren't amicable, to enter without raising a lot of questions.

The Tryp hotel in Cayo Coco was on the north shore of Cuba and we had to face a forty-five-minute ride on a bus to arrive at our destination. The woman with the tour company informed me that there would be no problem getting help to board the bus. Spanish is one language I have almost no knowledge of and I was happy to be able to dump my problem on someone who could communicate it to others. I was in for a big shock. The bus we were expected to ride on was very old and dilapidated. Two Cubans lifted me up and climbed the narrow stairs onto it. I got lifted in backwards and was a bit self-conscious about being the centre of attention and delay, but the other tourists didn't seem to mind. The interior of the bus wasn't much better than the exterior. The seat, which I had to myself, contained very little padding, was ripped in numerous places and stained as well. Once we got underway, it became apparent that the bus ran as well as it looked. The noisy engine made talking to anyone all but impossible and the smell of the fuel exhaust made me sick. It was clear that maintenance was either difficult or not a high priority. The suspension system was all but non-existent and the bumps literally caused me to jump from the seat.

As we drove along the narrow highway to the coast, the reality of the hardships that Cubans have endured during the years since the trade embargo started, became apparent. Farmers were carrying their goods in wooden wagons drawn by donkeys and what cars there were, seemed to be in various states of disrepair. As we drove past small villages, we could see that solving poverty hadn't been one of the successes of the revolution. The houses were not in good shape and from what I could tell so far, the whole country could've done with a coat of paint. The farm implements that the locals used were rudimentary at best and it appeared that most of the technological innovations of the twentieth century had left Cuba far behind. The countryside was little more than scrub brush and most of the farms grew sugar cane. It was a deep contrast when we finally arrived at the resort to gleaming white buildings and the excellent facilities that most of the western hemisphere take for granted, but are obviously not the norm for the local Cuban population. I was happy to finally get off the bus as my back and bum were killing me from the constant vibrations of the bus on the bumpy highway.

It took half an hour to finally be assigned a room and I was very pleasantly surprised at how spacious and wheelchair friendly it was. The large bed in the centre of the suite had lots of space around the sides, making it easy to get near and transfer onto it. I was a bit taken aback by the presence of two small geckos hanging from my walls, but I knew from my other trips to warm climates that the critters were actually a good thing to have around. Geckos are very quiet and eat insects, so if you want to limit the nuisance bugs, you're better off leaving them to their hungry business. I was provided with two large bottles of drinking water, which was a good thing, because the water coming from the tap was a bit scary—it was yellow. We were told that it was safe to wash up in, but that it wasn't advisable to drink it. When you're at an all-inclusive resort, there are plenty of more interesting things to drink than yellow water. The tub was easy to get in and out of, so showering would pose no problem and the entrance to the room had a small lip at the doorway, but was nothing a well timed "wheelie" couldn't cope with. My back and bum were killing me, so I thought that getting out of my chair for a while and stretching out on the bed for a few hours would be a good idea before supper. Only the geckos were watching as I drifted off to sleep.

It was late afternoon when I finally woke up and my sore spots were feeling a lot better. We'd each been given a plastic wristband at registration and mine was yellow, while others had blue ones. Yellow wristbands meant that you were entitled to breakfast and dinner, the blue ones included lunch. It didn't matter to me, as I usually don't even have two meals a day, at least when I'm home in Canada. I find that despite my best efforts to exercise aerobically for over one hour a day, I don't burn enough calories to maintain a proper weight. In fact, I like to eat oatmeal for supper a few times a week to keep a lid on the calories and help the heart out; besides, its quick and easy to cook. When I backpack, I burn more calories and am likely to have a breakfast of cheese and fruit and then another meal in the late afternoon.

I took a short tour around the property to see if it was "Walt friendly" and for the most part, it was. The only place I couldn't get to was the second floor of the townhouse units, which didn't matter and access to the beach was a bit restricted. There was a small wooden path to an outdoor café which overlooked the sand and was near the volleyball courts, so I knew I'd be spending a great deal of time in that vicinity. There was a huge cafeteria-style buffet kitchen and two small restaurants that required reservations for dinner. The pool was excellent and very clean with an outdoor bar attached. For once in my life, it seemed like I'd had some good luck with the travel agent in booking a place that was as accessible as had been advertised. I was outfitted with my old Tilley hat, some cheap green sunglasses, a blue chair, yellow shorts and skinny white legs that needed a tan. I must have looked quite the sight as I went to the bar and obtained a Legarto beer, the beach beckoned.

It didn't take long to meet some new friends. Around the pool, I quickly befriended a couple, Nadine and Jim, both of whom were in my age group, from the eastern suburbs of Toronto. At the beach, I met three younger vacationers from the west end, a couple, Tom and Julie, as well as another fellow who'd also come stag, by the name of Bruno. As the week progressed, I fell into the routine of meeting the younger guys for breakfast (I really hated the fact that the hotel didn't offer the guests a newspaper to read. I understand that Cuba is a Communist state, but censoring tourists didn't make much sense to me), then hanging out at the beach, while watching my new friends play volleyball, jet ski or swim in the water. Nadine loved to sun herself around the pool and Jim waited on her, bringing her the mixed drinks she craved. Jim and I got along quite well and discussed sports and current event issues. In the evenings, we all ended up at the Salsa lounge in the middle of the expansive complex near the pool, where we consumed massive quantities of alcoholic beverages and enjoyed dancing to the loud Latin beat of the Cuban band.

It turned out that my younger friends were as eager to get off the resort and meet a few of the locals as I was. Of course, we'd met many of the people who worked at the hotel, but they didn't seem to want to fraternize. I'm not sure whether conversing with guests was discouraged by the management, but it wouldn't surprise me. Sadly, there was an older gentleman we ate with one morning who bragged about getting friendly with the housekeeper and ended up giving her a small amount of American currency. To me that was terrible, but I suspect it happened frequently. Tom showed up one afternoon with an old, beat-up compact he'd rented from the front desk. Bruno threw the blue chair in the trunk and he and I got into the back, while the lovebirds sat up front.

It wasn't much of a trip of exploration. The others wanted to go into the nearest town and find a bar to grab a drink and talk to some of the locals. It only took about twenty minutes of driving along the bumpy road until we discovered a small village with nothing more than a main street and some sparsely scattered buildings running along its side. We parked the car and entered a dark, but noisy, tavern, which seemed full of life. Here, the currency of Cuba is the American dollar and not the local peso. I've always found this rather ironic, since over the years, Canada's been on friendly relations with Cuba, but the U.S. has not. It'd be nice to have a tropical island that accepted Canadian currency for a change, but with the Cubans in the States sending home their greenbacks to relatives in this country, it only made sense.

After ordering our beers, some of the locals came over and struck up a conversation. During our visit, a small U.S. plane had violated

Cuban airspace and had been shot down. The Cubans in the bar seemed to be very proud that their Air Force had stood up for their sovereign airspace. I tried to be diplomatic and looked at both sides of the story, but when I'm on vacation, the last thing that I'm looking for is a political discussion. We finished our drinks and decided to tour the countryside before making our way back to the resort. There really wasn't much to see. There were no major hills and the land was rather scrubby and unsurprising. We decided to make a beeline for the restaurant back at the Tryp and return our car.

Most of the days at the resort were very pleasant and the weather held out well. I fell into a lazy routine of food, alcohol, sun, food, sun and partying in the lounge with my new friends. In the evenings, I'd rest in my room, watching the Cuban World Series between Santa Clara and Industriales. I can't remember who won, but the crowd was extremely enthusiastic and the calibre of play was very high.

I hoped that when the week was over and we all returned to the frozen north, the Cuban authorities might restrain themselves and let our plane escape the sunny south without causing an international incident. Unfortunately, they did.

SUNRISE WITH A SORE BUM AND A BROKEN MOTOR

Despite many of the initial problems that I encountered at my resort in Bali, I quite enjoyed my holiday there. The staff went out of their way to do everything they could to make my stay pleasurable.

In the mornings, I'd transfer onto a wicker chair that was provided and use the flexible showerhead attached to the bath to enjoy a refreshing wash. I'd then spend a half hour on the porch, enjoying the morning sunshine as it began to make its way over the buildings. Mornings and evenings are, to me, the best times of the day in the tropics, because the equatorial heat and the high humidity are at reasonable levels, at least for a northerner such as myself. Then I'd go off to the buffet breakfast that was included in my package. The assortment of hot dishes was large and they had a chef cook up eggs or pancakes if you wished. The open patio, with its surrounding wonderfully bright and aromatic flowers, enticed the guest to relax and look out across the pool deck and the fence that separated the resort from the public beach. Beyond the fence and down a few stairs, the hawkers and vendors made every effort to peddle everything from miniature woodcarvings of dolphins to calendars featuring all the Hindu high festivals and promising to reveal your fortune. Beaches are all public in Bali and it's not prohibited to aggressively sell goods to the island's visitors. I noticed that this inhibited some of the older tourists from venturing out onto the black beach, but most of the younger ones, the few that were there, were used to it and knew that once you gave the wares a good look, they wouldn't hassle you again. When I visited, the Java Sea was quite calm, although there was a brief thunderstorm during my first morning. Usually a few puffy clouds would drift by, but beyond that, there were green seas and blue skies each and every day.

Following breakfast, I'd retire to my reclining lounge chair beside the pool facing the water. It was located under a tree and I enjoyed watching a pair of birds build a new nest above me. I made sure it wasn't right above me, otherwise I might be in for a messy time, but I was impressed by the progress the two of them made during the week I was there. It was nice to be out of my chair and I was only slightly self-conscious about my unusually skinny, white legs stretching in front of me from my bright yellow shorts. To the left was a little used exercise and fitness room, but that didn't seem to deter the trainers who worked there from trying to attract people to come in and work out. Just before the stone gate marking the perimeter of the resort, was another covered patio with tables and chairs piled up as if in storage. I assumed that they didn't use it during the lax season, but I'm sure that when the high season rolled around, the pool and patio were very happening places.

As lunchtime approached and the heat of the day reached its peak, I'd transfer back into my chair and make my way up to the room for a long nap and some French language TV, that included a half hour news broadcast from Québec. I'd make sure to eat a big breakfast that would tide me over until dinner. The front desk would deliver an English language paper from Jakarta to my door and I enjoyed spending the early afternoon out on the porch reading it, while sipping a cool beer. Before long, I was back on the patio in the late afternoon to see if any young beauties were in the pool for a refreshing dip.

As dusk approached around 6 p.m., I liked to make my way to the beach to watch what I could of the sunset. Most of the hawkers had gone home by then and the chance of getting hassled had decreased considerably. About twenty feet away from the shore and in knee-deep water, local fishermen with long poles were out attempting to catch either dinner or something to sell to local restaurants. It was a very placid time of day and the silhouette of the fishers against the salmon pink horizon with its purple clouds reminded me that I was very lucky to be fortunate enough to enjoy the sunset with them.

After a dinner of a very tasty personal pizza, which was much better than I'd expected in this part of the world, it was time to think about making an early night of it. One of the managers of the resort, Mr. Uton, the kindly gentleman with black-rimmed glasses who'd been in charge of erecting the homemade ramp to my room on arrival, had informed me that the next morning, a number of guests were going out to look for dolphins. The cost was only $7 U.S. so I decided that for that affordable price, it was something not to be missed. I asked if he thought I could do it and he smiled and said "of course". The one hitch was that I had to wake up at 5 a.m. because this was billed as "Sunrise with the Dolphins". It sounded memorable and it ultimately turned out to be.

I woke up to a bang on the door at the time we'd agreed on and rose to wash my face and brush my teeth. I'd showered before bed the night before, so I was relatively refreshed, at least as fresh as anyone could possibly be at that time of day. It was completely dark and I had to ring the front desk to ask someone to meet me outside my door to help me down the steep ramp. I arrived in the pool area and made my way to the steps leading down to the beach. I had proceeded as far as I could go on my own. There were a few other people there, but none of the hotel employees had arrived. We discussed the impending trip and everyone seemed quite excited at the prospect of viewing dolphins. Finally, right at 5:50 a.m., Mr. Uton and some of the other staff members showed up and guided the other tourists down to the beach to assign them their boats. He then returned and we instructed a few of the helpers in how to best carry the chair down the steps and across the black sand to my craft. It was important to me that they not drag the chair in the sand, since small grains can get into the bearings and totally wreck the spinning ability of the wheels.

I took one look at the boat, which was more like a canoe, and wondered if I should start crawling back across the sand to the resort on my own. It was very rough looking and the small engine at the stern didn't look to be in very good shape either. The boat was white, with some red designs painted on it, and was fitted with outriggers on either side to assist with stability and balance. I was lifted out of my chair and onto a seat that had been fashioned by tying five pieces of bamboo together. I wasn't even sure whether it had been properly secured to the side, but I didn't feel it move, so I guessed that it was OK. I was given the photographic gear from my chair and then my captain and I were off into the dark night along with a small flotilla of other thrill seekers in search of the promised dolphins.

It wasn't long before I wished I'd been fitted with outriggers for balance as well. I'm notorious for falling over in a slight breeze when out of my chair and this was really scary. I did the best I could to hang onto the side of the canoe while we were pushed out of the shallow waters near the shore. The first leg was a bit bumpy, but soon the outriggers were doing their thing and the ride seemed to improve. Fortunately, the seas were very calm that morning and there wasn't much pitch or roll. The captain of the vessel (and I use the term loosely) quickly sparked up the motor that was perched above the top of the rim of the canoe, in what I imagine was an effort to keep it from getting wet. The noise from the damn thing was deafening! I couldn't hear myself think and the stink from the exhaust was pretty horrible as well. After we moved a little further out, he turned the motor down and both those annoyances abated somewhat. In the distance, the first streak of morning light was beginning to awaken the exotic landscape and it was quite impressive being out there on the almost still sea with the sun just breaking the eastern horizon. Sea birds were starting to stir and many of the land-based species could be seen shuffling from tree to tree. To the south, the mountains began to appear out of the darkness and exerted their towering influence over Lovina's citizens. I did the best I could to hold my camcorder still in the gently rocking boat with my dreadful balance, while trying to enjoy the scene with my naked eye and not completely through the viewfinder.

As we continued further out, we made little progress in trying to spy a school of jumping dolphins. In broken English, the captain told me that they favoured these waters in the early morning at this time of year as feeding grounds, but he warned me that some days they didn't make an appearance at all. We both scoured the horizon in vain and as our little canoe ventured into deeper waters, we passed small, rustic floating platforms with little huts that the local fishermen used as daytime bases of operations.

I turned around and noticed that my escort had left our flotilla and had travelled the farthest away from shore. Just as I noticed that, our little motor conked out. This was not a good situation to be in. No radio, no companions, no method of propulsion, no Skipper, no Gilligan and no dolphins. I envisioned losing my balance and breaking my neck in the long fall to the bottom of the boat or perhaps falling overboard into the Java Sea and suffering an ignominious death, bumping into one of the fishy mammals on the way down. It hadn't been a good morning so far and worse for me, the bum numbing rocking of the boat and the bamboo I was sitting on, were beginning to take their toll. I was starting to lose feeling in my lower extremities.

It took about twenty minutes of trying to restart the little engine, but I must give the captain credit for diligence as he tinkered between each attempt and never gave up the effort. He finally got it going, although it sputtered a bit at first and then ran much smoother after a short while. The smell of diesel fuel during all his vain attempts had begun to make me sick, but once we got moving again, I was able to clear my lungs and my head.

We rejoined the flotilla and then someone yelled out excitedly that they'd finally spotted a dolphin! I looked around in the easterly direction they were pointing, but couldn't see a thing. Finally, my captain tapped me on the shoulder and pointed out beyond the right outrigger of the canoe. "Dol Pin" he shouted, slightly mispronouncing it, but knowing more English than I did Balinese. I looked out and saw four small dark forms riding slightly above the waves as effortlessly as a puff of smoke blows in the wind. They were quite a sight and best of all they seemed to be heading right across our bow. They stayed about twenty-five feet from us, but seeing them so close and being almost at their level on the water, made it a unique and exhilarating experience. Since we were late coming back to the crowd of canoes, we'd ended up in the best position to see them. The dolphins didn't stop. Instead, they continued westward towards the nearby town, but I think everyone felt they'd seen what they came for.

We looked for more dolphins for another hour or so, but by now, the sun was higher in the sky and most of us lacked proper sun protection or hats. The captain turned the boat around and we slowly made our way back to the resort. It seemed surreal as the shore, buildings and people came into focus. As we neared the shore, the sea began to flatten and I could see small rocks covered in seaweed. I relaxed a bit and dropped my hand into the Java Sea to feel its warm waters rushing through my fingers.

It'd been quite a good morning after all and there was the ever-smiling Mr. Uton, with his thick glasses, to greet our arrival. The workers came out into the water to retrieve our craft, as the captain cut the flaky motor. We were dragged onto the sand and then two men came to retrieve me and return me to my weather-beaten, but land-loving, blue chair. The feeling was finally starting to return to my bum and legs and I tipped the captain and thanked him for a memorable experience.

It had been great and I knew that when I enjoyed my breakfast, I wouldn't look out across the Java Sea the same way again. On the way out of the hotel, another tack found my chair. As I was out of tubes, I had to limp back to Australia on only one good tire.

Somehow, it seemed appropriate.

THE END OF THE WORLD AND THE START OF EVERYTHING

When I booked my various flights around South America I remember thinking that it would be outrageously expensive to visit Ushuaia, which is located in the southern tip of the continent on the island of Terra del Fuego and on the northern bank of the Beagle Channel, only 600 km. from Antarctica. I was totally surprised to find out that the round trip from Buenos Aires would be only a few hundred dollars. So, if I was going to be that close, I felt it would be a waste not to try to visit it anyway.

After the heat and sun of the middle of the Argentina, I was really looking forward to getting down south and to some cooler weather. I fretted each day during the week before my flight as I checked the weather at Ushuaia from the internet cafes as my visit approached. The weather was vile, rainstorms and temperatures that approximated late autumn in Canada. But, no matter what awaited me, I was determined to go.

My flight was quite pleasant. After three hours in a plane, the topography had changed dramatically as we flew along the Atlantic coast over the barely populated region of Patagonia. Rugged beauty surrounded us as we hugged the waterline and moved closer to landing. Snow capped peaks and sparsely spaced green vegetation dotted out of the dark blue waters. Once we landed I was happily surprised by the fact that the weather appeared to be clearing and though there were spots of rain on the plane window and an abundance of black clouds, there were also patches of blue sky and a hint of afternoon sunshine poked out to brighten the cabin.

Ushuaia is very pretty from the air, and it is also very small. It seemed as though there were only about six parallel roads ascending away from the harbour and the whole town was surrounded by the southern peaks of the Andes. I quickly escaped the modern airport and caught a taxi to my backpacker's hostel the Cruz del Sur, which I had found on the internet and had been corresponding with. They mentioned that for the most part it was blue chair friendly, so as usual, I hoped for the best and prepared for the worst.

The Cruz del Sur was located on the third street up from the waterfront, so it would be up and down two hills to get to the port and back. The sun had finally come out from behind the clouds and long shadows formed in the early evening daylight as would be expected at this latitude. Actually, the latitude is about the same as Holland in the Northern Hemisphere, but on most maps it seems extreme due to the fact that the equator is never centered properly. The hostel was painted blue and had two floors, the top level was easily accessible from the street and I was greeted by a pretty girl named Vicky who showed me to my bunk bed, just off the kitchen and near a washroom that was great for a chair except for the fact that it was up a step. I couldn't see it being a problem since getting help up a single stair is generally no big problem. Vicky even made my bed for me and invited me to join her and some of the other backpackers for a communal meal they all chip money in for and prepare together.

After about an hour, the owner, Luca, a friendly young Italian who spends most of his time in South America running the place and doling out advice to weary travellers. His hospitality was apparent right from the start as I was offered a homemade cappucino. As we talked about what there was to do in town, some other backpackers arrived looking for a place to crash. Luca mentioned that his hostel was booked up, but they were more than welcome to sleep for free on the floor in the lower dorms. On top of being nice, it was also good business, since after some bunks were freed up, they would probably end up as paying guests in the long run.

Before dinner I took the opportunity to head out and wheel around Ushuaia a bit. Actually, I could only wheel up and down the street that the hostel was on since most of the other streets were far too steep to use. There were some businesses on our road but for the most part there were small wooden dwellings and undersized hotels that seemed more like construction sites than places to reside in. From the high vantage point overlooking a space of green grass I could view the panoramic vista of the little village located at the bottom tip of South America. I had always wanted to visit and now the blue waters of the Beagle Channel surrounded by the glacier capped mountains were sights I could spend the next two days to enjoy.

The dinner at the hostel was a communal affair and Vicky, along with Luca and some of us staying, all contributed toward the ingredients. My contribution was a few bottles of wine I had picked up on my venture outside. The meal was mainly a meat dish of beef cutlets while we had a side salad as well. It was quite a pleasant time, as the Israeli contingent of backpackers, most of whom had just concluded their tour of compulsory military duty, were boisterous and really livened up the conversation. In addition to them were a pair of Dutchmen, Karsten, a tall friendly blonde guy with a huge smile and Geb, an engineer, who was waiting to head out into the Antarctic seas working on a Tall Ship that was heading to Europe via Africa. Boy, did I ever envy him for his job! I have to confess that I didn't stay up too long after dinner and some wine as the day's travels had caught up with me, so I quietly slipped off to the adjacent dorm room, inserted in my earplugs and quickly drifted off to sleep.

Next morning, after mooching a coffee from one of the other backpackers, it was off to the harbour. Luckily it was all downhill, although I did have to slalom lengthwise down the streets in order to descend safely and avoid the steep grade down to the port. The sun was out and I thought it would be a great day for a trip out to the Beagle Channel. I visited the ships that were moored, and armed with the promotional brochures that I had picked up and read the previous day, I finally found the correct vessel that was headed out for a day's trip on the open water. Although I was considerably early, as is often the case in my travels so as to avoid the crowds and scout out the accessibility options, the crew readily welcomed me on the deck about thirty minutes prior to sailing and from the stern I was able to record the wonderful panoramic view of the little town of Ushuaia, that was nestled against the foreboding mountains. It was a great view.

The ship was two-tiered, but the deck that I was located on was great because the cabin was on the same level and was complete with tables and padded benches for eating. Another fellow from the hostel, an Israeli named Alex, also was on the trip so it was nice to have someone else to share the experience with. Slowly the small ferry moved away from the dock and we gently moved down into the Beagle Channel. What there was of civilization in this part of the world quickly faded and we were left with only the Andes mountains as our companions. Even the mountains were of interest as the guide explained over the intercom that this was the only part of the range in which the Andes actually rose in an east-west direction.

We quickly came to a small island where a group of seals were lounging around. Although most of the animals were quite ambivalent to our presence, a few of the younger ones seemed to specifically jump into the water and approach our craft in an attempt to satisfy their curiosity. Most of us took the opportunity for photographs and filming and after a short while we abandoned the seals to their noisy existence. As we made our way further east into the channel I thought about how long I had looked at this point on the map and wanted to see this part of the world. To our left were the mountains of Argentina and on our right were the rough hills of Chile. After another half hour of drifting along, we were happy to finally approach a colony of penguins. As it was approaching the lunch hour I surmised that the penguins had already eaten their breakfast as, unlike the seals, they were all quiet and sleepy. One or two were near the shore but there really wasn't much activity at all. This is the first time in my life I had seen such a large penguin colony, though I had seen wild penguins a few sporadic times during my travels. We remained for over twenty minutes and it was nice to watch the excitement of the tourists at the penguin viewing.

As we moved away, I made my way into the cabin to try to get some lunch. The ship offered a waitress who took your order and then brought it to you, which was quite upscale compared to what I was used to. I shared a table with an older Scottish couple, Pam and Grahame, who were supposed to be on a world cruise, but their new luxury liner was stuck in Portsmouth, England with a broken engine. They had been housed on the ship with all their expenses taken care of, while the tour company tried in vain to fix the hapless machinery. Finally, they took matters into their own hands and booked their own trip around the world. They were a couple in their 70s and they had just arrived in Ushuaia from trekking to the top of the Andes in Peru! Quite a pair of wonderful travellers and just the kind of people you meet while backpacking to the distant corners of the world.

Our last stop on the agenda was an old farm and sheep ranch that had once been a productive enterprise and had now been converted into a restaurant stop and cultural centre. It was quite rough terrain going up from the shore, so I just remained on the ship's deck by myself to enjoy the songs of the aquatic birds and the wonderful scenery that the bottom of the world had to offer. We ultimately made our way back into the town's harbour and although it was late in the day, the sun was still quite high above the horizon due to the length of each day at this southern latitude. Alex and I disembarked and pushed our way back up the steep hills to the hostel to see about getting something to eat.

Luca, Karsten, Geb and Vicky had hatched a plan to have a bunch of us chip in again to buy groceries and booze so that would have a big dinner at the hostel. It sounded great to me and so they headed out to the stores to arrange the meal while I skulked off to bed for a quick nap and stretch. When I finally perked up the dinner preparations were already well underway, and although I offered to help with the chopping of the vegetables, I had to satisfy myself with a cold, dark beer and the sight of a pretty girl making my supper. We had a great dinner of shish kabobs, roast vegetables and salad as the conversations, many of which were in languages that I didn't understand, ran well into the early hours of the morning. I had to head back north the next day, so I quietly slipped outside for a breath of fresh air and a last look at the stars and lights of the quiet little town below my vantage point above the harbour.

In the morning I was all alone as I got ready for my taxi to the airport except for the energetic Vicky who had risen early to attempt to clean up the huge mess leftover from the evening before. She carried my bags out to the cab for me and gave me a big hug and kiss before I departed.

I had been blessed with wonderful sunny weather during my brief stay in Ushuaia, though it had rained torrentially before my arrival. As I sat in the plane looking out at my last view of the rugged landscapes on the other side of my window the raindrops began to hit the panes of plastic. I had really been lucky in many respects and I sat back and smiled wondering if I would ever be lucky enough to visit "Tierra del Fuego" or the Land of Fire again. I hoped so.

AFRICA ENDS WITH THUNDER, A THUD AND A CRACK

It had been over a decade since my previous visit to Africa and suddenly in early 2006 I got it into my head to explore that wonderful continent again. The only other time I had been there, I was visiting my friend Wayne, who had been working there. This time I was determined to backpack in Africa alone.

Following a brief nineteen hours in the air, on a pair of flights via Frankfurt, I finally arrived in sunny Cape Town, South Africa, just near the southern tip of the continent. I was quite tired, but luckily I had arranged to meet a bus to take me to the hostel and my long awaited reservation with a bed. The hostel was quite large and had a very friendly staff, and all had been expecting me. The facility was barely wheelchair friendly. There was a large step from the street into the hostel, but a security guard was always posted at the gate and willing to help. Once inside there were long hallways with one or two stairs, most of which I could negotiate with the assistance of another backpacker. I was located in the "Rhino room".

Despite the bleary state of my eyes and the temptation to lay down and sleep, I headed out by taxi to the famous Table Mountain that overlooks the city and the last bay in Africa. I took the cable car, which has a rotating floor and was really impressed by the magnificent vistas. The blue sky was magnificent against the azure oceans and the sprawling urban landscape was busily moving to the rhythms of the daily grind. The top of Table Mountain is a bit uneven but with some determination I was able to make it around to gaze at the distant beaches along the coastline and then trip over to the other side of the mountain slowly to see the city's skyline and the Lion's Head. It was 33C, so the cool mountain breezes were quite welcome and the lunch on top really hit the spot. I had finally returned to Africa!

The next night the hostel was offering a trip out to Newlands Stadium to watch a pro rugby match between the local team the Stormers against an Australian team called the Brumbies. Newlands was built next to the SAB brewery so we were enjoyed the game while smelling hops and munching on sausages on a bun. The fellow who ran the tour was named Ferdinand, and apparently he had won the first South African Big Brother TV contest. Ferdy was really out going, he said that if I could get to South Africa in the blue chair, he could get me up the steps to stadium. Of course the bus had broken down and so he had to shuttle the numerous backpackers around in his own utility vehicle and he graciously supplied the cans of beer for the thirsty trip to the stadium. The match finally ended in a 15-15 draw but it had been an exciting game for those of us who had never been to a live match before. Afterward we headed to an exclusive pub, where I met a fellow backpacker named Tony and Selene, a Dutch girl working at the hostel as part of her college training in international tourism. It had been a very hot day, and as we sipped our drinks and laughed into the night a cool breeze finally blew through Cape Town to give the evening a welcome chill.

The following day I simply relaxed by the amazing pool at the hostel which had palm and banana trees and an exceptional view of Table Mountain, not bad for 90 rand a night! I met a Swedish couple and their three children whom they had been taking through Africa for the previous 4 weeks. Sandra and Mikael invited me to visit them in Sweden, so hopefully I could meet them later in the year on my visit to Sweden to go out to their horse farm. During my stay at the hostel, I actually spent quite a lot of time laying on the couch facing Table Mountain and I'm sure many of the staff and other backpackers must have felt I was foolishly wasting my time, but it was my holiday after all and I think that if such a simple thing brings pleasure, why not indulge?

My buddy Rex, from New Zealand who now lives in Australia had asked me to look up his old buddy Bruce, whom he backpacked with in younger days and lives in Cape Town. I called Bruce and he was nice enough to take the afternoon off and pick me up in his car. We headed out into the area around the Cape as well as a few pubs. The two of us drove out to Hout Bay, and passed the magnificent Chapman's Peak, all along seaside roads that offered great sea vistas of the west coast of Africa. We then went into the National Park and down to Simon's Town, and finally past the Cape of Good Hope, the most southwesterly point in Africa. We then proceeded back north, up to Muizenberg, built on a marsh flat, and into a winery called Groot Constantia, which has the vineyards up the side of the mountain, where we enjoyed a relaxing late lunch. On the way back to the hostel, we finished at the first drinking establishment in Cape Town, Forrester's Pub, What a great afternoon drive it had been! As much as the places you see on the way, the great thing in travel is the kindly people you meet offering to help you out. Bruce was one of those guys.

The following day was slightly cooler but bright and sunny so I decided to take a taxi down to the Victoria and Alfred Waterfront. The waterfront pier was fully developed for tourists with an indoor mall, a food court, an outdoor walking path around the harbour to a fancy hotel and there was also a bandshell where a string orchestra was playing. It made for a great atmosphere. After pricing out some tours, I decided to take a small craft for a harbour cruise. As we pulled away from the docks the shops on the shore became smaller and the expanse of Table Mountain became framed against the city of Cape Town in the forefront. We saw some seals near the fancy hotel and then sped out of the inner bay and slightly up the west coast of Africa. We were lucky enough to spot a lone dolphin and it reminded me that I had been too late for the whale watching season in this part of the world. After we returned to shore I wandered around the V & A again and happened on a native Xhosa band which drummed out tribal rhythms in the afternoon's fading light. On my return to the hostel it was time for a traditional South African "braai" which included sausages, chicken kebabs, corn on the cob and snoek, a bony fish, that was quite good. My dorm buddy Mathias, from Denmark, brought along a bottle of wine that he shared and we enjoyed the food and conversation under the stars of the southern hemisphere well into the night.

Mathias and I, along with another fellow from the hostel, Gareth from Wales, decided to hire a car, so together the three of us piled into a small hatchback we rented as Mathias tried to master driving on the left side of the road, and turned on the windshield wipers numerous times in an effort to indicate turns. We headed down the M3 motorway along the east side of the Cape and made our way onto Boulder Beach where a colony of penguins makes its home. Mathis managed to help me onto the sand to get quite close for some pictures of the lazy penguins that were ambivalent to our presence for the most part, not taking any notice of us. We made our way right to the Cape in the National Park and the other two walked up to see the point. I was just about to purchase a ticket to take the tram up to the top when the hydro cut out for the umpteenth time and so I was thwarted in my attempt and had to settle for a photo by the signpost. The Cape had been having horrible rolling blackouts during my stay, but for the most part it hadn't interrupted my vacation too often. On our way home we ventured along the western side of the peninsula and past the scenic Chapman's Peak that I had seen earlier with Bruce, it was quite a sight for the three of us to end our day trip on.

A cool wind finally blew through Cape Town and so I just hung out at the hostel, enjoying the bikinis around the pool and the view of Table Mountain. An Irish fellow named Dave had taken up residence and he and I hit it off. In the evening the two of us simply sat around the pool with some other backpackers enjoying pizza and wine and some great conversation. The next day was hot so I finally asked Seline, the Dutch hostel student worker to order me a taxi with a trunk big enough for my blue chair and I headed out to Camps Bay Beach, which is the flattest of all the beaches in the area. Dave was off to climb Table Mountain, with Gareth and promised to join me in the afternoon. The beach was quite nice, but the water was far away from the access for the blue chair due to the large width of sand, so there was not too much ogling of the pretty girls. In the afternoon, Dave showed up and stretched out on the grass, as he lamented the fact that he had to shortly return to Ireland since he only had the weekend in South Africa after a work assignment in Johannesburg. He should be a therapist with all the deep questions he asks, "Walt, what is your most happy moment?" etc. Anyway we ended up with a great dinner at the beach and saw the sunset over the Atlantic with a few glasses of grog and wine. On our return to the hostel, we began drinking again with some European girls who were attending dance classes in Cape Town. I finally crashed at 12.30 am. after 3 glasses of red wine, as the Swedish barmaid, Kiki, passed around a book she titled the "Fabulous book of Kiki" that we were supposed to write something memorable in. Later Dave went out dancing until around 4.30 am doing Tequila shooters. Next morning Dave looked horrible and with his wonderful Irish accent complained, "Ah Walt, I'm totally shattered!! The drink is evil". He slept by the pool the whole day while I wrote postcards and admired the view of Table Mountain. We did finally shuffle off to trendy Long Street later in the late afternoon, for a veggie curry. There were some hippies seated beside us, but in the end they were bogus as they whipped out their cell phones and got into their Mercedes cars to go home. What a strange street in a wonderful land!

Monday arrived and most of us were heading out of Cape Town. I for the Gauteng, Mathias for Denmark, Dave for Ireland, Gareth and the two Claudias from Munich onto the Bazbus to drive the Garden Route up the Eastern Cape to Pt. Elisabeth. I promised all at the hostel I would return in a week and with that my new friends lifted me onto the airport shuttle and I shook their hands goodbye.

My flight to Johannesburg was booked on the cheapo carrier Kulula Air, but it was converted to British Airways, so it was a great flight. The hostel shuttle picked me up and when we got out to Pretoria Backpackers, they tried to shunt me out to the far away rooms a few blocks away, saying I was overflow. I protested saying I had booked a week ago and was not "overflow"! They relented and I had a room with a Peace Corp volunteer. The hostel is pretty but not that great access to get outside, only the interior was relatively barrier free. The hostel asked if I wanted to book any tours, which puzzled me since I thought I had already been booked for a Soweto tour and the game drive. Apparently my 3100 rand had not included the tours so I was getting really annoyed, but I booked anyway. The next day a small group of us headed to Soweto (short for South West Township) to see the area where five million people live and where rioting occurred in 1976. We toured the apartheid museum, which is quite good and I may be in a promotional pamphlet there, as a lady asked me to pose beside a picture on the wall for new literature they are putting out. The museum documents the start of apartheid after the Second World War until its demise in the '90s and the visit is not as depressing as you'd think. Soweto is not just about poverty, though it does abound, some millionaires live there too and white people are now moving in. Soweto boasts the only street in the world with two Nobel winners, Bishop Tutu and Nelson Mandela. We stopped for a tour of one of the squatters camp and it was sad, but they had gardens, a day care for kids and portable toilets on the street every five houses or so. I must say they seemed happy and frankly, I have seen worse poverty in Europe with the many Gypsies shacks in Eastern Europe. We ended at the Hector Peiterson Museum documenting the 1976 riots. He was the first fellow to be gunned down and it was quite moving. At the end of the day, our group stopped for lunch but I didn't know it would take an hour, so I remained in the van and cooked in the sunshine, while the rest ate! I was annoyed since the guide had previously instructed us to eat on our own, which I did at the Apartheid Museum at noon. Oh well, I used the time to simply watch African life go by, as vendors sold sausages called "walkie talkies", made from the heads and hooves of animals. Cy, a buddy of mine back home, thinks that I am quite adventurous when it comes to trying new food, but I didn't try any of these.

The following morning I was annoyed again as the game drive to Pilansburg National Park that I had booked, got cancelled since I was the only person interested and you need a minimum of two to go. But what really bugged me was that there was another drive they could have got me on leaving at 5:00 am. and no one notified me. For one of the few times in my travels no one cared enough to help me out and let me know. My time in Gauteng had been a fiasco for the most part, but soon I was heading to Zambia to see Victoria Falls and the Zambezi River and go on a game drive in Botswana. I found out that the tour the lady at the Cape Town hostel had booked me in Zambia for only for 2 nights and 1 full day ... so again circumstances had conspired against me. This time at least, the hostel changed my itinerary to 3 nights and 2 full days. Perhaps thing were looking up for a great trip to Central Africa?

Birgit, a German girl staying at my hostel, was also going up to Zambia on my plane so we got up early and the hostel dropped us off at the Johannesburg airport and we looked to find our flight. This is where it gets really interesting. The airline, Nationwide, was on strike and wanted to charge me $50 US to use a Personal Assistance Unit truck (PAU) to get on the plane. I protested saying it was discrimination and a form of apartheid. They wouldn't let me on without paying, but I stuck my foot in the gate door and no one could board the plane until I got through, on the bus to the plane stairs. At the foot of the plane, Paul, an English guy, helped me up the stairs and lifted me on the plane. Even the Nationwide lady helped as she couldn't take it anymore, when I started shouting my new slogan "Apartheid isn't dead yet in South Africa". What a frustrating day, but I didn't pay the $50 hostage fee!

We arrived in Zambia at the Jollyboys Backpackers, owned and operated by Kim, a Canadian girl from Comox, B.C. It was nice to be in the "real Africa", potholed roads and malaria all around. We were near Victoria Falls and after a Mosi beer, Birgit and I took a cab to the Falls and viewed the thunder of the falls and the deep gorge that it fell down into. At first I was surprised by the lack of infrastructure near the Falls, but as I stared out at the magnificence of the cataract with all the natural beauty around and the thunder of the water flowing over its edge, I realised that this is the way it should be. Birgit was pushing me along the path, but it ended and only dirt remained. Suddenly we hit a tree root and thud, I hit the ground falling out of the chair into the red Zambian soil. I usually do this on each trip at least once. This time, when three Zambians put me back in my chair I knew something was wrong as my right knee hurt and started to swell up. Something was broken!!! Crack!

What to do when in Zambia in a blue chair and a broken knee? The Zambians wanted to take me to the local hospital but some tourists said there was a clinic in the hotel nearby, so I was wheeled there, and rang Canada to let the insurance know the score. The nurse took my blood pressure and called Ihanda, the local ambulance lady who is an Africaaner from South Africa. Ihanda and her workmate took me carefully on the stretcher to the ambulance. As I was loaded into the vehicle, I looked over and saw two zebras munching grass. At least I had seen some wildlife on this trip!

Dr Shafik's private hospital in Livingstone, Zambia was nothing to write home about but Dr. Shafik took me right in and took some X-rays, applied a plaster cast, cleaned up my cuts, gave me an anti tetanus shot as well as some pain and anti-inflammatory pills. This was all accomplished in two hours of wonderful care and for only $220 US. During all the time Ihanda stayed with me, offering words of comfort and when we were done she took me back to the backpackers. Kim switched me to a private room and got me dinner and asked her worker to watch me throughout the night. The next day, Ihanda came back to tell me she would take me to the airport, as Kim got my flight rearranged to go back to Johannesburg, she asked if I wanted anything and I told her I didn't want to be a bother. She admonished me, saying "stop being so Canadian" and so she got me breakfast. What treatment by friendly people in Africa's boonies!!! Birgit had dropped by and was upset, but I told her that's life and I was OK and not in too much pain. What really upset me was that I would miss my game drive in Botswana!

So Ihanda dropped me off at the airport and I was back off to South Africa and then home. It was the end of my trip. Many thanks to both Kim, Dr. Shafik and Ihanda for all the compassion. Nationwide wanted to charge me again for a PAU and I couldn't argue, but instead the staff carried me off the plane and I saved the $50 again.

After 32 hours in planes and airports, I arrived back in Toronto and Wayne picked me up laughing at me and calling me a maniac. After swallowing some Canadian pain pills he had, and enjoying his wife Brenda's home cooked dinner, I drove my own car for ninety minutes back to Niagara. I called my brother John to help me struggle out of my car and onto the couch for some well deserved sleep prior to heading to the hospital the next day for some Canadian medical attention.

So that was the abrupt end of my return to the Dark Continent! Africa leaves you with something and takes something away from you. It left me with a broken right leg but a great feeling about people, and it took my heart and mind with all the struggles to complete the trip.

I hope to return to Africa some day, as this cannot be my final memory of the place, but if it is, I will only try to dwell on the happiest parts of what was definitely a very memorable adventure!

THE HAPPY ENDING

There are people you meet in your lifetime that change your life and sometimes, in a rare instance you meet people and change their lives (or so they say). In previous stories in this book, I met Luke in Thailand, an English fellow on his way home after his trip to Australia. Luke suggested I meet up with a Dutch girl named Esther, when I got to Melbourne, which I did and then took her to a Formula 1 race at Albert Park. During the race Esther kept talking about Luke the whole day long, even after the race when we went to an Australian Rules Football match. Once I got to an internet kiosk, I emailed Luke and mentioned that Esther was really hooked on him and that since he wasn't too far from Holland, that he should try to keep in touch with her. Later in the year, I received an email from them, and much to my surprise Luke was visiting Esther on the continent. They had gone to a few weddings together and now were planning to live together in Belgium. It is funny how life goes sometimes, isn't it?

Two years after my original meeting of each of them separately, they came to Canada as a couple for their vacation. They spent some time with one of Esther's friends in Toronto and then rented a car and travelled down the QEW to Niagara to visit me. I was living in a one-bedroom apartment in Welland and I moved onto the chesterfield, so they could have my bedroom. It was great to see both of them again and they made a marvelous couple. After some coffee and cakes and getting caught up on conversation, I suggested that even though they were a bit tired, it would be a great time to head over to Niagara Falls. It was evening and by the time we arrived, most of the tourists had left for their hotels to get ready for dinner. We even found a disabled parking space, which is a pretty rare event, I can tell you. I always love going to "The Falls" as we call it. The thunder of the torrent of water falling down is absolutely deafening and they were in awe of the magnificent cataract. Although both of them were experienced backpackers, I knew that visiting at night would be special since the Niagara Parks Department always illuminates the Falls with different coloured lights after dusk. Both Luke and Esther stood right at the edge to take it all in, before moving about to begin snapping photographs.

After a long sleep in the following day (Luke and Esther are famous for not getting up early) I hopped in the car to get some food and beer before they awoke. They had brought me a book about Belgium which I enjoyed with my coffee, and then finally Luke rolled out of the bedroom with a sleepy grin. Once Esther had showered, I decided to take them for lunch in Port Colborne at a small yacht club on Sugarloaf Harbour overlooking Lake Erie. The lunch was quite good and afterwards we ordered some ice wine, which Niagara is famous for. It was their first introduction to the sweet aperitif and they both enjoyed it immensely. After lunch, we browsed an exhibition of old cars that had been set up in the park adjacent to the restaurant and Luke was quite knowledgeable in his conversations with the various owners. We hopped back into their car and took the scenic route through the southern half of Niagara. This is where most of the War of 1812 was fought, the last time Canada and the U.S. were on opposite sides in conflict. In a few years from now, there will be many events planned to mark the almost 200 years of peace that we have enjoyed since.

It was back to Niagara Falls to enjoy the landmark with some sunshine and the two of them took the opportunity to go on the "Maid of the Mist", which is a small ferry that braves the rapids and whirlpools to venture as close to the Falls as a craft can get without getting smashed to bits on the rocks that have fallen below over the years. They asked me to accompany them, but I was not interested having been on the ride as a kid and not wanting to be a third wheel on a romantic voyage of possible death! Of course the fact that I didn't want to get soaked may also have entered into my decision. After a long tour of the vicinity, I suggested we start to head back and so we stopped off for an ice cream in the village of Fonthill. The settlement is so named because the hill is actually a glacial kame that left a small mountain of rocks and boulders when it crept as far south as it could and then started retreating north, marking the beginning of the end of the last ice age. It is amazing that I actually paid attention to that lesson in Grade 5 geography class. For supper it was off to a local pub to enjoy a few bottles of Moosehead and some chicken wings that were properly made. Living just over the border from Buffalo where the chicken wing was invented we know a good chicken wing when we taste one and both of them agreed that it was really tasty.

The following day was their last before heading up to Algonquin Park to try to howl with the wolves. We ate at a diner known for their tasty breakfasts (as you can tell, I'm not much of a cook) and then it was off to a winery in Niagara-on-the-Lake (the first capital of Upper Canada) for a tour and especially to learn about the making of ice wine. Of course we couldn't arrive without Esther stopping by one of the roadside stands to see what local fare she could stock up on prior to camping and the both of them also got some gifts for friends and family back in Europe. It seems that every country these days has a wine tour on offer but we are proud of the local ice wine. Apparently, it is a special grape that is used and the winery leaves a certain percentage on the vine over the winter. As soon as the temperature first drops to -8C or below, the call goes out to volunteer hobbits who emerge from their slumber in the middle of the night to commence the harvest in the bitter cold. In return the pickers receive free bottles of the sweet elixir after it is made. After the tour and learning about the process of wine making it was off to the wine bar for some free samples and then we exercised out wallets to sample some of the fantastic ice wines. Luke graciously bought me a bottle of a fabulous vintage and also bought others as gifts. They were now headed to Elora and Northern Ontario for the rest of the holiday and so we parted ways again with a promise from me to visit them in Belgium at the first opportunity.

The following spring I received a phone call from Luke, he mentioned that they had given up the lease on their flat in Brussels and that if I wanted to fulfill my promise to visit them, I would have to do it in the next few months. I decided to exercise the credit cards and make my way to Europe. It seemed that there were no cheap flights to Brussels, so, as usual, I did the trip the hard way. I flew into London's Heathrow around 6:00 am. one early April morning, and then still bleary eyed, found my way onto the rails to try to find the best route to Waterloo Station, which is located along the Thames River. It didn't take too long to get there but the problem was that I now had six hours to kill before my EuroStar train ride through the "Chunnel", which is the tunnel that was built under the English Channel between England and France. I had planned to do some sightseeing, but as was customary for this time of the year, it was raining, so that plan had to be put off for another time. I decided to have a cup of coffee and a steak pie and watch life go by, although by 11 am. it was all I could do to keep awake!

The EuroStar only takes about two hours to run from London to Brussels, ending in Amsterdam, and there is an alternate route that goes to Paris. I was located in the first class compartment, even though my disabled ticket was supposed to be in second class. The train was quite clean and spacious and as it rolled south out of the station I was surprised to see that the trees were already growing leaves and that flowers were blooming in backyard gardens, this was far earlier than back home in Canada. It was quite a strange feeling when we finally entered the Chunnel. Usually these tunnels are quite short, but this one took a long while and left me with an eerie feeling knowing all the water that was above us and the pressure it was exerting all around. In due course, we emerged unscathed to our first stop in "Lille, Europe"! I thought it was funny that they used the term Europe rather than France, but since the advent of the European Union, I guess that is the way it would be from now on. At meal time, when they got to me they had run out of meals! I'm not sure why I was the only one not getting anything, maybe it had something to do with the class of my ticket, but they did scrape together a dish of cheese and grapes. I can definitely see why the EuroStar is in financial distress if they can't even organise meals properly.

At the end of the journey to Brussels I was welcomed by the smiling face of Esther, who had arrived to meet me. Of course a reunion must be conducted properly and usually with my friends it includes mass quantities of beer. We started with a round in the railway station and then moved into the lounge of a hotel across the street. Esther rang Luke who was due into the same station from Frankfurt where he was working, but he said he would be late and would meet us at their apartment. So after a few more rounds and getting caught up on our lives the past nine months, we finally headed out. I was quite impressed with Esther's ability to handle the blue chair. It really wasn't that heavy but sometimes people who aren't used to handling it can become quite intimidated. Not Esther. She packed it up in her German company car and we drove out to the flat. There were a few steps to get up to the entrance but they were very wide stairs so Esther could easily manage helping me up one at a time, the problem was when we were in front of the elevator and she tipped my chair back to help me over a small lip, the weight of the backpack hanging behind my chair caused me to tip over and I ended up on my back looking up at Esther from the ground! She was dying laughing as was I, and so she phoned Luke to come downstairs and help me out. Luke finally arrived with a smirk and helped to get the chair upright again. The reunion had begun.

The next day, after a great sleep, I got a chance to scout around the flat. It was quite nice and on a quiet street. My room doubled as Luke's office when he worked from home and had a balcony. There was another balcony on the other side of the building off the living room, so I was quite impressed with the design. The toilet was a bit of a bother since it was small and the throne was around a tight corner. The washroom was in another room and I was just able to get in and close the door, though the tub was quite deep, and as a result useless to me. I would be washing with a face cloth again. No matter, I made a cup of tea while they slept in.

Luke and Esther were hosting a dinner party with a mystery theme so for the following evening I was to play a brash American from Texas. This is not really my cup of tea, but I thought I would give it a try. In the meantime we had a chance to drive through Brussels and tour around while purchasing some items for the dinner. Brussels, though with a reputation for being rather dour by European standards for large cities, was rather charming in my opinion. It was clean and orderly and the architecture was quite pretty. I thought it was quite modern since you could take an underground tunnel with your car and the tunnel seemed to pop back up above ground just in time to exit or make a turn before heading back underground for a few minutes in your express journey into the heart of the city. We drove past the palace, but unfortunately the King of Belgium was not around to greet me. I always have terrible luck with royalty. We found an underground parking spot and then proceeded to tour around with Luke and Esther alternating turns at getting my chair over the cobbled streets. One of the major points of interest is a fountain in the form of a boy peeing water. It was quite the attraction and everyone was taking pictures. We stopped at a cafe right on the Grand Place and had a view of the magnificent central square with its beautiful churches. It was just wonderful to have now been with Luke and Esther over three of the world's continents! I'm not sure if it was the beer or the thrill of going downhill to the car once we got back to the parking spot, but Luke slipped and my chair tipped again with me tumbling out for a second time and so we all laughed hysterically.

The dinner party went quite well and it was really nice meeting such an eclectic assortment of friends that they had. Esther had prepared various courses and the main dish was duck, which I had previously only had once. It was quite good. I was a terrible actor but we all had fun and after dinner Luke broke out the Canadian ice wine from his supply and the others who hadn't tasted it before, seemed quite impressed. The following day after a long sleep and some cleaning up from the party, Luke did some work at home and Esther and I headed off to an art museum. We had a late lunch at one of her favourite restaurants and she was quite strong to lug me up about five stairs to get inside. The museum was featuring an exhibition entitled "Birth, Life and Death", which would seem to just about cover it all. I was starting to get depressed by the end of each room since at the end we would be at the "death" pictures after starting with the birth pictures. I suggested that we go in the opposite direction from the other viewers of the remaining rooms, so that we would be more upbeat by the end of viewing each artist's efforts. It made for bumping into some other tourists but we decided to rename the show "Death, Life and Birth", and it seemed to work out a bit better.

The weekend was over so I decided to head out the next day for a bit of backpacking until the following weekend. On the Monday, Esther drove me to Louven, which is where Stella Artois beer is brewed though I was unaware of it at the time. The weather was still rather drizzly but the town was quite pretty with a wonderful Gothic church in the main square, where I enjoyed lunch. I loved watching all the Belgian schoolchildren coming and going from their studies on bicycles. I slowly wheeled my way to the train station and got a ticket to Mechelen, which was where my friend Kathleen whom I had met in Cordoba, Argentina, was from. Mechelen was a nice Flemish town and the hostel, though a bit sterile was rather centrally located to the main square. I was able to have dinner with Kathleen on one of my evenings there and she gave me a tour of some of the points of interest, including St. Rumbold's Tower, which at one time was one of the tallest buildings in Europe.

My next stop was in the other half of Belgium, the french speaking part known as Wallonia and the town of Liege. The train moved along through green pastures and rolling fields until we finally arrived in a town where I could once again read the signs as my knowledge of French is much better than my Dutch. The hostel was quite a distance from the station but luckily for me the buss es were all wheelchair friendly and again the hostel seemed to be in a very good location. I ended up with my own room though there were another five bunks in it. I guess Belgium is not a big backpacker destination during the rainy springtime. Liege was not as neat and orderly as the Flemish towns I had been to but it had a unique charm of its own. There was a larger Arabic and African population, probably from some of the french speaking former African countries that Belgium had formerly colonised, so it seemed a bit more diverse. I wandered around the old part of the city, rode the bus around to see a bit more of it and spent a rainy day sipping coffee and reading a paper while watching life go by. In the evening I wheeled through a small festival that was happening in the evening which included rides for the children.

The week was over and as Friday rolled around the sun finally made an appearance just a I was heading back to the capital to see my friends again. I was determined not to call either of them for help as I wanted to see if I could make it back to their flat on my own. I did quite well until I took the subway to the stop near their place as the station had no elevator. It didn't matter as I simply asked one of the passersby to hold the blue chair steady while I hopped on the escalator to the surface. It was only two blocks from the apartment so I had made it back all in one piece. Yeah!!

The next day the rain reappeared and Luke and I accompanied Esther to her field hockey match. We had gone with good intentions to watch her play but the good Belgian beer and the cold and wet conspired against us. We did plod out for a few minutes to make a ceremonial appearance whilst we huddled together under a tiny umbrella, but it didn't take long before we scurried back to the bar, once we knew Esther's team had the game well in hand.

In the evening we met some more friends, Louisa and Andy, and we toured around the Grand Place again prior to finding a cozy restaurant where we enjoyed some fine food and conversation. Later it was off to a bar called "Monks", where you can sample literally hundreds of beers brewed by Trappist Monks. I guess that is what they do when they aren't praying? Anyway we hooked up with Luke's buddy Aksel and some more of Esther's friends from her Dutch club in Belgium, one of whom was named Heidi. Late into the evening the five of us finished the day with some Belgian fries with a spicy mayo dressing that the country is famous for. The following evening was my last and the five of us got together in the nearby town of Ghent for a walkabout and dinner. It was quite fitting for me as every Canadian schoolboy knows that it is the town where the "Treaty of Ghent" was signed ending the War of 1812 between the then British colony of Canada and a young, upstart country called the United States of America. I wonder if the guys signing that treaty ever wondered what those two countries would ever amount to?

Just over a year later, in June of 2006, I would be on the other side of the pond once again, this time in England for Luke's stag and the couple's wedding. Once again I rode the rails away from the airport but this time to the little town of Farnham in Surrey, just south of London. I had arranged to meet Esther at a pub near the railway station after she got home from work. We had decided to watch England play a World Cup football match. Esther brought along her next door neighbours Owen and Joanne and Jo's sister, and we proceeded to watch the game and get caught up on wedding arrangements while we waited for Luke to arrive from his work in Slough. England won the match and it was great to be with my friends again in advance of such a happy occasion and with all the cheering in support of the football team. On our arrival to their home, the neighbour, Owen invited us to a barbecue in their backyard, which was a great way to kick off the visit. The house that Esther and Luke were renting was quite nice and on a quiet street, but not the friendliest for the blue chair, so I was sleeping on the couch, which suited me fine. In fact I ended up being so tired that I forgot to undress and slept in my clothes!

Esther was heading out to Amsterdam with her friends for a "Hen's weekend" and the fellows were heading west to Luke's hometown of Bristol for his "Stag Doo". On the Friday afternoon, Luke's buddy Martin arrived, armed with a few large tubes of beer and after carefully entering the back of the car with my leg in a cast, that I had broken a few months earlier in Zambia, we began the journey and I even got a chance to glimpse the ancient ruins of Stonehenge as we travelled the green English countryside on that late Spring day. Luke's parents, his mum Denise and stepfather George were away in their caravan, so the boys had the house to themselves. The house wasn't great for the chair, but the main floor was OK, only the "loo" would be a bit of a bother. An assortment of Luke's friends proceeded to arrive during the course of the evening, There was Guy, Craig, the best man named Vince, Owen arrived late, one of Luke's brothers named James, and another fellow with the unusual nickname of "Toggy", which I actually never got the story on. Anyway, they were all very friendly and welcoming and we overindulged in frozen pizza and beer while chatting well into the night as the boys kept a bonfire roaring outside in the backyard.

The following morning, near lunchtime, most of us finally awoke and Craig had taken charge of the breakfast duties in the kitchen. Vince had arranged a day of paintball combat for the guys, so I just went along for the ride and watched the kids have a go at the nearby dirt track on a hot sunny Saturday afternoon. By late afternoon, the fellows were quite tired but all agreed that it had been quite a bit of fun. We had to quickly get home to get cleaned up for the pub crawl in a few hours. I washed outside in the backyard with the garden hose and then changed into something semi-respectable for the bar scene and then we all made our way to Bristol's waterfront, for the first stop in the pub crawl. Vincent had rented "The Big Blue Bus" which would ferry us around town all night. Guy and James became quite adept at pushing my chair and James made sure that I always had a pint in my hand when we arrived at a new pub. The bus was double decker and on the top floor were a bunch of girls attending a stagette. A lady on the bus ran the whole thing and there was music included. By the end of the evening the guys got quite raucous and funny. Luke was getting quite drunk and we all made a point of making sure it stayed that way. By the time we hit the last bar on the bus route, I was getting annoyed, since I had previously been unable to complete a pint before it was time to get back on the bus. This time, James, Craig and Guy made sure the bus waited outside until I could finally complete a pint! After the bus left, we all decided to hit one last after hours bar, but it was up some stairs and the bouncer wouldn't let me in due to "fire regulations", I was drunk and really annoyed but I held my tongue and we gave him a bribe to let me in. I really hated that but I didn't want to ruin Luke's evening. On the way out afterwards, my chair almost ripped Vince's finger off getting down the stairs and I think it was well past 4 am. before we hailed the taxi back to the house. All in all, a very successful way to kick Luke into married life!

Two weeks later I went back to Surrey, this time to the village of Haslemere, where everyone was staying and the reception would be held. It was another hot, but beautiful English weekend. I was finally able to meet Esther's parents and extended family as well as her sister and many of her friends from my visit to Belgium. In the evening we all sat around outside anticipating the next day's ceremony and recounting tales of past experiences with the happy couple.

July 1st was Canada Day, so it was quite nice because Luke's mother, Denise was Canadian having been born in Manitoba, before coming to England. Also, I didn't realise that that day was also St. Esther's Day, so it made for a triple meaning to me! George and Denise were in charge of transporting me to the wedding and Aksel, who had been unable to attend the stag, and was to be the master of ceremonies, was also coming with us. The ceremony was to be back in Farnham and it was quite funny because there was all sorts of traffic and we got stuck behind an old fire engine on its way into town. We made it to the church with plenty of time to spare and Esther looked spectacular in her white gown. Luke also looked rather dashing in his tuxedo but I must say I was disappointed not to see him in a top hat. At the end of the ceremony, we all joined the choir for a round of "He's got the whole world in His hand" and then moved outside to the churchyard among the gravestones for some cake.

In England they have a "wedding breakfast" in the early afternoon, I think it is called that since it is the first meal after the wedding and I was really honoured to be sitting right next to Esther. Each of the tables were appropriately named after a continent or region of the planet in keeping with the travel theme that brought the two of them together in the first place. Louisa and Andy were also beside me so we were having fun chatting and drinking our beer on such a hot day. After the curry soup the main course was my favourite, lamb, and I even got seconds when Andy gave me his as it was a bit too rare for his taste. Excellent! The toasts were made, the champagne and wine was sipped and a few speeches were recited. It all made for a wonderful wedding day for Luke and Esther.

In the late afternoon we all moved out to the grounds to try out some croquet or just mingle under a tree away from the hot sunshine. I skulked away for a brief time to stretch out on the bed, but it wasn't much relief as the radiator in the hallway outside my room was on and the towel warmer in the washroom was also on. Oh well, my leg in the cast was starting to swell a bit so the rest did me some good anyway. When I got up most of the guests were in the pub watching England play football again, but this time they lost on penalty kicks to Portugal so that put a brief damper on things. Later it was time for the reception and the band they had hired was quite good. Luke and Esther made for a very handsome couple and as I looked around the room at all their admiring friends and family from all over the world, I could only wonder at the adventures that their future together had in store for them. They say that two heads are better than one and I definitely know that two hearts are better than one!. Who knows where it will all lead? Perhaps one of these days the small item in their backpack on one of their trips will be in frequent need of fresh diapers!

This story is entitled "The Happy Ending" and it also marks the last story in this book. Like most endings, this is also a beginning, both for Luke and Esther in their lives together and for me in new adventures that hopefully await in other travels not yet undertaken.

I just wonder if the old blue chair will be up to it? I know that I will.

APPENDIX

NORTHERN LAND

Northern Land, Northern Land

When I recall
my home, away
I think of years gone by

Of mapled stands
on snowy lands
and western mountains high

Far from me now
but near in my heart
I long to return once more

First Nations' earth
my place of birth
Many cultures 'tween our shores

Canada, Canada

When times are hard
you open your arms
to those who seek a peace

Grained patchwork fields
with golden yields
and bounties that never cease

I've travelled far
And seen the world
There is no land that I compare

Your northern lights
that steer my sights
will guide the hopes we share

Northern Land, Northern Land
I'll return to you again

Northern Land, Northern Land
I'll wake in your morning then

Lyrics by Walt Balenovich
Whilst homesick in Perth, Australia 2002
(Song with no music—as of publication)

978-0-595-46149-3
0-595-46149-2

Printed in the United States
136732LV00001B/2/A